Beyond All Reason

BEYOND ALL REASON

The Limits of Post-Modern Theology

John Reader

Aureus

Aureus Publishing 144 Marlborough Road Cardiff CF2 5BZ.

ISBN 1 899750 02 9

Contents

Acknowledgements

I would to thank Sue Granger whose questions and ideas about Post-Modernity created the initial stimulus for the book.

I would also like to thank colleagues in the church and the academic world whose support and advice was offered at key moments. These include John Atherton at Manchester Cathedral, Christopher Rowland and Lord Plant of Highfield at Oxford, and the Right Revd Dr Rupert Hoare, Bishop of Dudley.

My gratitude extends to the people of the Four Square Parishes in Worcestershire and particular friends from Shropshire and beyond who have been party to the background discussions. This includes the artist Lin Brown who has allowed me to use one of her paintings for the cover.

Finally I would like to thank my wife Christine, and my children Kate, Simon and Thomas, for their forbearance during recent months.

J.R.

I

The Changing Nature of Religious Belief

Introduction

R eligion is back on the agenda. This might come as something of a surprise to the pundits of a previous generation who were eager to herald its imminent demise. The announcement of the death of religion has been premature. Yet, as those familiar with arguments about the definition of words will realise, there is no one thing called religion. I am not going to attempt a definition here but merely to offer a thumbnail sketch of contemporary developments to highlight the growing interest in the study of religion.

Whose agenda might prove of interest? Politicians find it difficult to ignore religion. In parts of the world religious leaders play a prominent role in political matters, either in support of the status quo or as a focus of resistance. Nelson Mandela and Desmond Tutu in South Africa grounded their opposition to apartheid in their Christian faith. Ayatollah Khomeini combined the revival of Iranian nationalism with that of Islam. In the years leading up to the collapse of communism in the Eastern bloc churches provided a meeting point for the resistance movements. In Latin America priests have been murdered because of their opposition to oppressive regimes.

Religious differences and divisions are still significant in many contemporary conflicts: Jews and Arabs; Serbs and Croats; Unionist and Loyalist in Northern Ireland - the list can be multiplied across the globe. The rise of fundamentalism is seen by some as the greatest threat to world peace. Even in Western countries such as the United States and Great Britain where the society is portrayed as largely secular, religion retains an influence at the highest levels. It would be a brave politician who would declare the death of religion.

For institutional religion and the major world faiths the picture is confusing.

1

Some elements of Christianity, for instance, display clear numerical decline, if the statistics are to be believed. Yet Islam is often cited as being the fastest growing religion. Even more difficult to unravel are the strands where people are moving between the world religions and sometimes combining facets from a number of them, or from outside influences. The boundaries are beginning to get blurred in some instances and yet more sharply defined in others. It seems as though there is movement in opposite directions.

Even in the academic world religion is proving to be a more popular subject, possibly because of this unstable but exciting climate. There is so much going on that there are lots of different facets of religious life to be studied and researched. It is not just a matter of covering the same old ground knowing in advance what is likely to be discovered. It is as if, for the first time since the rise of professional academia, there is the possibility of something new being said in this field. Until recently science was on the frontier of human exploration. Suddenly it is not so obvious that it stands alone on the boundary between past and future.

The parasitic world of journalism has been quick to spot the potential of storyline in these new developments. Rather than merely harassing or exposing the official representatives of religious institutions, reporters now delight in infiltrating obscure religious sects that proclaim new divinities or advocate alternative lifestyles. Occasionally they offer more considered comment on what might be happening in this world so recently returned to life. I offer as an example an article from a British Sunday newspaper published in December 1993 (1).

Under the title 'Faith, hope - but not too much clarity', the article suggests that churches are losing out on the one side, to do-it-yourself faiths and, on the other, to a growing fundamentalism. Even though 15 million people attended church in Britain over Christmas in 1993, the following week worshipping figures would slump back down to normal. Yet this does not represent an abandonment of faith.

'In the post-modernist Nineties, where the consumer is champion and personal choice is everything, many people are making up a faith for themselves. This is the era of do-it-yourself faith or making your own god. Today people are not god-fearing just god-interested.' (2).

Examples are offered of high profile public figures such as Richard Gere disappearing to Tibet in search of a greater deity and Boy George eschewing drugs in favour of Hare Krishna. The Glastonbury festival attracted 80,000 people, many sitting in stone circles and practicing dowsing or white witchcraft. In a lot of bookshops one of the busiest sections is that entitled

Spirituality or New Age, or Mind, Body, Spirit, covering such subjects as personal psychology, alternative health, mythology and astrology. The orthodox texts of Islam, Judaism or Christianity are getting squeezed into an ever tighter corner.

This is described as 'pick-and-mix' religion, constructed by the individual from the fragmented components of the declining major religions and the unorthodox offerings of previously marginalized beliefs. Corporate worship, statements of faith and adherence to doctrine are out, privatized spirituality is in. Quite commonly there are links with a growing awareness of environmental issues and the search for an ecological ethics.

At the other extreme is the growth in fundamentalism, particularly in Islam and Christianity. The apparent explanation for this is a search for certainty and community in a world where both have been undermined, the first by science, and the second by capitalism, individualism and liberal democracy. The only other type of formal churchgoing to flourish is that which offers people a renewed acknowledgement of personal religious experience and straightforward ethical teaching. Liberal faith traditions rest increasingly uncomfortably between the greater freedom of the pick-and-mix and the greater certainty and security of the fundamentalist approaches. Both extremes could be seen as a reflection of the growing disillusion with the great god science, now taking the blame for some of our worst contemporary crises. Perhaps they could also be interpreted as a backing away from democracy where people are expected to act in consensus, but without any external controlling force. It is easier either to 'go it alone' as in pick-and-mix, or to hand the decision-making power to the authority of an external tradition, as in fundamentalism.

The article concludes with a quote from Grace Davie, whose work will be referred to later in this chapter. 'We do not live in a secular society... (but)... a society in which belief is drifting away from orthodoxy to no one knows where, in which belief is floating, disconnected, without an anchor' (3). The abandonment of religious institutions does not mean the abandonment of religious faith. If this is an accurate description of what is happening then it leaves much to be explained and poses immense questions for theology.

Perhaps the only thing that can be said with certainty is that the picture is more complex than even before. This should not come as a surprise given recent advances in technology and communications and the greater knowledge that we now all have of each other. In many countries it is very likely that we will regularly encounter those of other faiths or beliefs, or indeed those who hold no belief. The options proliferate as people travel, watch other corners of the globe from their own living rooms and are prepared to debate ideas that were previously accepted without question. The result, according to some, is a heady mixture of beliefs and practices, often combining in unexpected ways. Religious institutions appear either to be losing their grip in the face of rampant heterodoxy or to be attempting to re-impose forms of orthodoxy by employing contemporary methods of coercion or persuasion.

We now need to return to the question of why the pundits of a previous generation would be surprised that religion is still alive and well, albeit in rather varied forms. If today there is naive talk of a classless society, what grounds did our predecessors have for predicting a religionless society? Most commentators would offer one apparently simple explanation: the Enlightenment. In fact this encapsulates a number of separate but related strands, some of which will be returned to in greater detail in later chapters. For the moment I will present only a basic picture.

The Enlightenment is the term that is used to characterize a new way of thinking about the world that dates from the Seventeenth Century. This movement involved a number of key thinkers including Voltaire and Montesquieu, themselves influenced by the British philosopher John Locke and scientist Isaac Newton. Their ideas were further developed by Hume and Rousseau, culminating in the philosophy of Kant. As with all such terms it is a generalization covering a number of different thinkers and approaches and must be viewed in this light. However, certain central themes do emerge: an emphasis upon the primacy of reason as the correct way of organizing knowledge; a concentration upon empirical data accessible to all and a belief that human progress was to be achieved by the application of science and reason. This new way of looking at the world placed a question mark against the role of tradition in determining knowledge. It is no longer what others in the past have said that shapes our beliefs but that which we can now work out for ourselves.

The Enlightenment could thus be viewed as the triumph of reason over tradition. In other words, the first replaces the second as the source of our knowledge about ourselves, our world and anything that might lay beyond it. When we ask such questions as 'What do we know?'; 'How can we know?' and 'What meaning can there be to life?', rather than turning to a particular tradition for the answers we now presume to be able to answer them for ourselves. We do this through the power of human reasoning; our abilities to observe, calculate, theorize and discriminate. We think it all out for ourselves rather than relying on an external authority or tradition to provide predetermined answers. It is this supposed flowering of human reason through the arts, philosophy and of course science, linked with the political upheavals that began with the French Revolution, that are deemed to have sounded the death knell for formal religion.

The argument is admittedly crude, but so often repeated in theological circles, that it has to be attended to if we are to understand the potential significance of Post-Modernity. Given that the Enlightenment is seen to be both the beginning of the modern era and to provide the intellectual foundations for what we call Modernity, if we are now moving into a period where the Enlightenment has been undermined or superseded, there may be fresh hope for religious beliefs. As people began to exercise their own judgement so the authority of religious traditions began to decline. Science and reason replaced religion as the way of understanding and interpreting both the natural world and human existence. The development of capitalism and the move towards more democratic political structures also challenged the social position of the religious hierarchies. The sacred is pushed back into the farthest recesses of human life and increasingly equated with myth and superstition while the non-religious or secular spreads across politics, the economy, intellectual and artistic pursuits and even the sphere of morality. As scientific explanations of the world take over we enter a disenchanted world, where religious views have less purchase upon reality. Explanations dependent upon reference to an external power or metaphysical principle - God - are relegated to a previous stage of human development when people still believed in some form of magic.

Thus the Enlightenment was expected to herald the end of religion, as the latter would no longer be needed or trusted to provide answers to the most important questions about human existence. The Enlightenment would be the tradition to end all other traditions and thereby the hope that the divisive forces of religion and superstition would be overcome once and for all. When everybody used their powers of reason global agreement would become a reality and we would all learn to live peacefully together. The fact that this now sounds incredibly idealistic and naive explains, in part, why the Enlightenment tradition is itself under suspicion. The reality is somewhat different.

If the Enlightenment is now being brought into question and the Modernity which has been built upon it is perceived to be far from secure as we move into this Post-Modernity, then religious belief might be back in the frame. As the newspaper article hinted, a disillusion with science could easily lead to a return to religion as people search elsewhere for meaning.

During the dark years, the wilderness decades since the birth of the Enlightenment, religious belief has clung on beneath the surface awaiting the opportunity to re-emerge. Now the tide has finally turned as we move into Post-Modernity where the modern certainties are revealed as no more than convenient myths or the power-plays of particular groups and the even older certainties of religion take fresh wing. At least, that is the argument. Unfortunately it leaves too much unexplained and pins its hopes on a set of ideas that create more questions than answers. The task of this book will be to examine the key ideas of Post-Modernity and to suggest their real implications for theology.

However, before moving on to these arguments, there is a prior question to be addressed. How accurate is the picture of changes in religious belief offered by the popular view as illustrated by that newspaper article? In order to develop a more rigorous approach we turn to the work of three contemporary sociologists of religion. One thought at this stage: if religion, in whatever form, has survived extended contact with the Enlightenment and Modernity, can it now claim to return to a Pre-Enlightenment self-understanding? Perhaps what begin to evolve are different patterns of religious belief and practice. This is what one might expect if there is substance to the idea of a Post-Modernity or Post-Enlightenment.

Yet is there anything significantly new happening in the religious sphere or is it all media hype or academic backchat? The evidence needs to be carefully and critically examined.

Believing without belonging

The first example of changes or developments in religious belief and practice emerges from research carried out into religion in contemporary Britain (4). Immediately we encounter difficulties both of definition and of generalization. What is to count as religious belief? Are there particular factors peculiar to the British situation that rule it out as a basis for further argument? Both questions arise from the presupposition that there is going to be one overall and overarching understanding of religious belief that carries over all cultural and temporal boundaries and against which particular examples can be measured. I suggest that this would be difficult to justify. Far better to accept, for the moment, that we can examine only individual cases and what they might have in common with other instances left open to question.

What Grace Davie's work appears to show is that although formal or institutional religion is in decline in Britain and has been for a number of generations, the incidence of people claiming some sort of religious experience or belief in the sacred is not. It is worth noting that this evidence undermines the secularization arguments of a previous generation of sociologists, the idea that a disenchanted world would lead to a weakening of the claims of religion. Has this sense of meaning and purpose remained despite, or because of, the increasing dominance of a view that sees the world as a machine operating by a system of regular natural laws?

It is perhaps dangerous but nevertheless important to speculate here. Not all scientists subscribe to such a straightforward understanding of the world. Some give a greater emphasis to the limitations of scientific knowledge and see science itself as a fallible human enterprise (5). Outside the scientific community there is unease at the effects of dominant scientific claims upon human life and the environment generally (6). Both of these tend to undermine the confidence that has been attributed to that aspect of the Enlightenment paradigm. In which case it is perhaps not surprising that religious beliefs have not been swept off the board after all. In fact they might be seen as an essential component of an anti-science reaction, or, at least, a potential site of resistance alongside others.

There is an ambiguity here though. On the one hand there is an argument that religion itself is being swallowed up by and churned out as yet another product of a consumer culture. On the other it might be seen as a potential protected space where the rules of that culture do not apply. Thus they provide places where alternative values and world views continue to lodge, in the crevices of a hostile culture. Or are they both in fact the same thing? One could say that this is what religious belief is now turned into and yet it can still be marketed within the culture as an anti-culture product. It could be that a sensible cultural system would retain some spaces where intransigents or subversives could lodge, preferably on the margins where their views carry little weight and can do no real damage to the dominant structure. There is always the possibility of religious believers being guided into a corner from which they believe they can criticize the culture, but that is in fact controlled by that very culture.

This argument will return. In the meantime a little more on the apparent demise of institutional religion in Britain. The statistical evidence available supports the view that, with the exception of certain sectors, notably evangelically inclined congregations, religious institutions have been experiencing a steady decline. However, belief in God remains more common. One may conclude from this, as Davie does, that non-institutional belief is thus rendered vulnerable to a wider range of external influences as people encounter ideas and beliefs from other traditions (7). Without the boundaries and constraints that belonging to a specific faith community normally provide, one would expect to see a greater variety of religious beliefs and indeed an increasing eclecticism. Hence what is now called New Age, that is perceived to contain an unordered mixture of beliefs and practices culled from just about anywhere.

Once again caution is required. There is no one New Age religion with clearly identifiable beliefs and boundaries. It might be safer to use the term to refer to a general approach to religion rather than to any specific content. The external caricature of New Age is that it is pick-and-mix religion, highly individualistic and existing on the margins of, or well beyond, institutional religion in Britain. The reality is by no means so clear cut. There are a number of people who are engaged in so-called New Age practices and beliefs who are also worshippers within the official institutions. So the phenomenon does not just exist on the margins. There are instances of New Age worship techniques being employed by congregations within the institutions. For instance, the *Nine o' Clock* service in Sheffield that fell into disrepute in 1996 when it emerged that its leader, Revd Chris Brain had been using his position of power to seduce female members of the congregation. It was argued by the Church of England authorities at the time that this was an isolated incident and that similar attempts to combine high technology worship techniques with traditional Christian practice were perfectly legitimate.

The New Age label is often used by those within the institutions to identify others who do not conform to their particular definition of orthodoxy. Further, if what is supposed to be new about the New Age is people deciding for themselves what strands of religious belief they will adopt, drawing upon a wide variety of sources, then it becomes increasingly difficult to justify calling this new at all. It would seem that people both inside and beyond institutional boundaries have always been able to respond to and appropriate new ideas as they are encountered. One only has to read of the poet and visionary William Blake and the religious groups of that period in Eighteenth Century Britain to see that beliefs are formed and reformed with considerable freedom and imagination. Traditions are not solid and static but flexible and organic. If the use of New Age as a label does indicate some new phenomenon in the religious world, it is not immediately obvious what that might be.

Defining and de-limiting what is meant by both institutional and non-institutional religion is far from easy. As Davie points out the non-institutional dimension has itself spawned a number of terms that attempt to describe it: privatized; invisible; implicit; popular; common; folk; civil or civic religion are all to be found in the literature (8). They indicate an amorphous and shifting pattern of belief and practice that has tenuous links to formal religious institutions. Is there now greater flexibility than ever before, with more people exercising individual choice in this area? The temptation is to accept this, but how much has this to do with the language of privatization that is prevalent in British political life? Everything is being privatized so religion must be too. The evidence is not that conclusive. For many there remains a shared or collective dimension to their beliefs. Beliefs rarely occur in a vacuum.

There is still in Britain a strong civic or civil dimension to religious life. In part this stems from the particular relationship between the Church of England and the political constitution, however, it is now more broadly based. The role of the churches generally in providing a liturgical and ritual focus on important national or local occasions or at key events must be taken into account. Recent examples include the role of the Anglican and Roman Catholic bishops of Liverpool following the Hillsborough tragedy when 94 football supporters died, and Manchester Cathedral hosting a civic service for the expression of feelings of shock and hope after a terrorist bombing in the city centre. One suspects that there is sometimes a discrepancy between the civic perception of the role of institutional religion and the institutions' own self-understanding, particularly as the latter define their identity in terms of adherence to a specific set of beliefs or doctrines.

Neat conclusions about what is happening are not readily convincing. It is tempting to see believing without belonging as a typical form of Post-Modern behaviour, enabling the individual to select their own personal package of beliefs from the enormous range of options now on offer. Yet this description does not easily fit the reality. In Britain it is more often a case of intellectual inertia where people cannot be bothered to put much mental energy into thinking through their beliefs and would rather settle for what is immediately to hand. In some ways there is a deliberate shying away from choice as individuals prefer to delegate such decisions to a 'higher' authority, be that an institutional church or a particular sect.

Davie is not convinced that describing the evolving patterns of religious belief and practice as Post-Modern is helpful. The particular British habit of believing without belonging seems to be less a self-conscious selection from the various goods on offer and more of a passive fall-back position when there is neither the incentive nor the energy to make a positive decision. Perhaps the classic example of this is the continuing popularity of certain forms of media religion in Britain. Viewing figures remain high but there is a general vagueness about and even indifference towards the doctrinal content that would be of greater concern to the officials of the religious institutions. Within those institutions there is evidence of a narrowing of theological perspective related to both a financial and intellectual retrenchment. Religion in Britain is not disappearing but rather mutating and the exact relationship between cultural and religious change is difficult to define.

Religion as a cultural resource

Another potentially fruitful way of interpreting the role of religion in contemporary Western society is to see it as a cultural resource. The suggestion comes from Beckford, another sociologist of religion who is concerned, like Davie, that sociological models of religious belief and practice need to be brought into line with current notions of cultural and industrial change (9). Like Davie he believes that the institutional framing of religious beliefs is now of less significance. Nevertheless '...religious forms of sentiment, belief and action have survived as relatively autonomous resources' (10). So, for instance, they retain the capacity to symbolize ultimate meaning, infinite power, supreme indignation and sublime compassion. It is perhaps this capacity that explains the civic religion behind the Hillsborough and Manchester examples. Religion can provide both the space and the means for the public expression of deep emotions, either individual or collective. Even in a supposedly secular society such a function remains of value.

I believe that Beckford's idea is suggestive, but requires further research and substantiation. It is not difficult to identify further examples. Perhaps more clarity on the term cultural resource is necessary. One wonders what might not be counted as a cultural resource in the broad sense of something upon which one draws when trying to cope with life. Sport, the arts, the media, close personal relationships could all be cultural resources in this sense. What is to be gained or learnt by placing religion into this category? Nevertheless, I think the idea is worth pursuing.

In what other ways could religion be seen to be a cultural resource? For some clearly, particularly those who attach themselves to a religious institution, it can provide the function of belonging or integrating into a specific group or community. This, despite Davie's comments about the prevalence of believing without belonging, remains a great attraction of more formal religion. It could be argued that, for some, the need to belong is heightened by the sense of rootlessness or alienation engendered in Western societies. Perhaps this is a partial explanation for a growing narrowness or fundamentalism where people strive to hand their freedom over to an external authority that will make all their decisions for them. Overwhelmed by choices and options one could choose to surrender that choice to a religious institution. In which case one is likely to defend the doctrines of that institution with considerable ferocity to compensate for that abrogation of personal responsibility. Once again this is not a particularly new phenomenon.

Another cultural function played by religion is that of legitimating the status quo. Perhaps much civic religion has fitted into this category in the past. In other words, religious beliefs and practices actively support and confirm a mind set that is essential to a particular group or society. This is close to a Marxist interpretation of religion. Religion can be used to help keep certain groups subservient, either because they accept a moral and social hierarchy or because they are prepared to postpone emancipation to an indefinite or eternal future. Whether this form of legitimation is so common now is possibly doubtful, but there are other forms of cultural change that may turn to religion for legitimation. Environmental movements are an obvious example. The gathering of world religions in Assisi in 1986 was organised by the World Wide Fund for Nature in an attempt to forge a lasting alliance between religion and ecology. This has been followed up by further events including the Festival of Faith and the Environment at Canterbury Cathedral in 1989. What is the attraction of such alliances with the world religions? Part of it at least is surely to gain a wider credibility and legitimation for environmental concerns.

Another area into which religion is being increasingly drawn as a cultural resource is that of personal development. This is again a Western idea, originating probably from the human potential movement, but now mutating through its widespread employment by commerce and industry. I am thinking of the use of the Myers-Briggs Personality Indicator, the Belben Self-Perception Inventory and the Enneagram, just the tip of the iceberg in the attempts to understand ourselves that are now a growth industry. Each of these employ some version of a psychological theory then developed into a questionnaire or series of workshops that aim to identify the key personality traits of the person in question. These are often used as pointers towards a person's suitability - or lack of it - for a particular role or function within an organization. This whole area is now beginning to be taken seriously by sociologists (11). The interesting phenomenon is that the very same techniques and language are gaining a hold in both formal and informal religion. People retreat on Myers-Briggs weekends to determine their personal spirituality or their preferred style of worship. This could be seen as one way traffic, cultural developments invading the religious world, but it is more subtle than that. Elements from within religious traditions are resurfacing in the guise and language of personal development and beginning to exercise an influence of their own. We will return to this issue in the chapter on the Self and Post-Modernity.

Finally, religion has the capacity to become a site of resistance. If one examines the role of Liberation Theology, for instance, in Latin America and contextual theologies emerging from other Third World countries, it is clear that local churches and congregations can provide a focus of resistance to oppressive regimes. The events of the late 1980s in Eastern Europe reveal that churches played a role in sheltering and then releasing resistance to Communist regimes. One of the interesting factors is the recent decline in support for institutional religion in some of these countries now that particular battle has been won and political events have moved on. From time to time religion can provide alternative spaces or legitimation for radical social and political movements. It is also possible to identify parallels between radical religious movements and what are called New Social Movements both in terms of structure and content (12). Example of New Social Movements would be feminism, the various environmental groups that have emerged in recent years and people engaged in local community development issues.

Beckford's idea is clearly of value for this discussion. What those inside religious institutions might find difficult is the suggestion that religion either is, or should understand itself as, subordinate to the service of cultural change. That is the perspective of a sociologist of religion, not a theologian. Religions might want to see themselves as more than simply another cultural resource.

The Rise of Fundamentalism

There is little doubt that this is the single most significant feature on the contemporary canvas, not just because of what it represents for the major world religions but for its implications for global politics. One could say that the features examined so far are minor figures tampering with religion close to the frame, whereas the resurgence of fundamentalism is a mountain range dominating the foreground and demanding the attention. The title of a recent book on the subject sums it up succinctly, *The Revenge of God* (13). As hinted at earlier in this chapter what is now beginning to emerge is not a further accommodation between the Enlightenment project and religion but a complete reversal of roles with the latter once again reasserting its dominance. This relates directly to the debate about Post-Modernity as this is seen as conclusive evidence that Modernity is undergoing not just a temporary crisis of confidence but is approaching its nemesis. As Kepel says, fundamentalism represents a 'disillusionment with secularism' (14).

It is not possible to rehearse all the arguments in an introductory chapter, but key features do need to be drawn out. It is often the general experiences of powerlessness and contingency that re-open spaces for religious questions. From the mid-1970s onwards an optimism about human progress based on the supposed capacity to control or restrain both political and natural disruption, has been replaced by a pessimism sometimes shading into fatalism. It is no longer possible for humanity to convince itself that through the application of scientific knowledge or the spread of liberal democracy the world can progress smoothly towards a state of prosperity, security and political equilibrium. The ills of society and of human nature have indeed returned to haunt us. The oil crisis of the early 1970s; a growing awareness of the possibility of an ecological disaster; the re-emergence of militant nationalism in Eastern Europe following the collapse of the Communist bloc; the instability of the Middle East; genocide once again in Africa and so on . All of these suggest to some people a time-bomb ticking away beneath the complacency of the Western world. At least, that is the argument. Given that context it is to be expected that people will search for alternative sources of hope and meaning and see the Enlightenment and Modernity as a dead end.

Even so, it would be dangerous and arrogant to read back into the last three decades a necessary movement of human thought and politics in a particular direction. It was not bound to be like this and we should not assume that events are pre-determined to continue in this fashion. Cultural pessimism is a not unknown phenomenon as humanity approaches the turn of a century, let alone entry into a new millennium. The resurgence of fundamentalism in different religions and in different parts of the world require explanations specific to the particular context. There is no one explanation even though that might have become part of the anti-Enlightenment rhetoric.

For instance, in the case of Islam, it was the aftermath of the Arab-Israeli war of 1973 that triggered the initial revival. A shift in the balance of power on a global scale is part of the picture. Western economies became more aware of their vulnerability to the oil-producing states who, in turn, used their riches to buy themselves a leading role in world affairs. According to Kepel this led to a decade of revolutionary Islam and attempts to seize political power from above, to be succeeded by a very different strategy, a re-Islamization from below (15). The latter requires the reinfiltration of Islamic traditions and beliefs into everyday life through essentially local networks. It could be interpreted as an attempt to recreate identity and meaning in a world that appears hostile and confusing.

This movement has happened not only in Muslim countries, but also within Islamic communities in Western Europe, in each case being partly shaped by the specific economic and political circumstances of that country. There is no one inevitable movement and local factors will continue to influence the forms that fundamentalism will take. A major difference from Muslim countries is that the issues will be worked out in a largely democratic political environment.

The case of the United States is different once again. In the twenty years after the Second World War it was the small fundamentalist groups collaborating with the extreme right who were most actively concerned with politics. The Evangelicals put more emphasis upon the individual and concerned themselves with the family and civil society. The first group had little effect upon the nation as a whole, while the second, spearheaded by such figures as Billy Graham and Oral Roberts, had more of a lasting impact. In recent years the emphasis of the Evangelicals changed to become more overtly and aggressively political and they played a part in the elections of Presidents Carter and Reagan. The fundamentalist movement of the New Christian Right claimed the credit for Reagan's success in both 1980 and 1984 on the basis that they had been able to bring to the polls 2 to 4 million evangelicals who had previously taken little interest in politics. The claim may be overstated, but it clearly illustrates an attempt at re-Christianization from above that was not in evidence a decade earlier.

Since then the emphasis has shifted once again as rifts began to appear between the politicians and the religious groupings. Characterized by the career of Jerry Falwell, the victory over secular humanism has been carried

14

onto the cultural field, utilizing the weapons of the mass media. Falwell began by trying to exercise a direct influence over politicians and policy making but later decided to concentrate his energies on the more informal and cultural level. Influencing the next generation through such institutions as Liberty University, working from the inside, appears to be the chosen way forward. Kepel describes this as Christianizing modernism (16). The internal contradiction in this strategy is that it is the techniques of the very secular humanism that is under attack that are employed in the fight. Does this irrevocably damage the integrity of the message and mean that it is a sophisticated form of self-deception or political manipulation?

A final example that could be offered is that of Jewish fundamentalism, but a similar pattern emerges of an attempt to re-impose religious values from above shifting to a more subtle attempt at grass roots influence, building upon the infiltration of family and civil society. Does any of this pose problems for those beyond the confines of liberal academia in those countries? The answer must be that it does because of the political power that is now being exercised by these religious groupings. They may all be reacting against the wasteland created by reason and Modernity, but they do not share a common vision of what should be the basis of a new world order. The power will rest with their own faith community and culture at the expense of every and any other. There appears no room for compromise or accommodation. One could suggest that the remedy seems more fatal than the disease.

Conclusion

The argument has reached a point where the future appears to be bleak and religion as much a part of the problem as a solution. It is at this stage that a way is required of steering between two extremes. There would seem to be a battle between a form of secular humanism or reason that, carried to its logical conclusion, strips not only the world, but humanity itself of any purpose or meaning. The practical outcome of this could be a species rushing headlong towards its own self-destruction at the mercy of a technology gone out of control. At the other extreme is what is claimed to be a reversal of this brought about by a return to and revival of the universal world views of the major world religions. The problem is that they will be in direct competition with each other and with the weapons of mass destruction at their disposal. This is what is described as being between a rock and a hard place. Surely there must be an alternative?

15

There is indeed a third scenario, not the exclusive property of any one religion, but not unrelated to religions either. To catch a glimpse of it requires first that religious fundamentalism be placed in a wider context. As Giddens has suggested, fundamentalism cannot be restricted to the religious environment (17). Rather, a fundamentalist is 'someone who seeks to defend tradition in the traditional way - in circumstances where that defence has become intrinsically problematic' (18). What is significant about this recent phenomenon is the manner of the defence of the tradition, the fact that it is a reaction against a world of interrogation and dialogue. 'Refusing the discursive engagements which a world of cosmopolitan communication tends to enforce, fundamentalism is protecting a principle as much as a set of particular doctrines' (19).

I believe this highlights the real challenge to both religion and theology. In a world of cosmopolitan communication where positions adopted and held must be defended through critical discourse and dialogue rather than by bland assertion or coercion, can religion be open and self-critical enough to stand the test of interrogation? Those who fear it will not either abandon it totally or retreat into forms of fundamentalism. The third way is more risky and unsettling since it requires that religion open itself to the critical challenge of other discourses. But then, it also means that those other discourses open themselves to the critical challenge of religion. The outcome is certainly unpredictable, but hopefully more creative than the alternative.

I want to describe this as the democratization of religion. I do not mean religious truth and doctrine being put to the vote, but rather that willingness to engage with other ways of understanding humanity and the world. This requires not only more open debate across traditions but also a capacity to be reflexive and self-critical within traditions.

This may sound like one way traffic, the imposition of an alien cultural paradigm derived from the Enlightenment upon the religious dimension. I do not believe this is the case. It could be argued that religions have no choice in fact. Now that people are free to choose which religion they might belong to, or to transfer to another religion, or to combine elements of a number of different ones, the question inevitably arises of how such a choice might be made. What criteria could there be behind such judgements? Remember that this includes choosing to submit oneself to an external authority or tradition. Is such a choice essentially arbitrary, a matter of where one is born or which culture one inhabits, or what one feels like on a particular day? If there were criteria then one could defend both to oneself and others where one stands and why. I believe that this approach will have to develop if religion is to progress beyond the passive background faith described by Davie or not to resort to a form of fundamentalism. I describe this as exercising the critical consciousness in the sphere of religious belief (20).

The other point is that it may be possible for some religions at least to offer a positive contribution to the form and content of the dialogue. So, for instance, some of the resources for the public expression of feelings and hope; the capacity to create spaces and opportunities for the discussion of moral and spiritual values; sites of resistance for the telling of alternative narratives; as ideas for personal and spiritual development. Perhaps these are cultural resources, but does it matter what they are called if they contribute to an essential process?

Finally, there is a growing awareness that what is required if humanity is to avoid the scenario of self-destruction, is the willingness to exercise self-limitation at a personal and collective level. This argument will be further developed in a later chapter. For religions it will mean a tempering of claims to possess the whole truth and therefore of the right to impose that upon others. It will mean the same humility from other scientific and cultural disciplines. It may be that theology can find within itself a resource to justify that self-limitation.

To return to the statement at the start of the chapter: it would seem that religion is alive and well and adapting to cultural change in a variety of ways. Its mutation into forms of fundamentalism is perhaps the most significant and disturbing of these. The central issue here for theology specifically is its relationship with the Enlightenment project as realised in Modernity. Is Post-Modernity a complete reversal and rejection of these or rather a way in which the key questions the Enlightenment raises are kept sharp and active? So far it has been seen as the first of these. The objective is to argue for the second through a more careful assessment of Post-Modernity itself.

2

Theology and Post-Modernity

Modernity and Post-Modernity

Now that religion is securely settled on centre stage it is time to introduce the other major theme in this contemporary drama, Post-Modernity. In the previous chapter there were hints as to the meaning of the term but we are now almost ready to usher Post-Modernity out of the wings and into the full spotlight. However, just before the grand entry it is necessary to introduce more fully the notion of Modernity itself. We can only understand what comes next if we have already grasped what has gone before. This must be particularly true for a term that has the prefix 'Post'. It is the meanings of Modernity that define the scope and content of the debate about Post-Modernity. Within this chronological or evolutionary structure there is also Pre-Modernity and the same comment applies: interpretations of Modernity are the controlling factor.

It is important to be clear on how these terms are being used. They are a shorthand method of drawing attention to certain identifiable developments that are assumed to be characteristic of a particular era. As such they are, inevitably, generalizations and points of detail are always therefore going to be open to dispute. So, for instance, if somebody claims that Modernity began on 14th July 1789 with the Fall of the Bastille and came to an end on 15th February 1946 with the formal dedication of the first computer, we might be inclined to say that they have misunderstood the way the word is used. Yet both could be seen as significant symbolic dates. It needs to be recognized that social theorists and historians are reading back into events a pattern or meaning that has been constructed in retrospect. That makes Post-Modernity a particularly difficult concept to handle as it represents an attempt to describe developments that are still unfolding. One might wonder whether the jury is going to be out on this verdict for another generation or two.

Building upon the ideas formulated in the previous chapter what more is to be said about Modernity? It is clearly a term intended to describe a distinct stage in the historical development of human society. Pre-Modern refers to a time when agricultural production was the dominant feature and human control over the natural environment was limited, to say the least. Close-knit family relationships, enclosed communities, a feudal structure where everybody knew and accepted their place in the social hierarchy and dependence upon a religious view of the world are further features of the Pre-Modern period. With the beginnings of the Industrial Revolution much of this begins to change. Humanity assumes increasingly greater control over the physical environment and a series of technical innovations, mechanized farming and the introduction of machines into the production of cotton for instance, transform both economic and social life. The population begins to shift from the countryside into the towns to work in the factories, themselves now organized by a new entrepreneurial class. Greater social mobility, raised expectations and expanding opportunities for travel and education take their toll of relatively static communities and what remains of the feudal system. Under the weight of these changes traditional cultural practices and religious beliefs come under increasing pressure. As Marx described it: 'All that is solid melts into the air, all that is holy is profaned and man is at last compelled to face with sober senses his real conditions of life and his relations with his kind' (1).

The concentration of population within cities and industrial conurbations begins to take shape, creating the requirement for further technological change and the now familiar cosmopolitan environment for artistic and cultural life. Modernity is not just a series of developments but a radically new situation in which continuous change and development become the norm. Yet there is both threat and promise involved: 'To be modern is to find ourselves in an environment that promises us adventure, power, joy, growth, transformation of ourselves and the world - and, at the same time, that threatens to destroy everything we have, everything we know, everything we are' (2).

As has already been pointed out the intellectual basis for this revolution is a new self confidence built upon the belief in human reason. Reason now becomes the sole reliable means of access to the world. It is through the power of clear and logical thought and the human capacity to observe, analyse and then construct hypotheses and theories that greater control is assumed over the external environment. If there is a problem to be solved or an obstacle to be overcome then switch reason on in the brain and the solution will be found. Every aspect of reality is deemed to be susceptible to this reasoning process to the point where experiences that cannot be fitted into this framework are treated with suspicion or incredulity. So religious experiences can find no home within this increasingly narrow and hostile environment and are categorised as either superstition or myth. The success of reason in the field of scientific and technological innovation is taken as a sign that it will have similar success in other fields. From now on all the possible tunes have to be played in this one particular key.

Truth is no longer the prerogative of existing traditions and institutions but rather that which is to be shaped from the cauldron of philosophical and scientific exploration. The future is open; ways of life can be changed and new relationships forged. Instead of a world determined by an external force - either God or nature - there is a world to be determined through human effort, intelligence and skill. The old certainties are to be swept away for ever to be replaced by constantly shifting and provisional conclusions. It is not so much a matter of replacing one god by another but of emptying out the place where God used to be and leaving it knowingly and deliberately unoccupied. The hypothesis of God is no longer required. Explanations of life derive from elsewhere.

Another consequence of this process of modernization is that areas of life that were previously integrated become increasingly split apart and specialized. The explosion of knowledge and the growth of working functions initiated by an industrial society require this differentiation of skills and expertise. Lawyers, teachers, engineers, scientists, managers, builders, assembly line workers and the like become distinct and specialized spheres each needing their own approaches and understandings. Bureaucracy and administration take on a vital servicing role. The result of this is that religion, instead of being the train in which everybody travels, becomes just one carriage among many - often the one tagged on at the end because nobody else knows what to do with it. The officials of religious institutions start to lose their status and influence as society begins to progress quite happily without the insights and the guidance of faith and social functions are taken on by a series of new professionals, teachers, health care and social workers.

All of this is probably reasonably familiar. It is essentially the story of how we got to be where we are now. The modern world founded upon science and technology, big business and bureaucracy relying upon rapid travel and communications, in the West being organized into some form of capitalism and democracy and moving towards a complex and expanding global economy. What are often not so explicit, but nevertheless vital for an understanding of Post-Modernity, are the underlying intellectual assumptions of

Modernity. These could be summed-up by the phrase 'Big is Beautiful'. This could be applied to ideas, theories, projects, organizations, ambitions and even buildings. It is the big ideas that become the focus for the philosophical attack launched by Post-Modernity.

There is a technical term for these big ideas; they are called either Grand Narratives or metanarratives. I would describe them as universal world views. In other words they are interpretive frameworks or ways of understanding the world that are claimed to have a truth or validity that crosses all spatial and temporal boundaries. They are true for all people, at all times and in all places. They are true yesterday, today and forever. So, for instance, Marxism and Christianity are both Grand Narratives to the extent that they claim a universal validity. Behind Modernity lies a Grand Narrative, that of the triumph of human reason, that through the application of science and technology humanity can achieve mastery over the natural world and create a prosperous and peaceful global society.

There is an increasingly strongly held belief that human history is moving inexorably towards a particular form of society. According to this theory of social evolution, once the forces of myth and superstition associated with religion had been driven from the field, the capacity of humans to work life out for themselves would yield a rationally ordered and thus peaceful world. Religion seen as irrational prejudice was believed to be the major source of conflict and thus the stumbling block to real progress. Reason would spell agreement on the best and most profitable ways of organizing economic and social life. The way forward would be a one-way march towards a more affluent world. This is the Grand Narrative of the Enlightenment that inspired the successive waves of industrialization and has brought us to where we are now.

There are other ways of describing this particular big idea. What we all have in common, what unites us as human beings, are our powers of reasoning. Contrast this with the Christian Grand Narrative that would say that what unites human beings is that we are all children of God, unique members of Creation. Modernity also assumes that there is a potentially identifiable rational structure to the natural world, hence its susceptibility to scientific exploration and explanation. There is an order to life that is to be discovered by the exercise of our rational and critical faculties. So there are theories and structures that can account for everything of significance; everything can be brought together under the same ideas and categories. Modernity assumes an underlying identity or commonality of human life and meaning across all traditions and cultural boundaries. As commented earlier, it is the tradition to end all other traditions; it claims to swallow everything up and create a new unity. It is these central claims and assumptions that are at the heart of the philosophical criticisms that are placed under the heading of Post-Modernity.

At this stage of the discussion I offer one key point about Post-Modernity without further elaboration. One of the philosophers responsible for the whole debate has described Post-Modernity as 'incredulity towards metanarratives' (3). In other words all big ideas, all Grand Narratives or universal world views, including that of the Enlightenment, are now under suspicion. The very attempt to establish a metanarrative of any description is to be treated with the utmost caution. The reasons for this will be offered in due course. For the moment suffice it to say that Grand Narratives assume too much and claim too much and, in so doing, oppress and marginalize those who cannot be contained within such universal categories. No one big idea can possibly encapsulate all that can be thought or written or that is of significance for humanity. So, put crudely, small becomes beautiful once again.

If Pre-Modernity is the period when what is true is externally determined - by either nature or tradition - then Modernity is the era during which truth is determined internally, by human beings exercising their powers of reasoning. Post-Modernity becomes the time when truth is indeterminate, when there are no longer any trustworthy criteria for making such judgements. Order is undermined by chaos; the supposedly rational by the irrational. One further comment before pressing further into the subject. Is this a way of describing what is actually happening, or is it social theorists and philosophers prescribing what ought to happen? This question becomes critical as Post-Modernity takes centre stage.

Post-Modernity

It has already been suggested that the prefix 'Post' creates problems for it is a judgement made while events are still unfolding. Is there not a danger of deciding too soon exactly what is going on rather than waiting for a period of time to elapse? But this is not the only difficulty engendered by the prefix. Does it mean that Modernity is decisively and definitively over? If it does there are further questions. Has Modernity been reversed, overcome, undermined and overturned, the clock somehow turned back to before the Industrial Revolution? Or does it suggest that human society has progressed to a further stage, building upon Modernity but moving beyond it? There are no clear answers to these questions within what is now a wide-ranging and complex body of literature on the subject. There are elements of both an anti-modernism or rejection of Modernity and a new modernism in the sense of a going beyond. Theology, as will be illustrated in due course, is inclined to steer towards anti-modernism, particularly where it perceives the Enlightenment as a major threat.

However, it is necessary now to give some attention to the varied strands that make up the subject matter of Post-Modernity. I am going to draw two distinctions that will assist this process. First, I want to separate the philosophical arguments about the breakdown of Grand Narratives from the specifically cultural aspects of Post-Modernity. This section will offer a review of the cultural as a background to the philosophical, but it is the latter that form the focus for this book. Second, I want to keep in mind the difference between description and prescription. So, does Post-Modernity merely describe what already exists, in which case judgements can be made about its accuracy, or does it embody certain values and thus begin to prescribe the way things should be? It is easy to slip from the first into the second without realizing it and discussions about Post-Modernity seem particularly prone to this difficulty. With those distinctions in mind let us turn the spotlight on Post-Modernity.

Self-Identity

If a figure were now to appear on the stage it might well be that of the global tourist or perhaps the international business executive. Both of these characters are constantly on the move, only staying in one place long enough to consume the local scenery or to strike another deal. Then on to the next place of interest or set of potential clients, changing clothes, moods and even personalities en route in order to adapt to the next situation.

The argument is that the Self has moved through those stages of being externally determined in Pre-Modernity, internally determined in Modernity and is now radically undetermined in Post-Modernity. So, in the good old days everybody knew who they were because identity was predetermined by their social roles and membership of a family, clan or tribe. Identity crises were still a thing of the future simply because there were no questions about who one was; it was given in advance. In Modernity however, identity becomes more mobile, flexible and subject to change. Social roles are still important, but individuals are more likely to be called upon to play a range of different ones, as family member, part of a workforce, volunteer and these will change over time. Identity does become an issue because it is more self-consciously constructed, but within certain recognizable parameters. There is a limit to what one can become, even though the guidelines of say religion or class carry less conviction. In Post-Modernity there are supposedly no limits or guidelines; the field of self-creation and re-creation is radically open, thus the figures of Michael Jackson and Madonna tailored to the market but open to reconstruction at a moment's notice. There are no good reasons why one should become or remain one specific thing rather than anything else. There is no fixed identity, merely a flitting from one to another much as one might switch through or surf the channels with a T.V. control. In fact it is very much like that, for the options are probably presented by the media or by the shapers of consumer culture. Pick-and-mix personality is now on offer.

This may sound extreme but one can recognize elements of truth in it. Life and lifestyle options have increased, even if they are often determined by commercial interests. But of course the options are only available to those with adequate access to financial resources, so there is an inherent elitism in operation. In some parts of the world Pre-Modernity may still seem closer to reality - no choices, merely survival. So, is this tourist an accurate portrayal or just itself another media creation?

Culture

If we turn now to a rather different field, that of architecture, a similar process can be identified. The term 'Post-Modern' made its first serious appearance in architectural studies back in the 1970s. 'Some observers even fix the advent of the postmodern architectural age at 3.32p.m. on July 15th 1972, when that symbol of modernist ideals, the Pruitt-Igoe low-income housing project was demolished by the city of St Louis' (4). For some this particular project embodied the ideals and hopes of a rational and ordered approach to planning and design and the epitome of social engineering. Its failure to achieve a calm and stable living environment undermined these hopes.

The Post-Modern means the end of standardized, functional and essentially boring buildings and the introduction of greater flexibility and a deliberate mixing of different styles, often in the service of consumer attraction. Theme restaurants, theme malls and theme parks are all examples of this. Out are the faceless housing estates, huge hospitals, office complexes and tower blocks of the 1950s and 1960s, to be replaced by a consideration of social context and local history. Design and development are meant to be on a more human scale. A new, more subtle and differentiated use of space is characteristic of Post-Modernity. Both the content of architecture and the forms in which it is now expressed emphasize difference and a reaction against the large scale unifying forces of Modernity. Again, to what extent this is an accurate picture or whether it overplays the elements of freedom and flexibility must remain an open question.

In the arts more generally Post-Modernity is used to describe this same deliberate breaking up of established forms and practices and the advent of a random and often ironic mixing up of styles. The division between high and low culture, so beloved of a previous generation of cultural critics, is under attack on the grounds that it perpetuates an elitist approach to art and restricts the scope for creative development. Classical music is now used regularly in commercials. Pop stars appear alongside classical artists at fund-raising concerts. Pavarroti and Domingo abandon the opera houses to bring snippets of culture to the masses at more 'secular' venues, earning themselves 1 million dollars a night into the bargain. Anything goes now - or so it would seem. The purists amongst us may wriggle uncomfortably in our seats but the reality is that, if somebody can make some money out of it, it will happen, however bizarre or unlikely. Culture is just another product, to be packaged, marketed and sold to the highest bidder.

The Business World

One final glimpse at the tourist before we move on to consider why any of this should be of interest to theology. He - or she - has a lap-top computer and can tap into the World Wide Web at a moment's notice to respond to the next invitation. Information Technology is an inescapable part of the picture because it increases flexibility, speed of response and the exchange of information. It allows people to operate from anywhere at any time. This will enhance the capacity of commerce and industry to flatten hierarchies within organizations, subcontract more functions and reduce its permanent overheads to a central core of staff - at least, this is the argument, the evidence for this is perhaps somewhat limited. The days of huge plants, heavily Unionized labour-intensive industry probably located in the same space since the Industrial Revolution appear to be numbered. Instead we are entering a contract culture where people can be expected to have a portfolio of careers and where qualifications are increasingly transferable across previously impermeable boundaries. That is the hype at least, to make it sound good for employees. The truth is that it is probably more advantageous for employers, a way of cutting down on permanent labour costs. However, the term Post-Modern is applied to this because it displays the same fragmentation, increased choice and radical indeterminacy. Where it is all leading nobody can really be sure, but the pace of change is certainly accelerating.

In each of these different fields it is possible to recognize most of these changes that are labelled as Post-Modern. However, attracting and exciting though they may appear to be, it is not convincing to argue that they represent the whole picture. They are trends, possibilities perhaps, but if they are inherently unstable their long-term effects may yet prove to be ephemeral. In many respects they appear to be just a reaction against what has gone before - the big ideas and structures of Modernity. But both are themselves still very much in evidence and are far from conceding the game. It would seem premature to judge the final outcome at this early stage. Yet, for those with a vested interest in seeing the back of Modernity there is a temptation to do just that. The links between theology and Post-Modernity now need to be clearly brought to the surface.

Theology and Post-Modernity

Why does theology have a stake in the debates about Post-Modernity? I am going to suggest five reasons for its interest in this subject. First, Post-Modernity represents a critique of the myth of progress encapsulated in the Enlightenment project and put into practice in Modernity. Second, and closely related to that, it challenges and even undermines the significance of both reason and science. Third, its descriptions of the Self raise challenges for a Christian understanding of human nature. Fourth, Post-Modernity has a concern for those who are marginalized, who do not fit neatly into the categories of modern society. Lastly it provides the basis for a critical commentary on contemporary culture and offers a contribution to understandings of power. The objective at this stage is not to enter into detailed argument as these themes will form the subject matter of later chapters but merely to establish that theology does engage Post-Modernity at these strategic points.

The Critique of the Grand Narrative

The big idea or Grand Narrative behind Modernity is that humanity is now on an upward path towards peace and prosperity, essentially without reference to God or to the Christian faith. This is the story to end all stories; the victory of capitalism and liberal democracy across the world. Although this sounds increasingly like a dated example of cultural arrogance and Western imperialism, the idea is far from dead. In recent years the debate has been re-opened by the American scholar Fukuyama in a provocative article and subsequent book proclaiming the end of history (5). By this he means that it is difficult to see a viable long-term alternative to the spread of liberal democracy and capitalism across the globe. His argument has been readily dismissed as out of step with the current pessimism about the future, but it does have some force. We have to ask ourselves what alternative forms of economic and political organization we are seriously prepared to work towards or might envisage.

Nevertheless, this appears to be exactly the Grand Narrative that Post-Modernity claims to have debunked. The hopes placed on human reason and the continuous improvement associated with Modernity have backfired. In a recent book on the subject of Post-Modernity the Canadian theologians J. Richard Middleton and Brian J. Walsh state why this is good news for Christianity.

'On the most ultimate level we need to confess that the cultural pain and confusion of postmodern culture is the doing of God. Just as God confused the speech of the tower builders and scattered the tower dwellers in Genesis 11. 7-8, so He has brought judgement upon the arrogant culture of modernity' (6).

Strong stuff, but echoing a biblical theme that is now frequently used in this discussion; the tower of Babel.

There is certainly an enticing fit between that biblical story and the debate about the collapse of Modernity. In both stories human beings attempt to establish control over the world and to answer all the important questions without reference to God. Human autonomy is at the heart of both accounts. In the biblical version God decides that humanity is getting above itself, trying to become too much like him, and so he confounds their speech so that they are no longer able to communicate with each other. The resulting confusion and distress sound like the fragmentation of individual identity, culture and society described by Post-Modernity. Humanity gets too big for itself so God takes revenge, and causes utter confusion, thus putting humanity back in its place.

Modernity is a Grand Narrative gone wrong, hence the catalogue of disasters in recent years and the decades of genocide that seem to constitute the Twentieth Century, Rwanda, Cambodia and the ethnic cleansing in Bosnia being some of the most recent examples. Even more than that it is difficult to imagine any theory of world history that could carry conviction at the moment. As Lesslie Newbigin says 'In the closing decades of this century it is difficult to find Europeans who have any belief in a significant future which is worth working for and investing in' (7). Thus Christianity and Post-Modernity become equated with an extreme cultural pessimism.

There is of course an immediate problem here. Post-Modernity is incredulity towards all Grand Narratives, not just that of the Enlightenment. Most theologians who welcome the undermining of the Enlightenment do so because they want to replace it with the Christian story - itself a Grand Narrative according to the accepted description. There is, to say the least, an inconsistency here. The analogy with the tower of Babel and its reversal at Pentecost breaks down at this point. For Post-Modernity there can be no restoration of communication, no re-unifying language. The space for God remains unoccupied. For Christianity however there is Pentecost and thus the hope of a world made whole again.

Reason and Science

Following on from this is the relativization of the Enlightenment project wrought by Post-Modernity. In other words, it is revealed as just one tradition amongst others, one more big story alongside all the rest. It is an account of human life offered by a particular culture at a particular time and ignoring alternative contemporaneous accounts. It is the story of Western capitalist liberal democracy told as if it applied to everyone. Unless Fukuyama is proved correct and a global society emerges along these lines such a universal claim is unacceptable. For the American theologian David Tracy:

'Modernity...has become that which it most opposed and feared - one more tradition. The honest desperation of many modern secular thinkers reveals the pathos of liberalism in our period: the forces for emancipation set loose by the Enlightenment and the great modern revolutions may end trapped in a purely technical notion of reason from which there seems no honourable exit' (8).

Reason, particularly through its manifestation in science had apparently replaced religion; it had taken over the whole train and relegated religion to the guard's van. It too has been relegated in turn, having failed to produce a world of peace and prosperity. This appears to face theology with two options. It can either try to re-stake Christianity's claims as the only universally valid world view, discounting reason and science along the way, or it can works out ways of standing alongside them as just another debunked tradition. For Stanley Hauerwas the temptation is too great.

'...it is my contention that Christians would be ill-advised to try to rescue the liberal project either in its epistemological or political form. The very terms necessary for that project cannot help rendering the church's challenge to the false universalism of the Enlightenment impotent' (9).

The only way forward is thus to state that salvation can come only through the church. As I have said I am not attempting to do justice to the depth of these arguments at this stage, but just to establish that theology has a stake in these debates. A fuller consideration of some of the views expressed is reserved for later.

Self-Identity

The picture of the person painted by Post-Modernity has to be both disturbing and challenging for theology. The scenario where apparently anything goes and individuals are free to create and re-create themselves as they go along without reference to any external guidelines or criteria would seem to undermine a Christian understanding of the self. This radical indeterminacy of self-construction has been helpfully described by the Post-Modern social theorist Bauman. He suggests that we are all now either vagabonds or tourists (10). A vagabond is a pilgrim without a destination, always on the move and engaged in a journey but without any clear sense of direction or any specific goal. Hence also the tourist, consuming different identities or ways of being and switching from one to another and back again as boredom or frustration set in. What hope can there be for stable relationships or coherent communities if human life is so fragmented and random?

This could be seen as autonomy taken to its extreme. Humans have the freedom to become anyone they wish to be, regardless of the consequences for others. However, that is only one side of the picture portrayed by the Post-Modern thinkers. This apparent freedom turns out to be more an illusion than a reality. The problem, as hinted earlier, is that the options for self identity are invariably those offered or determined by the culture industry. For instance, what one wears is deemed to be a key factor in the image of oneself to be created or projected. Yet much of this is dictated by those who create and manipulate contemporary fashion and that, as we all know, is about making money. The same applies to all other consumer items that are part of one's image - cars, houses, holidays, computers and so on. So the freedom to create oneself is more apparent than real. The possibilities and the boundaries are still externally determined.

Some of the Post-Modern writers interpret this as the overturning of autonomy and the potential destruction of human agency (11). Rather than objects existing for the benefit of humans, the humans have begun to serve the existence of the objects. Children become video fodder as parents become obsessed with filming every significant moment of their lives. Rather than relating directly to their child a parent will retreat behind the the video recorder and watch the offspring consume the latest toy or 'play' in the carefully designed theme park. It is as if we exist for Disneyworld, not the other way round.

Even when it comes to the more serious business of life, the spheres of commerce, politics or social welfare, there is a view that the languages or discourses of each of these areas possess a power over human agency. It is almost as if we become trapped within the words and ideas that we use and fail to exercise any real freedom or critical thought. All human activity is merely a mask of power, sometimes that of a particular group trying to manipulate or control, sometimes that of the language itself determining human thought and action. Whether this is an entirely accurate interpretation of what the Post-Modern writers are saying will be investigated more fully in a later chapter. The point for the moment is that this view is expressed by theologians such as Anthony Thiselton :' the postmodern self perceives itself as having lost control as active agent, and as having been transformed into a passive victim of competing groups. Everyone seems to be at the mercy of someone else's vested interests for power' (12).

If this is the case, then theology might want to respond by re-asserting a view of human agency both given and directed by God. In other words, humans are pilgrims after all, gaining their value as unique members of God's creation and finding a purpose and direction for life through being co-creators with God. This could be seen as the only way of combatting the loss of freedom that results from the indeterminacy encouraged by Post-Modernity.

Difference and the Other

The fourth major area where theology appears to share some common ground with Post-Modernity is the latter's concern for the marginalized.

A vital objection to any Grand Narrative is that it excludes all those who do not conform to its accounts of reality. Various groups could be said to have been pushed to the edges of Modernity, given its Western, male, heterosexual and capitalist bias. For instance, those of other races and cultures who are on the outside of the system and particularly women and those who might be deemed non-productive but are on the inside of it. It could be argued that the most significant social changes of recent decades have happened as a result of such marginalized groups struggling to assert their rights and separate identity against the over-arching power of those who benefit from and control Western capitalism. The feminist movement is the obvious example (13).

The problem with the Enlightenment view is that, once again, it claims too much. If what makes us all human or establishes our common identity is our power of reasoning as defined in a particular way, then anybody who does not think or reason in that way is labelled irrational and excluded from power and participation. How often have women been dismissed as emotional or irrational and therefore denied access to the political or economic processes? Members of other cultures who do not happen to share the Protestant work ethic are branded as lazy or irresponsible and thus not entrusted with significant responsibility. There is still a stigma attached to unemployment, even when it is involuntary. Those with various disabilities are prevented from participating in certain activities because the majority cannot be bothered to make the necessary adjustments.

The picture is clear. Much has improved over recent years as a result of the raising of awareness of these sort of issues. Is this Modernity making some necessary adjustments and correcting some of its inadequacies or do these movements represent a more radical questioning of its approaches and assumptions? Whichever, there is certainly a case to be made that Christianity has traditionally expressed a concern for the excluded and the marginalized. Its own record is admittedly patchy, particularly in countries where it is closely identified with the political establishment but, as suggested in the first chapter, churches often become a focus of resistance or a safe haven for those who are perceived as outsiders. Thus if Post-Modernity in any way champions the underdog one might expect theology to express a level of solidarity.

Culture and Power

Finally then the critique of contemporary culture. From the descriptions earlier in the chapter it will be seen that Post-Modernity has much to say about recent movements in art, architecture and music as well as about the fields of commerce and industry. These could be viewed as a valuable resource for theology as it attempts to come to terms with and analyse changing patterns in society. The exact relationship between Gospel and culture is a live issue, particularly for those theologians who see Post-Modernity as a potential ally. Can Christianity distance itself enough to offer a prophetic voice or is it so bound up now with the myths and values of the age that it has nothing distinctive to say? This is a permanent tension for theology. The current position is probably more ambiguous than is often acknowledged. American Evangelists utilize modern technology to communicate their message and religious T.V. programmes reach a wider audience than local churches. Does this compromise the content of the teaching and mean that Christianity has already conceded too much ground to Modernity? The alternative might be to risk losing touch with contemporary life and to abandon credible communication of any kind.

As suggested earlier, the Post-Modern interpretations of culture should not be accepted uncritically. They describe part of what is happening but do not give the whole picture. Theology needs to be particularly wary of areas where the commentators slip from describing to prescribing. There is much in the use of the media and Information Technology that Christianity might want to remain critical of, notably the free play of images and access to material that could degrade or corrupt.

Beneath each of the foregoing areas rest questions of power; the power of one group to impose interpretations or Grand Narratives upon others; the power of those at the centre to suppress others at the margins; the power of big business to exploit the latest technological advances at the expense of workers or consumers. It could be argued that Post-Modernity has provided a more subtle analysis of power and helped to make its operation more visible. This analysis could be applied to theology itself and indeed to all religious institutions. Who is excluded and why? Thus it could form part of an internal critique as well as being applied to the surrounding culture.

Whether all these possible links between theology and Post-Modernity can be so straightforwardly understood will be discussed in later chapters. For the moment it can be said that there are clear points of contact. If Modernity is about to expire Christianity may want to be in at the death. If it is merely developing further Christianity will still need to reconsider its own self-understanding.

3

Modernity on Trial

The story so far is this. The study of religion is of increasing interest to the academic world and indeed more generally as beliefs and practices continue to adapt to social change. A major way in which these social changes are currently described is as a movement from Modernity to Post-Modernity. Five significant areas of common concern between theology and Post-Modernity have now been identified. However, in what might be termed the trial of Modernity the key philosophers normally associated with the case for the prosecution have yet to be called to the witness box. It is also important to give a hearing to two major thinkers who offer an alternative interpretation of these social changes. These will be defence witnesses.

Chapter Three will introduce these contributors to the debate. However, as their work is complex and wide-ranging it is necessary to limit the scope of the discussion. As the specific focus of the book is the relationship between theology and Post-Modernity I will continue to centre the discussion around the themes isolated in the last chapter. This approach is inevitably schematic but far from arbitrary. While it is the case that each of these philosophers has painted on a broader canvas, it will also become clear that they have given significant attention to at least one of these major themes. The objective at this stage is still to lay out the territory, not to engage in more critical discussion. This will follow in the later chapters.

The chapter will be divided into the following headings. The breakdown of Grand Narratives and the work of J-F. Lyotard. The changing view of reason and science and the particular contribution of Richard Rorty. Understandings of the self in Post-Modernity and the writings of Michel Foucault and Jean Baudrillard. Concern for difference and the marginalized linked to a discussion of Jacques Derrida. These will be followed by an introduction to the alternative interpretation of social change in the work of Anthony Giddens and Jürgen Habermas.

One hint before these witnesses take the stand. It is reasonably safe to say that every original thinker is motivated or driven by a central issue or question. Sometimes there may be a number of these, but the point remains valid. To begin to understand their work one needs to become aware of the central question or questions that each has been trying to answer. Only then do the pieces of the jigsaw puzzle start to fall into place. Confusion sets in when others approach their work with different questions and mistakenly assume that the concerns are the same. Ideas are then appropriated and sometimes misappropriated, often being distorted in the process. This is a particular warning for theology and especially for those theologians who approach the subject of Post-Modernity with their own agenda, notably in anticipation of the demise of Modernity. In the desert of Modernity are these philosophers offering an oasis where theology can, once again, flourish in safety, or is Post-Modernity a mirage born out of wishful thinking?

J-F. Lyotard and the Breakdown of Grand Narratives

Lyotard was born in Versailles in 1924 and studied philosophy and literature at the Sorbonne. His early written work in the 1940s and 1950s centred on political themes. He taught in Algeria just before war broke out there and this experience seems to have contributed to his increasingly radical political stance. On returning to France he became involved with the French anti-war movement. Philosophically he developed a critique of Marxist theory, which he felt no longer adequate to describe the contemporary world. As his political views shifted away from more direct involvement so he moved into an academic career becoming a lecturer at Nanterre University. However, he was still in evidence during the May 1968 student protests - a significant date that will turn up again in this chapter. In the early 1970s he became a philosophy professor at Vincennes University where he has been a popular teacher and written many of his best known works. The book that is often seen as the starting point of the Post-Modernity debate, 'The Postmodern Condition' (1) was published in 1979 and was in fact a work commissioned by the Province of Quebec on the topic of knowledge. It was in this that Lyotard brought into question the Grand Narrative of the Enlightenment.

I think it is important to begin with some brief biographical details of each of these thinkers so that we can gain a sense of where they are coming from. For Lyotard we can see that his early political involvements and his search for a theory beyond Marxism represent a concern for justice. There is also an interest in knowledge as his academic career progresses and a particular concern for the ways in which knowledge has been determined by the big story or Grand Narrative of the Enlightenment. The two concerns are intimately connected. How can there be justice for those who do not fit into the categories and schemes of the Enlightenment? What is to be done for those who are excluded from the normal political processes? To what extent are 'truth' and 'knowledge' merely the result of a very particular view of the world that has been claiming too much for itself?

As one would expect of a thinker of this calibre there are significant shifts and developments in his work. However, the battle between the big, over-arching and all-inclusive theories and stories and the small,subversive and individual accounts remains a constant and is fought out on a number of different fronts. Before 'The Postmodern Condition' was published Lyotard attempted to identify sites of resistance in the visual and the sensual. He tried to oppose the visual to the dominance of words in Western culture, and the sensual to the dominance of the purely intellectual. Both, he believed, could be challenged and undermined by the power of desire, an intensity and strength of feeling that cannot be contained within a rationalist straitjacket. Lyotard describes the heroes of this rebellion:

'Here are the 'men of profusion', the 'masters' of today: marginals, experimental painters, pop, hippies and yippies, parasites, madmen, binned loonies. One hour of their lives offers more intensity and less intention than three hundred thousand words of a professional philosopher' (2).

This somewhat romantic idea of the subversive role of an intensity of feeling is then abandoned as Lyotard shifts the battleground to the more concrete territory of language and theory. Yet the basic intention remains the same, to establish political justice for those who are excluded by the rationalism of the Enlightenment project. So the targets of his attack become the languages, discourses (I will offer a technical definition of 'Discourse' in the section on Foucault), bodies of knowledge and theories that claim to dominate and determine what is accepted as truth and knowledge. For instance, masculine discourse needs to be subverted by feminism and Lyotard calls for a patchwork of minority discourses - ways of speaking about important things differently.

The basis upon which Lyotard launches his attack is that all these dominant ways of talking are in fact narratives, stories told about the way things are rather than incontrovertible theories built upon empirical evidence. As such, none of them can claim to be the last word on human history, grounding all other ways of understanding the world. Any notion of a theory that might ground or provide a foundation for other interpretations is brought into question. There are thus no privileged narratives, immune from criticism or holding sway over all other possible alternatives. Claims to universal truth or to absolute criteria of judgement must be questioned and justice can only be local, multiple and provisional, always subject to contestation and transformation. Big is ugly, small is beautiful. Each case has to be judged according to its merits and then these judgements can only be made from within a specific context. There is no overall rational framework that provides means of making those judgements at all times and in all places. So there is a plurality and multiplicity of narratives and discourses and no one of them can be attributed with universal validity.

An important comment at this juncture. Lyotard does not offer an analysis of Modernity now become Post-Modernity. His is a more abstract discussion on the conditions of knowledge rather than a fully developed social theory. There is no description of Post-Modernity as such but rather a critique of all narratives that claim too much, a philosophical discussion based on his concern for political justice. This will need to be registered in the assessment of the importance of these ideas for theology. In his later writing Lyotard himself questions the periodization suggested by the term Post-Modernity and argues that neither Modernity nor Post-Modernity can be defined as clearly circumscribed historical entities (3).

Lyotard's later work becomes, if anything, even more abstract and focusses on the philosophy of Kant, perhaps surprisingly given that the latter is often regarded as the Enlightenment rationalist philosopher. However, his essential concern remains the same: that which cannot be captured or described by the dominant narrative of the Enlightenment, as potentially pointed to by what Kant had called the aesthetics of the sublime. This is not of direct relevance to the theological discussion but it is important just to note as it is consistent with the general direction of Lyotard's work. For the moment it is clear that caution must be exercised in the examination of this particular thinker. While on the witness stand his main preoccupation is with justice and the ways in which forms of truth and knowledge hamper justice being done. Whether this feeds directly into the theological interest in Post-Modernity we will return to in the next chapter.

Richard Rorty, reason and science

Richard Rorty is an American philosopher who stands broadly within the pragmatist tradition, the most famous previous exponents of which have been William James and John Dewey. This results in a very particular slant to his work that will be identified in a moment. Rorty's contribution to the Post-Modernity debate is, superficially at least, encouraging to the anti-Enlightenment lobby within theology. There is sometimes a tendency to subsume the other Post-Modern writers under the Rorty banner whereas there are in fact significant differences between the various philosophers.

Rorty was born in New York City in 1931, educated at Berkeley and Yale and gained his doctorate of philosophy from the latter in 1956. His first important book 'Philosophy and the Mirror of Nature' (4) appeared in 1979, the same year as Lyotard's 'The Postmodern Condition'. Since 1982 Rorty has taught at the University of Virginia.

In the opening pages of 'Philosophy and the Mirror of Nature' (5) Rorty suggests that Dewey, Heidegger and Wittgenstein are the three most important philosophers of the Twentieth Century. His reason for doing so is that each of them has exercised a therapeutic role in the field of philosophy by showing that certain traditional debates are no longer worth bothering with. Like Dewey, Rorty expresses a strong commitment to liberal democracy and the need to construct communities that are both tolerant and concerned about civic virtue. In other words, his major aim is to break down the boundaries between different forms of life by showing that the differences between them are not as hard and fast as had been imagined. Their big stories or Grand Narratives are cut down to size and can no longer be interpreted as providing a foundation for life that is secure and incontrovertible.

Liberal democracy and the civilized lifestyle that goes with it will flourish best in an environment where nobody takes their own ideas and perspectives too seriously and is prepared to see them as just another set of stories that we tell about ourselves and the world. The role of the philosopher is that of a sort of amateur cultural critic, chiding and poking fun at the pretensions of colleagues who believe they are engaged in a more serious activity - solving the problems of the universe or whatever. We see parallels in this with Lyotard's objectives to cut the Grand Narrative of the Enlightenment down to size, although Rorty's political starting point is quite different. He is carrying on the pragmatist commitment to liberal democracy through the attack on grand theories that claim to provide firm intellectual foundations.

It is from this background that Rorty launches his critique of science and reason that has aroused the interest of some theologians (6). Whether they would share his attraction to the American form of liberal democracy is perhaps a rather different matter. How does Rorty approach the pretensions of science to have provided a foundation for our understanding of the world?

The popular view of science is that it offers hard, objective truth, a direct access to a reality 'out there'. Rationality, objectivity and truth are terms frequently used in the context of scientific explanation. We establish objective truth by using our powers of reasoning and identifying our ideas and theories with the real external world through a process of observation and analysis. Within philosophy this is described as a realist viewpoint, built upon the correspondence theory of truth. Our ideas correspond in some way to an external reality to which we have direct access through our senses. It is this supposed privileged access to reality leading to its application in scientific criteria and methods of operation that some see as having undermined a religious interpretation of the world. The credibility of some key aspects of Christianity, for instance, is undermined by scientific research. Miracles are an impossibility because they contravene the laws of science. The Resurrection likewise falls on the same count. Science tells us that such things can just not happen so Christianity must be pure fairy story.

What Rorty does is to take apart the correspondence theory of truth. The common sense view that truth is the correspondence between our words and an external reality is replaced by the notion that truth is what it is good for us to believe. The justification for the first part of the argument is that language and the outside world are just different sorts of things so it is impossible to know in what sense they could be the same or correspond. The replacement is a version of what is known as the consensus theory of truth. Truth is actually no more than a particular group of people at a particular time agreeing on what is to be known as true. This theory is often criticized on the grounds that it merely baptizes the status quo, allowing no scope for new ideas or for external criticism. However, despite the fact that Rorty reduces truth to solidarity between people, he argues that it is always possible for somebody to come up with a better idea, so truth can be changed or extended. Rorty, with his support for democracy and pluralism, does not envisage enclosed communities but rather people constantly engaged in the 'ongoing conversation of mankind' (7).

It follows from this that an alternative understanding of rationality is also required. Within the scientific paradigm it has come to mean applying criteria and making decisions and judgements in an ordered and consistent way. Being rational means using a method that is deemed valid and appropriate in all circumstances. The problem with this is that it does not capture what many research scientists do in practice. It leaves out of the account the exercise of intuition, the leaps of the imagination, the spontaneous and sometimes random ways in which theories are devised. It is a reductionist view of science that describes a process that is more neat, controlled and orderly than is often the case. We note that there is, within the philosophy of science, a view that attributes advances in knowledge as much to the influences of propaganda, political pressure and personal rivalry as to objective and ordered research (8). It also needs to be said that there appears to be common ground here with Lyotard's concern for that which does not neatly fit the Enlightenment description of reality.

Rorty wants to redefine rational as meaning civilized (9). By this he means an agreement within a culture to operate with tolerance, a respect for the opinions of others, a willingness to listen and to rely on persuasion rather than force. Being rational requires discussing any topic in a way that eschews dogmatism, defensiveness and righteous indignation. The idea that there are historical and universal procedures that constitute rationality and are employed in scientific research and debate must be abandoned.

In Lyotardian terms science cannot be a privileged narrative or discourse. It is just one way that humans have devised for describing the world. Thus the claims of Enlightenment reason underlying Modernity and the scientific enterprise are thoroughly relativized - along with those of all other potential Grand Narratives. So how do the different views of reality that humans think up relate to one another in this relativist environment? Rorty describes this process as the reweaving of beliefs (10). As we never get outside our heads to an external reality all that we do is to play around with the various ideas and beliefs that we have and occasionally re-form them into new configurations. So there is no inherent reason why science and religion, for instance, might not come up with a new shared understanding of the world. This is an attractive proposition, but whether it will withstand scrutiny is an issue to be returned to later. Does Rorty sell the pass to a form of intellectual anarchy by relativizing reason and science to this extent? Would a theology that adopted his views also be committed to his non-realist view of truth and would that be acceptable? Much remains to be answered.

Foucault, Baudrillard and the self

I have to admit that attempting to condense any discussion of Foucault and Baudrillard into one section focussing on the subject of the self is not a satisfying prospect. The justification for it is that the scope of their respective works goes well beyond what could be described in a brief introductory chapter and that, from within the theological domain, it is in the context of discussions about the self that one is likely to find reference to their work (11). Placing the two philosophers together might also suggest a commonality of thought and purpose that is definitely not the case. There is in fact a well-documented and heated debate between the two in the course of which Baudrillard recommends that we should 'Forget Foucault' (12). With those reservations in mind we turn first of all to Foucault.

Once again we are back in France. Michel Foucault was born in Poitiers in 1926. He studied at the Ecole Normale Superieure and gained his doctorate in 1960. However, his path to becoming one of the foremost French intellectuals was somewhat tortuous and included spells teaching abroad in the early part of his career. From 1964 to 1968 he was head of the Department of Philosophy at the University of Claremont-Ferrand, although he was on the faculty at Vincennes in Paris during the student upheavals of 1968. This date is to be noted and we also acknowledge that, as with Lyotard, there is a very particular political background to Foucault's work. There is considerable evidence that there was a growing commitment in later years to stand alongside marginalized groups (13). Foucault died of A.I.D.S. in 1984.

It is not easy to fit his work into familiar philosophical categories and that makes it even more difficult to appropriate it to a theological perspective. As I believe will become clearer as we move through this chapter, it is often a case of theologians latching onto selective and apparently helpful ideas taken out of their wider philosophical context. Although Foucault's emphases appear to change more noticeably even than Lyotard's, his major and abiding concern is with human knowledge and the forms in which it is constructed and expressed. Questions about the self - although perhaps of great personal interest to Foucault (14) - could be seen as subsidiary to that one major concern. In one of his final comments Foucault states that his whole objective has been to create a history of the different modes by which, in our culture, human beings are made subjects (15), but, if taken out of the context of the rest of his work, this can be misleading. However, theologians are inclined to see this as his most important contribution to the Post-Modernity debate and to ignore his work on knowledge (16).

Foucault's first published works represent an attempt to develop what he calls an archaeology of knowledge and are on the subjects of mental illness, the growth of interest in public health and the ways in which understandings of crime have changed (17). The term archaeology is instructive because it points to Foucault's central method of digging up references from texts and sources that have otherwise been neglected. By doing this he aims to be able to describe the various discourses that have developed around the subject under investigation. A discourse is a group of statements which provide a language for talking about a particular kind of knowledge or topic. The problem is that Foucault, after much struggle and attempts at definition (18), abandoned this approach. Whether or not he did produce valuable or valid insights in this period is open to debate.

One can see a certain commonality of concern shared with both Lyotard and Rorty in that Foucault was questioning the linear and straightforward accounts of the development of human knowledge and practice offered by the Enlightenment. Rather than a neat and seamless process of change guided by rational principles and methods, Foucault unearths, through detailed historical research, that the paths of human knowledge are pitted by discontinuities, disruptions and factors apparently beyond human control. In essence he is telling a different story about the ways in which contemporary culture have come into being, one that challenges the rational gloss imposed by the Enlightenment Grand Narrative. It is almost as if the discourses or languages ascribed to the fields he is investigating have a life of their own rather than being the conscious and deliberate creation of human agents. Each of these discourses is a social construct, not an objective reality. They are a story that could have been told differently. What interests Foucault is why they were told in the way they were.

It is here that we begin to see how the debate about the self can emerge from Foucault's work. In his early writings he attempts to bracket out any reference to human agency as he examines the development of the particular discourses. This could be seen as an almost perverse way of establishing a degree of objectivity more characteristic of the natural than the human sciences. Yet Foucault abandons this approach and moves to what he terms genealogies to replace the archaeologies of knowledge. As this is not of direct interest to this particular discussion I will not go into the details of this.

It is in the developments of what were to become Foucault's closing works that we find a clearer focus for theological interest. He begins an investigation into the subject of sexuality and historical research into how different understandings of the self came to be constructed (19). The clear implication is that there is no essential self, no permanent way of understanding what it is to be a human being, merely the different stories that come to be told over time. So, for instance, the Enlightenment view that what makes us all human is our faculty of reasoning is, once again, relativized. It is just one more story that has been told, no more and no less.

However, this raises the further question of how and why such narratives or stories about the self develop as they do. It is at this point that Foucault introduces power as an explanatory concept. This has created enormous confusion for those not familiar with Foucault's methods. Most of us probably interpret power as something exercised by the few while the rest are powerless. Power is a finite resource of some kind. Shift it towards x and y will have less of it. So when Foucault begins to use the concept of power in relation to the formation of the self, people jump to the conclusion that he means that some group is manipulating another. So those who control the media and advertising, for instance, are forcing a self-image upon a naive and unsuspecting public. We all have to drive a Porsche or holiday in the Bahamas and eat smoked salmon for breakfast in order to be successful and fulfilled people. That is an argument in its own right but it is not what Foucault is saying. He does not divide people up into the powerful and the victims.

Foucault has a very distinctive understanding of power. Power is not a thing that some possess and others do not. It is more like a permanent web that runs through all social and political life (20). It is ever present like the air that we breathe and cannot be the exclusive possession of a particular group. We are all implicated in the exercise of power understood in this sense and the objective of further analysis can only be to see where particular individuals or groups stand within the networks or webs of power. Foucault suggests that there is always power and counter-power, that resistance will often emerge and that political activity of a subversive nature will be focussed on local critiques of the negative use of power.

Once again Foucault's approach is difficult to grasp because it by-passes more familiar interpretations. He is taken to mean that the self is merely a product of external forces, determined by the manipulators of images in the free-for-all of Post-Modernity and the consumer culture. If there is no essential self and all the traditional views such as the Christian one have been revealed as just another social or cultural construct, then there is no basis upon which distortions of the human spirit or instances of exploitation can be resisted. In fact, while this view could be attributed to Baudrillard it does not accurately describe Foucault's position. Foucault does not destroy, undermine or deconstruct the self but continues to bracket it out of his intellectual investigations. He will not use human agency as a way of explaining the ways in which knowledge is constructed through discourses because this would only disguise the other factors that Foucault wishes to highlight or bring to the surface. Nor does he see power as one way traffic, even when it comes to discourses about the human subject. He leaves questions about human agency deliberately open and this does create problems for the radical political stances that he himself adopts. But Foucault is no victim and those who are tempted to read this interpretation into his work are in danger of imposing another agenda. Perhaps they would do better to forget Foucault.

So, we call Baudrillard to the witness stand to listen to his charges against Modernity. Baudrillard is undoubtedly the infant terrible of Post-Modernity. Another child of the inter-war period he was born in 1929 and has pursued an academic career, currently teaching sociology at Nanterres. As with Lyotard and Foucault he has to be seen against the background of the French post-war intellectual environment. The writing for which he is now famous - or perhaps notorious - seems some distance from where he began in the 1960s. His early work centred on an attempt to develop a Marxist critique of contemporary culture. His Marxism is now long forgotten but what remains is his interest in culture and attempts to describe forms of domination within it. Both have taken a rather extreme turn, to the point where much of his writing appears 'over the top'. Is Baudrillard serious in what he says or is he being deliberately provocative in order to make a point or to stimulate further debate? The man himself is not inclined to answer this question.

Many of the caricatures associated with the cultural aspect of Post-Modernity as described in the last chapter, are derived from Baudrillard's writing. Here is a world where reality and illusion are so intertwined that it is impossible to know which is which. The rapid expansion of Information Technology; the image-creating machine of the mass media; the application of science to the fields of recreation and culture and the deliberate fusion of different styles all contribute to what Baudrillard terms hyperreality (21). What we have now is the more real than real not simply an illusion. Everything has been taken to its nth degree, to the point where it turns back in upon itself, or implodes.

We are surrounded by simulacra or simulations of past culture, now set free from their original moorings and floating freely within a completely open market of signs and meanings. So scenes from history now become part of theme parks, entertainment bites to be consumed and then recycled. Baudrillard's most recent controversial comments have been on the Gulf War (22). Did it really happen or was it an invention of the media fought out by politicians on computer screen and visual projections and consumed by everybody else via their T.V. sets? This seems so clearly an absurd suggestion and offensive to those who did suffer as a result of the conflict and it has caused a violent reaction amongst Baudrillard's critics (23). However, one can see what he is getting at. Baudrillard takes an element of truth and magnifies it out of all proportion. His point surely is that this is what Post-Modern culture does all the time.

How though does this impinge upon understandings of the self? Recalling the notion that Pre-Modernity represents life's external determination - by either God or nature - and that Modernity is an internal determination by humans themselves, then Post-Modernity is a radical indeterminacy. Nobody is in control of what is going on. What Baudrillard suggests is not that version of Post-Modernity but rather a reversal of Modernity. So, in the latter it is human subjects who determine the shape and meaning of objects. In Post-Modernity it is the objects that increasingly determine the shape and meaning of the human subject. This is where even Baudrillard starts to differ from the caricature of Post-Modernity. Objects now have the power to overwhelm and to seduce human beings (24). Baudrillard sees evidence of this in the development of commodities; capital; fashion; the sexual object; the media; politics; information and other characteristics of contemporary culture. Our lives are now subject to and completely under the sway of the objects that were once our creation. Children exist for video cameras, not the other way around.

Baudrillard is taking an extreme position once again and one that it is all too easy to refute. Of course there is an element of truth in the suggestion that people are allowing their lives to be determined by the objects of culture. However, any satisfactory explanation would have to continue to include some concept of human agency. Humans partly determine and are partly determined by these objects. Perhaps Baudrillard deliberately paints a nightmarish science fiction scenario to draw our attention to the dangers inherent in the world we are now creating. A world where the self could be obliterated or else shackled by the image-creating moguls. Michael Jackson is one of Baudrillard's examples here: is this person real or some sort of clone of a new composite reality? Can we tell the difference any longer? I suspect that we can.

In the sense that he is drawing out the possible consequences of this hyper-development of Modernity for human beings Baudrillard is offering to the anti-Modernity and anti-Enlightenment lobby some important arguments. Yet simply because he carries the arguments to such an extreme and moves from plain description into theories about the future - notably on the dominance of the object - his work must be treated with some scepticism and caution. He does not offer either a description or a theory of Post-Modernity that theology could take on board uncritically. It is certainly hard to imagine that theology could accept the total destruction of human agency that is integral to Baudrillard's description of the self in Post-Modernity. As with Foucault it is difficult to identify the self as victim of consumer culture or political manipulation that some theologians have latched onto as being an essential insight of Post-Modernity.

Derrida, deconstruction and difference

In this trial of Modernity the witnesses called so far have to be seen as something of a mixed blessing as far as theology is concerned. Either the evidence provided has not been quite what the anti-Enlightenment lobby had expected or else it has been against the background of other ideas that might be as threatening to Christianity as the Enlightenment. For instance Rorty's non-realism and Baudrillard's total negation of human agency. Our final witness will also prove confusingly ambiguous. Like the previous four Derrida is concerned for that which does not fit the Enlightenment picture, that which remains outside, in excess of, beyond its scope or not taken into account. Derrida draws our attention to that which is concealed, hidden beneath the universal claims and terminology of a rationalist approach. The shadow side of Modernity if you like.

Jacques Derrida was born in Algiers in 1930 - already an outsider looking in. He studied at the Ecole Normale Superieure in Paris and then at Harvard. From 1960 to 1964 he taught at the Sorbonne, becoming professor of the history of philosophy back at his alma mater the following year. He has a world-wide reputation and is particularly highly regarded in the United States where he has been a frequent visitor. His first significant publications date from 1966 and are often seen as heralding the arrival of what is referred to as deconstruction.

What is deconstruction? It is a very particular way of approaching the understanding of texts. I think I can best describe it as a means of taking into account that which remains hidden or lies beyond the boundaries. Even this may sound hopelessly enigmatic. Every word, concept, sentence or theory that we employ is an implicit setting of boundaries, a way of including some things in terms of meaning and of excluding others. This is in the nature of language. Any interpretation of a text is likewise selective, unable to give expression to all the possible meanings. In our culture, given the intellectual assumptions derived from the Enlightenment, we tend to approach texts in a relatively straightforward manner, assuming an identity between the language and a particular meaning. Remember that the Enlightenment view of rationality is that thought proceeds in a linear and exact fashion from point A to point B and so on. It was this notion of the development of knowledge that Foucault set out to challenge and disrupt. So the meaning of words and texts is assumed to operate in a similar fashion. One reads a text and the meaning follows as one reasons from point A to point B. Thus the obvious meaning and the language are assumed to be identical. Again, this parallels the correspondence theory of truth of which Rorty is so critical. The meaning A somehow corresponds to the language B.

Derrida's project of deconstruction appears to be designed to show that other options for meaning are always possible. Interpretation A does not exhaust the possibilities. There are however two potential ways of understanding this idea and it is here that confusion sets in. An extreme view is that Derrida is saying that you can make a text mean anything you want it to, there is a free-for-all of interpretation in which anything goes. There are no boundaries any longer; anything and everything is possible. Deconstruction means the destruction of any agreed criteria of interpretation. This is what Post-Modernity is often portrayed as saying. It becomes a form of both intellectual and personal anarchy.

The alternative interpretation is perhaps more difficult to understand and thus tends to get lost beneath the Post-Modern hype. According to this there is no free play of interpretation, but always the hidden presence of some other options. The word absence is possibly more suggestive here: that which is a possibility but is not offered in the interpretation. Derrida's version of deconstruction is not a destruction of the text to the point where it can mean anything - and therefore nothing - but a concentrated and skilled effort to bring to the surface or to light that which remains hidden. Thus much of his work consists of a very detailed and closely argued attention to particular texts - much too much like hard work for the playful and eclectic Post-Modernist. It needs to be noted that there are those who claim to be following Derrida's lead and yet are engaging in the anarchic form of deconstruction.

It is crucial to grasp the distinction that is being made here. If it were the case that Derrida subscribed to the 'anything goes' approach he would also be agreeing with the non-realist notion of truth suggested by Rorty. In other words, there is no external reality to which terms refer, either directly or indirectly, and that thus sets boundaries on what those terms can mean. Rorty himself finds Derrida ambiguous on this. He identifies in Derrida's writings both a fellow free spirit who plays around with words and concepts unconstrained by a world outside and a more old-fashioned opponent who still assumes that there are limits and boundaries to meaning (25). Rorty prefers to see Derrida as having finally moved away from the Enlightenment notion that there are criteria - agreed and justifiable ways of establishing interpretations. Another major commentator, Christopher Norris, believes the opposite and argues strongly that Derrida is not over-turning or destroying the exercise of reason but rather broadening its scope through an internal critique (26).

This is a very detailed and contentious argument that cannot be fully entered into let alone settled in an introductory chapter. However, we do need to register that there is a disagreement here and conflicting interpretations of Derrida's work. The only way to resolve this for oneself is by direct access to Derrida's writing. I have to say that my own inclination, on the basis of reading Derrida, is to support Norris' interpretation.

The importance of all this is that we come to see that Derrida is concerned to bring to the surface of texts that which is different; the other in the text that is inevitably suppressed by any one interpretation. The objective is not to achieve a reversal of interpretation; so before x was right and y was concealed, now y has been revealed and x can be seen as wrong. This would be to miss the point of what he is saying which is that other possible meanings are always already inherently present.

Although this may appear to be an obscure philosophical argument, merely the province or playground of academics, it does have ethical consequences that are of potential significance for theology. Naming and interpreting are both ways in which groups or individuals exercise power and impose a certain view of truth upon others. As we have already seen, those on the margins of contemporary society, women, gays and lesbians, ethnic minorities and so on are disempowered through the use of language. Derrida's deconstructive approach is a way of releasing the subversive meanings that can describe and do justice to the feelings and experiences of these groups. This is not in order for these alternative meanings to then become the established ones but to display the tensions built into the language and to widen the range of possible meanings. Derrida's work does not destroy all boundaries but questions the existing and accepted ones. It does not lead to the radical indeterminacy of Post-Modernity but widens the circle of those engaged in determining meaning. Such is Norris' interpretation and - I would argue - therein lies the ethical and political significance of Derrida's work. Concern for the other, for the outcasts and the marginalized are values to be found within the Christian tradition - amongst others. Derrida offers a way of doing justice to the other by drawing our attention to the shadow side of the Enlightenment.

Is it possible to reach some provisional conclusions following the evidence given by our five foremost Post-Modern writers? First, there are significant differences between them. On a crude spectrum of Modernity through to Post-Modernity, Rorty and Baudrillard appear furthest towards the latter while Foucault and Derrida could both be interpreted as still retaining at least vestiges of an Enlightenment approach and an interest in reason. Lyotard is more difficult to place, perhaps floating across the spectrum over time. Second, each has to be seen against the background of the political and philosophical context in which they have been working. Lyotard, Foucault, Baudrillard and Derrida share connections with radical French politics and were close to the events of May 1968. Rorty speaks from the very different setting of the United States and with a firm commitment to liberal democracy. For the others there seems to have been a movement away from and beyond Marxism. Third, the major questions that they address in their work are also revealing. Concern for knowledge, for justice and for the recognition of marginalized groups are characteristic of the French writers. They also attempt to establish critical perspectives on the existing structures of thought and power believed to be founded upon the Enlightenment Grand Narrative. Rorty however seems more concerned with preserving the American way of life.

At this stage in the trial of Modernity it is certainly possible to say that the key themes of interest to theology are present in the work of these thinkers. However, no clear picture of Post-Modernity as it is portrayed within theology at the moment emerges. It may be that the picture of a free-for-all, pick and mix, anything goes and nothing is sacred philosophy where Modernity is supposed to have completely broken down is itself a social construct, produced largely by media hype and then adopted by some theologians as matching their anti-Enlightenment tendencies. It is certainly very difficult to see how this view can be read directly out of the writings of the key thinkers who are deemed to be the intellectual gurus of Post-Modernity. This may not be a problem for theology if the arguments about Post-Modernity stand in their own right. Perhaps the picture is accurate anyway. But is it? In order to throw further light on this question we need to call two witnesses for the defence of Modernity. If their case begins to look convincing then maybe Post-Modernity is more of a mirage than an oasis and theology will need to think again.

Giddens and the radicalization of Modernity

The first witness for the defence is Anthony Giddens, a social theorist rather than a philosopher. Born in 1938 he has pursued an academic career teaching sociology in the University of Cambridge. Since 1985 he has been professor of sociology in the faculty of economics and politics. As such he inevitably approaches the subject of Post-Modernity from a slightly different perspective.

The importance of his work for this chapter is to show that it is possible to interpret the phenomena already identified in a different way. Giddens is unhappy with the Post in Post-Modernity because of its largely negative connotations. He is prepared to see a more positive side to current social change. Thus he prefers to talk about the radicalization of Modernity - the carrying of certain trends to a further degree of their development. Post-Modernity, in Giddens' view overemphasizes the elements of discontinuity and rupture with what has gone before. If there is some validity in his interpretation then it suggests that the anti-Modernity lobby within theology have some serious thinking to do. The announcement of the death of Modernity may be premature and theology will have to continue to critically engage with a Modernity moving into a new stage of its development.

Giddens vividly describes where we are now as like riding a juggernaut (27). The word has a Hindu background and is used to describe an idol of Krishna that was taken through the streets each year on the back of a large vehicle. People would throw themselves in front of this and often be crushed to death in the process. Not exactly a cheering prospect perhaps, but Giddens' point is that Modernity has become a runaway engine, almost out of control, carrying human beings along but nevertheless still within our capacity to steer to a limited extent. Those who try to resist it certainly risk being crushed as a result. Those who ride it do so with a mixture of exhilaration and trepidation. The engine may lurch in an unexpected direction at any moment, so there is fear and insecurity but its forward momentum is exciting and stimulating. There is an essential ambivalence towards what is happening. It is not all good, but it is not all bad either.

Giddens examines each of the four areas we have already identified in the light of this image of the juggernaut. He acknowledges the break up of the big stories or Grand Narratives and admits that this is where the image suggests a coherent and unified movement that may not be the case. Modernity is indeed fragmented in the sense that it contains a plurality of interpretations of the world and a variety of social and ethical systems. He cautiously welcomes the emerging emphasis upon locality and context but does not see them as leading to a complete breakdown or reversal of modern life. Rather, each has a series of feedback mechanisms and also ways of contributing to each other and to a greater, if somewhat more confused, whole. Giddens does not see society splitting into a number of radically different fragments each pursuing its own values and lifestyles regardless of the rest, but a world in which people can and will devise new ways of relating across different cultural and religious boundaries. Thus there are current attempts to do justice to these differences within many Western societies. However, there is always the possibility that these fragile agreements will break down as in the renewed ethnic conflicts in Europe and Africa. Giddens' point is that alongside such failures there will also develop new ways of coping and that both are characteristic of our current situation.

The picture of science and reason is also one of ambiguity as far as Giddens is concerned. Both have been relativized in the sense that they no longer have peoples' complete and explicit confidence - if they ever did. People are aware that the future cannot be tightly controlled or directed, either by science or reason. They are also clear that both have created certain risks and dangers, for instance, the possibility of a nuclear war or of an environmental catastrophe. Yet scientific exploration remains a key means by which we relate to the world and will continue to do so. Most people are not about to return to Pre-Modernity in practice, however much they may complain about the consequences of reason and science. Giddens suggests that the notion of trust is important in this context. It is a fact of life that we have to place our trust in both certain abstract systems and in particular experts. So we trust that the car will start in the morning, that the commercial world will continue to function and the goods we demand be available in the shops and that the doctor we visit has some understanding of the functioning of the human body. We do tend to listen to what the scientists have to say on various issues, although with the increasing awareness that there can be conflicting interpretations within science and that its conclusions are provisional and fallible. Without a certain degree of trust we could not function in the world as it now is. Yet we continue to keep this trust under review and undergo crises of confidence in both experts and systems when things go wrong. So, once again, the picture of our relationship with science and reason is more ambiguous than the caricature of Post-Modernity suggests.

When it comes to the self Giddens is prepared to offer a more positive interpretation of what is going on than that which we have encountered so far. We have already seen the difficulties in identifying a clear theory of the self in the key Post-Modern writers and, when one does begin to emerge, as in Baudrillard, it seems to deny any sense of human agency. Giddens counters this with the notion of reflexivity (28). This is his way of acknowledging that we are both partially determined by external events and structures and can partially determine them through our thoughts and actions. We are not totally in control, but we are not totally controlled either. Our main purchase on reality is the initial reactions we have to external events and then the capacity to stand back, reflect upon and develop ways of coping with what is happening. While we can be overwhelmed by the scale and scope of what is going on around us we can also use such critical tools as sociology itself to help us get a handle on reality. An obvious example of this is that sociology informs us of the high incidence of marriage breakdown and this then becomes part of the data on the basis of which we make a decision about whether to enter such a commitment. There is a sort of recycling of information and knowledge that contributes to our decision-making.

Giddens has also recently drawn attention to the increased reflexivity in our personal lives (29). He interprets the growth of counselling and the greater numbers now involved in self-help groups as evidence that people are aware that they need to manage themselves, or to adapt more quickly in order to function effectively in a rapidly changing world. So we are likely to encounter and have to be able to relate to complete strangers at a moment's notice, either in our working or social lives. We need to know and understand ourselves better if we are to gauge our reactions and guard against damaging these fleeting but important relationships. In addition to these face to face encounters it is now possible to sustain relationships over spatial and temporal boundaries through the use of telephones, fax machines and computers. We are in fact learning new and positive ways of relating to one another. There is still the possibility of failure and breakdown but also the increased reflexivity in the exercise of human agency.

On the issue of difference and doing justice to those who have so far lost out in Modernity, Giddens develops the concept of Life Politics (30). This is the suggestion that we are seeing a new focus for political activity in the development of groups centred around minority interests. Thus for instance feminism, the rise of environmental groups, those opposed to specific developments in their locality in addition to the longer established cultural and ethnic groupings. These both cut across and feed directly into the traditional political domains of conservative, socialist and liberal, republican or democrat. They represent the attempts of these groups to gain a hearing on very particular issues that have previously been suppressed or ignored. However, whether they have the capacity or the will to overturn existing political structures and replace them with something new must remain open to doubt. So, Life Politics is a way in which a radicalized Modernity can take into account the voices and needs of those who have so far been marginalized. It is more a matter of adaptation than revolution.

If Giddens is correct then what we see is Modernity developing new ways of coping rather than being transformed into Post-Modernity. Christians are presumably faced with two options: either to ride the juggernaut along with the rest or to join the sacrificial victims waiting to be rolled over. There may be a precedent for both of these.

Habermas and the unfinished Project of the Enlightenment

The second and final witness for the defence of Modernity is the philosopher and social theorist Jürgen Habermas. Born in 1929 in Dusseldorf he has become one of the most prolific and intense writers of his generation. From 1971 to 1983 he was director of the Max Planck Institute in Frankfurt and is currently professor of sociology and philosophy at Johann Wolfgang Goethe University in that same city. His intellectual background was shaped by his involvement with what has become known as the Frankfurt School, a loose formation of critical thinkers that included Horkheimer, Adorno, Marcuse and Fromm, each of them engaged in employing and adapting Marxist theory in establishing a Critical Theory of contemporary society (31). In different ways they attempted to move beyond Marx and to identify the processes through which relations of domination were created and sustained by culture itself, rather than by purely economic or political means. Habermas has broadly carried on this tradition of Critical Theory, although he has included in his work ideas from a much wider range of sources, for instance the sociologist Talcott Parsons, the pragmatist philosophers Peirce and Mead and the psychologist Kohlberg (32).

Clearly it is only going to be possible to provide a thumbnail sketch of his work. Habermas' most direct contribution to the debate about Post-Modernity stems from his discussion of reason. Put briefly, his argument is that Modernity as it now exists is the result of the development of a one-sided and even distorted view of reason. Returning to the key thinkers in the early years of the Enlightenment notably the philosopher Hegel, Habermas believes that it is possible to identify a broader and more satisfying concept of reason that has since been lost to view (33).

There are historical and sociological explanations for this that we will come to shortly. What Habermas wants to do is to revive this broader concept of reason and thus put the Enlightenment project back on course. Parallelling those who would say that democracy is a good idea but that it has not been properly tried yet, Habermas would agree that the Enlightenment is a good idea but that it has yet to be properly implemented.

So, what is this narrowed understanding of reason that now holds sway and how has it reached this exalted position? The idea that Habermas shares with other Critical Theorists is that we now have a purely instrumental reason. In other words, reason has been reduced to a method of calculating the most effective means of achieving a particular end. As such it appears to be a neutral tool, morally indifferent towards what it is being used to achieve. It is the supposed neutrality, impartiality and objectivity of Enlightenment reason that Foucault, Derrida and Lyotard challenge in their work, but Habermas does not acknowledge this possible common ground. So reason operates a bit like a computer programme. You feed a problem in at one end and out comes the solution at the other. Reason can be used to find a cure for A.I.D.S. or to work out the most efficient way of exterminating your enemies or to advise you on how to play the stock market. It is just a logical, ordered way of doing things that assumes an identity or correspondence between language and reality.

How has this situation evolved? As can be gathered from the earlier discussions on Modernity the application of this type of reason has been of great significance for the development of our industrial, commercial and scientific culture. A logical and controlled progression of thought verifying certain possibilities and excluding others has contributed immensely to the growth of Modernity. Most scientific research and most business and political decisions are supposed to be made in this way. The assumption is that any right-minded person employing logical thought would reach the same conclusions given the same circumstances. Questions about the accuracy of this as a description of how things work, even in science, are now familiar from the comments of Rorty in particular. However, this is still the popular and therefore the effective concept of reason.

What has been happening in recent years is that this narrow instrumental concept of reason has been so successful in what Habermas calls the Systems World of big business, bureaucracy and power politics that it has now begun to encroach significantly into other areas that had previously been organized by different criteria (34). This Habermas refers to as the Lifeworld, meaning our social and personal lives and the background assumptions that lie behind them. So, for instance, in a number of Western countries areas such as public health, education and housing provision are now being run increasingly according to strictly financial criteria. The idea that they are public services and thus to be subsidised because they contribute to the social good has been abandoned. Similarly in our own personal and family lives the influence of the Systems World becomes more prevalent as decisions are ordered around financial criteria rather than on the basis of what is good for people or their relationships. Leisure and recreation are now big business and even religious institutions are listening more to their accountants. The effect of this invasion of the Lifeworld by instrumental reason is to create a counter reaction. Habermas interprets the rise of feminism, the environmental movement and various community groups to a resistance against this narrow view of reason. Once again there is a different way of explaining some of the phenomena of interest to the Post-Modern writers.

We can see that Habermas is very close to the ground that all the others in this chapter find of interest: the Grand Narrative of the Enlightenment distorted this time by the rise of instrumental reason; the growing disillusion with science and reason as reflected in the protest movements and explained by the invasion of the Lifeworld by the Systems World; a perceived loss of agency felt by those who are marginalized by the dominance of instrumental reason in society. However, Habermas is highly critical of the Post-Modern thinkers and believes that they represent a purely anti-Enlightenment reaction. We have already seen reason to question this interpretation in some cases, but the detailed debate must be reserved for later.

The alternative concept of reason that Habermas offers and that he traces back to Hegel he calls communicative reason (35). In the early 1980s he wrote two large and complex volumes trying to explain this, but I shall try to limit myself to a few sentences. Communicative reason takes seriously the fact that human beings are conscious agents engaged through language in communication and inter-subjective activity. We are not lone beings working out our lives and problems in a vacuum but in the context of a life shared with others. As we use language to engage in the various interactive tasks of life it is possible to see that there are certain rules or criteria of engagement that hold good across all cultural and temporal boundaries. These rules or criteria of communicative competence as Habermas calls them are what is left of the big story of the Enlightenment, the only universals, the things that unite us in human society and that we all have in common. They offer a procedure, a way of operating that can be used when communication breaks down or when one group is trying to suppress or dominate another. So they retain the hope for a Critical Theory of society as first outlined by the Frankfurt School.

In any human communication there are four criteria that can be employed to work out what is going on. Four questions can be asked. Can I understand what the other person is saying to me? Is what they are saying true? Are they being sincere in what they are saying or perhaps deliberately trying to mislead me? Is it appropriate for them to be saying that? If the answer to all or any of those questions is negative then communication is breaking down and people can identify the reason for this and attempt to restore effective communication. For instance, if I cannot understand what you are saying I can stop you and ask for clarification or explanation. If I have reason to believe that you are lying to me in order to protect or further your own interests I can challenge your motives. These four criteria form the heart of Habermas' concept of communicative reason.

As might be imagined with such an ambitious and complex theory it has provoked extensive debate and no little criticism. As a result of this Habermas has continued to refine and redefine his theory. These reformulations lie beyond the scope of this chapter. What does need to be registered now is that Habermas has provided probably the most important attempt to reshape and revive the Enlightenment project. There is thus more to the Modernity - Post-Modernity debate than initially meets the eye. Further chapters will return to these discussions in greater detail. For the moment we would have to say that the case for the demise of Modernity is far from proven. Is this necessarily bad news for theology?

4

Christianity: Metanarrative or Major Narrative?

Introduction

The scene has been set, the main characters introduced and the key themes given their initial airing. So Act One proper can now begin. We have already caught a glimpse of the theologians who seem anxious to embrace certain aspects of Post-Modernity. Each of the next chapters will focus on contemporary theology that represents this position in order to offer a critical evaluation. What exactly is it about Post-Modernity that appears so attractive to theology? Does this Post-Modernity exist in the form in which it is portrayed by theology? If not, is theology in danger of heading down a blind alley and can a more creative direction be identified? These questions will continue to echo from the wings.

It will be recalled that the first key point of contact between theology and Post-Modernity is the latter's idea of the breakdown of all Grand or meta-narratives, in particular that of the Enlightenment. This in the light of the supposed crisis of Modernity that is built upon Enlightenment presuppositions. For those theologians who interpret the Enlightenment tradition as being Public Enemy Number One this seems like good news. So, for instance, Nicholas Lash, Professor of Divinity at Cambridge (England), is clear that there is a sense that Modernity is on its death bed.

'Some world is ending now, whether its death knell was sounded with the demolition of the Berlin Wall, with Auschwitz or Hiroshima or Vietnam, or even with the outbreak of the First World War. And one name we have given to this world now ending is the 'modern' world - hence all the talk these days about 'postmodernism' ' (1).

The nature of this ending stems directly from a deconstruction of key features of the Enlightenment (2). In particular the idea that there is some single overarching system or description, some single narrative with a beginning, a middle and an end, has been abandoned. In its place is an awareness that life is fragmented, without a true centre and that all claims to provide one are merely a mask for power or prejudice. The Enlightenment project of placing reason upon a secure and universal foundation is to be seen as no more than one particular set of 'local' circumstances, those of Seventeenth Century Europe (3). The tragedy of Modern Western culture is that its achievements in the fields of science and technology, education and communication, have to be set against the background of the cost in human suffering and the devastation of the planet. It also consists in 'the length of time that it has taken us to learn that there is no neutral vantage point, no universal standpoint...from which truth may be discerned and the pattern of right action estimated' (4).

Lash believes that the ending of Modernity may make it easier for Christian theology to return to its proper task: 'the consideration of our identity, our duty and our responsibility, in relation to an eternal Word once uttered in a particular time and place' (5). In other words, Christians need no longer be distracted from the central task of preaching the Gospel by the concerns of a world already on its way out.

It is important to register how prevalent this cultural pessimism has now become in contemporary theology. Lash is the distinguished tip of an ever-growing iceberg and the sentiment that the modern world is coming to an end reverberates down to local congregations. More detailed examination of the arguments follow later in the chapter, but a number of preliminary comments can be made. It is significant that Lash offers a series of human catastrophes that have occurred this century. Presumably after, or even during each one of them people felt that something was indeed ending or collapsing. The apparent demise of communism and the symbolic destruction of the Berlin Wall appears to have been the particular event that inspired Lash to this view. However, we can legitimately ask whether any of these events did herald the end of the modern world and exactly what such a claim might mean.

It is one thing to pick up on the fleeting moods and sentiments that accompany key events - and that is something that preachers are prone to do as they attempt to reflect the concerns of the moment. It is another to extend these feelings to form the basis of an intellectual argument and to start making sweeping claims about the future. There is a gap here between social comment and scholarly interpretation and it is a tendency of the theologians we will be examining to leap that chasm with the assistance of the arguments about Post-Modernity. Whether those arguments are secure enough to carry that weight is a question that we must now ask.

Another apparent weakness of the position represented by Lash is that it fails to make clear whether the end of Modernity means a return to pre-Modernity or a movement towards another stage of human social development. It is an inherently negative comment upon the current state of affairs. It would be easy to describe this as prophetic and thereby avoid the responsibility of suggesting a positive alternative to Modernity. This is in fact what seems to happen, but one could argue that this form of theology then represents a withdrawal from engagement with the wider world, a refusal to take seriously those who continue to struggle with Modernity and a retreat into a community ghetto that believes itself to be immune from the general collapse. It has to be questionable whether, if Modernity is coming to an end, religious communities could seal themselves off from the catastrophe. Can it be that this is only happening to them and not to us? Is there such a strict division between Christians and everybody else?

The cynical observer might say that theology has a vested interest in the debate about Post-Modernity. If Modernity has been bad for Christianity - and that again is a view that is open to question - then Post-Modernity, in whatever form, might well be a better environment in which to be operating. So how much of this jumping on the Post-Modern bandwagon is merely wishful thinking? What if this Post-Modernity should prove to be even more hostile to religious thought and practice than its predecessor? It could be a case of out of the frying pan and into the fire! Beware philosophers and social theorists bearing gifts.

Finally - and this will lead into the more detailed debate - how can theology be sure that the philosophical arguments underlying Post-Modernity are secure and reliable. Theologians do not necessarily make good philosophers - and vice versa. Perhaps the desire to see the back of Modernity and the Enlightenment tradition might lure theology into yet another minefield not of its own making. The previous chapter offered a guide through the labyrinth of Post-Modernity and revealed significant differences between the key players and some alternative interpretations of current events. We must now return to these paths before we can be sure what theology has to gain from this debate.

Lyotard and Metanarratives

In the introductory section on Lyotard in the last chapter it was established that this philosopher's main concerns have been justice and knowledge. What now counts as knowledge is the result of the metanarrative of the

Enlightenment, the big story told about humanity and the world. The problem with this has been that it has been based upon a particular understanding of reason then portrayed as a universal facet of human existence. Those who do not fit neatly into this category are thus excluded and marginalized from the mainstream of Modernity and Lyotard's concern is how justice is to be achieved for these groups and individuals. The serious philosophical debate about Post-Modernity began in 1979 with the publication of Lyotard's 'The Postmodern Condition' in which he suggests that the monolithic understanding of reason is being superseded by a variety of different discourses and that the claims of the one to ground or to provide criteria for all the others have been undermined.

However, in order to grasp the full significance of this position it is necessary to pursue the discussion back into the history of philosophy and to the early stages of the Enlightenment. Only then will it become clear how much is at stake in this debate.

So much of the story of the development of the Enlightenment really goes back to Kant - and this aspect of it is no exception. As has already been noted Lyotard himself has spent much energy on studying Kant in recent years (6). The reason for this is probably that the issues he is struggling with are first defined by Kant. One might almost say that much of the Post-Modern debate stems from the way in which Kant sets up the debate about reason. Or, at least, Kant is attributed with the responsibility for bringing into being the particular understanding of reason that is the target of Lyotard's critique.

Inevitably the reality is more complex than that and I want to highlight this complexity at the outset because it throws an important light on the subsequent theological appropriation of Post-Modernity. The crucial point is that Kant himself does not reduce reason to one particular set of operations. Far from it. In fact he identifies three - and sometimes four - different types of reason. In his very last work not to be published until 170 years after his death, he talks about 1. theoretical-speculative reason, 2. technical-practical reason, and 3. moral-practical reason (7).

In a further differentiation he offers speculative, practical, technical-practical and moral-practical reason (8). Earlier in the same section he makes it clear what the real significance of this interpretation is to be:

'There is, however, apart from sensible representation, yet another faculty of knowledge...namely, understanding, judgement and reason. The latter can be either technical, intuition-constructing reason or moral-practical reason...Moral-practical reason, if it contains laws of duty (rules of conduct in conformity with the categorical imperative) leads to the concept of God' (9).

The purpose of administering this hefty dosage of Kant is to show how the Post-Modern problematic can be traced back to this point. The argument is that one strand of reason - as defined by Kant - has gained dominance over the others. Technical-practical reason, the way of working out the best and most effective means of achieving a particular end, particularly in its application through science and technology, has relegated both speculative (philosophical) reason and moral reason to the sidelines. This is what Lash and his fellow cultural pessimists are referring to when they talk about the human and ecological costs of the developments of Modernity. This is the Grand Narrative of the Enlightenment, the notion that the application of this particular understanding of reason will lead to ultimate peace, harmony and prosperity for the human race. In fact, it appears to have led us to the brink of destruction - or so the argument goes.

Two things need to be noted before the discussion moves on. First, Kant himself does not subscribe to the dominance of technical-practical reason, but sees it as only one aspect of human understanding. However, by once dividing reason up in this way he inadvertently takes the lid off Pandora's box. It is impossible now not to identify some version of this division as central to modern life. Habermas, for instance, talks about the cognitive (scientific), the normative (moral) and the aesthetic (10).

Second, the heritage of this division is a poisoned chalice for both philosophy and theology who now have to sort out where they stand in relation to this three-fold pattern. On one reading, philosophy becomes merely a handmaid to technical-practical reason. On another it still has a contribution to make to the moral and aesthetic spheres. Theology fares even worse, being totally displaced by science as a source of secure knowledge and increasingly losing out in the sphere of the moral as secular theories take over. It becomes confined to the aesthetic, the realm of the subjective, the individual or the artistic. As such, it loses its status in public life and even its credibility in the academic world. We will see later in the chapter how important these arguments have become.

There seems, for the moment, to be no way out of this maze. Any claim by either philosophy or theology to take over the role of the dominant strand of reason is subject to the Post-Modern critique, that it is merely a disguise for power or prejudice. The same critique applies to any attempt to re-unite the three strands under a new single heading - it excludes difference thus creating injustice. On the other hand, for either philosophy or theology to be determined or positioned by any of the other strands, would be to undermine or to abandon their claims to truth and autonomy.

Is there yet another way of either or both coming to terms with Modernity or Post-Modernity. In the final part of this chapter I will hope to show that there is.

At this stage we move forward in time to Lyotard in order to see exactly what his position is. We noted in the last chapter the significance of the wider political context in which the French philosophers were operating, in particular the student uprising in Paris in May 1968 and the subsequent failure of Marxism to create substantial political change. Certainly both Lyotard and Baudrillard began their intellectual careers as Marxists, but the failure associated with May 1968 led to a growing disillusion with this approach and the turn towards what has become known as Post-Modernity. For both perhaps Marxism was the ultimate manifestation of the metanarrative of the Enlightenment, the hope that the exercise of reason through direct political action would create greater freedom and emancipate those who were losing out within the capitalist system. With that hope undermined there was a retreat from direct political action. A fellow French philosopher, Cornelius Castoriadis sums up this mood of disillusion:

'When the movement in France didn't have any success in the factual or even real-political sense, when May 1968 didn't take over power, many people who now talk about postmodernism, and at that time more or less attached themselves to the movement began a discourse such as 'Therefore there isn't any politics anymore: therefore politics is botched; therefore all projects are myths and we have left the epoch of this myth or these myths behind us.' ' (11).

The purpose of quoting this is to establish that Post-Modernity viewed as the breakdown of metanarratives, originated as a response to a particular situation. Rather than being a strict philosophical argument it began life as a piece of social commentary founded on disappointment. This is supported by Lyotard himself in an interview given in 1988. Commenting on the reception of 'The Postmodern Condition' by the philosophical community he says:

' 'The Postmodern Condition' was received by them rather as a book which sought to put an end to philosophical reflection as it had been established by Enlightenment rationalism. But what is certain is that 'The Postmodern Condition' is not a book of philosophy. It is rather a book which is very strongly marked by sociology, by a certain historicism and by epistemology' (12).

Even more significantly and disturbingly for the current theological interpretation of Post-Modernity, Lyotard states: 'I have said and will say again that 'postmodernism' signifies not the end of modernism, but another relation to modernism' (13). This is not a matter of splitting hairs but rather a clear indication that Lash and his colleagues have misconstrued the nature of the debate about Post-Modernity.

So, what was Lyotard trying to get at? In this same interview he admits that the philosophical aspects of Post-Modernity were not properly elaborated until the publication of his book 'Le Differend' in 1984 (14).

'I think that, in effect, a part of the attack against the position developed in 'The Postmodern Condition' - my critics not generally having read my other works - bears the marks of a summary and totalizing idea of reason. I would oppose them simply with the following principle (which seems to me much more rationalist than they think); there is no reason, only reasons' (15).

Lyotard goes on to explain that he is very much following the line of Kant in identifying different types of reason. So theoretical reason differs from practical reason and both from either moral or aesthetic reason. It is never a matter of one massive and unique reason, which can be nothing but an ideology, but a question of plural rationalities, each with their own autonomous sphere of operation (16). Even the doubts about the dominance of a scientific or technical-practical reason have to be set in this wider context... 'the crisis of reason has been precisely the bath in which scientific reason has been immersed for a century, and this crisis, this continual interrogation of reason, is certainly the most rational thing around' (17).

I believe there are two points here that are crucial for an accurate interpretation of the philosophical debate about Post-Modernity. Both make it clear that Post-Modernity is neither simply the end of Modernity nor a total undermining of the Enlightenment project. As Lyotard says, it is about identifying plural rationalities in the manner of Kant and the continual interrogation of reason. Carrying out that interrogation is a continued refinement of the Enlightenment project. What has been abandoned by Lyotard is not the attempt to further develop these plural rationalities but the naive belief that they can be directly translated into emancipatory political action. This is very different from saying that the Enlightenment project was a dead end and must now be replaced by something entirely different. That is what some theologians would obviously like Post-Modernity to be, but wanting it won't make it so!

Lyotard himself does carry the discussion further in a direction that is of concern to theology. What he is interested in are the different ways, or genres of discourse as he calls them, in which human beings now operate and the relationship between them. He clarifies this in an interview given in 1985 (18). There can be no synthesis of these different spheres of operation. So, one minute you are a philosopher dealing with a difficult passage in Kant, the next you are trying to draw up a budget for your department and then you are listening to a friend who wants to talk about a personal problem. The difficulty comes in switching from one genre to another:

'This kind of flexibility; the capability to switch from one genre to another, is demanded of us today, and is in the meantime the situation of all humans in whatever domain they are working. Precisely because of this they are stressed... That's the true Modernity' (19).

The only thing that holds these different domains together is money. That is the only universal go-between, the only medium of exchange between the different spheres of operation. Lyotard's other point is that there is a certain probity or integrity about staying strictly within the rules of each specific genre of discourse. He draws a parallel here with Wittgenstein's notion of language games (20) each of which has their own distinctive rules of operation and require strict adherence. What has disappeared is the notion that there is some universal reason that does cross all the boundaries of the different discourses, providing a decontextualized set of criteria for judging between them. There is only what there is within each discourse, in other words there are only a series of separate rationalities.

Thus we are back with the Kantian problem. Where can Christianity fit within this schema? How can claims of religious groups to have identified a universal way of living or meaning to life applicable to all people continue to be maintained in this context of plural rationalities? If genres of discourse or language games are that watertight then they can make no claims beyond their boundaries. The idea that only money can cross those divides is surely anathema to both theology and traditional philosophy. There are no more metanarratives or big stories that carry conviction now, but merely a disparate series of local narratives or discourses, each with their own set of rules and clearly defined boundaries. Philosophy, either in the form of the Enlightenment project or in any other, is merely a local narrative. But then, so indeed is Christianity.

This is surely the real challenge for theology to face if it is determined to take seriously the philosophical arguments surrounding Post-Modernity. It is not that Modernity has somehow come to an end or that the challenges of reason have been driven from the field. It is how Christianity is to fit into a situation of plural rationalities where no one discourse can claim dominance over the rest. What is so interesting as we now move on to examine the way in which certain contemporary theologians respond to this is that they use Post-Modernity to relativize all other narratives but only in order to reassert Christianity as a metanarrative. Are these the only alternatives: either a metanarrative or a series of local narratives confined to their own private worlds?

Theology and Metanarratives

What I intend to do now is to summarize the positions of three contemporary theologians as they relate to this specific issue. The strange thing is that each of them is concerned to present an interpretation of Christianity distinct from the ideas and influences of the wider culture, but can apparently only do so on the basis of a philosophical argument external to the Christian tradition. I want to argue that it is the inherent perversity of this approach that makes it clear that Christianity is no more watertight than any other tradition and that in its encounters and relationships with other ideas and traditions it is possible to find alternative philosophical arguments more appropriate to the theological task of interpreting and communicating the Christian faith. First however we need to locate these three theologians within the concerns of this chapter.

George Lindbeck is an American theologian from within the Lutheran tradition and is currently Pitkin Professor of Historical Theology (emeritus) at Yale Divinity School. He was a Protestant observer at the Second Vatican Council and edited the reports drawn up by his fellow observers. It was this experience within the ecumenical work of the churches that led him into the theological approach that is of interest to this book. He was also profoundly influenced by the work of Hans Frei, a fellow theologian concerned with the subject of biblical interpretation (21).

Frei has attempted to reverse what he sees as the Enlightenment influence on the way Christians now use the Bible. Briefly, the latter led to people trying to fit biblical stories and ideas into the framework of their own lives rather than allowing the biblical narratives to shape and define a life of religious belief and practice. This stems from the Enlightenment emphasis upon the autonomy of human reason replacing the authority of any external tradition. The Enlightenment big story of human autonomy and progress dictates terms to the Christian story as encountered in the Bible. Which should take priority or be the dominant narrative, the supposedly universal reason of the Enlightenment or the biblical narrative itself? This question is central to the work of each of our three theologians.

Also crucial to this approach is the notion of narrative itself. Frei has argued for a reading of the biblical narratives as narratives, as stories similar to those recounted in a novel. So there is an overall story being told in the complete text of the Bible and also a host of smaller narratives within that whole, each with their own linguistic rules and integrity. Essentially, the biblical narrative is a story for Christians to dwell in, not a text to be interpreted to and for people who live outside its narrative and the world of the text.

Immediately we begin to hear the echoes of the ideas suggested by both Lyotard and Wittgenstein of a series of separate and distinctive discourses or language games, each possessing their own internal rules and integrity. In fact Lindbeck expands Frei's argument using Wittgenstein's notion of language games. He applies this not just to biblical interpretation, but to the whole realm of Christian doctrine. According to Lindbeck, doctrines are communally authoritative rules of discourse, attitude and action, specifically with regard to those beliefs and practices considered essential to the identity and welfare of the Christian community (22). So Christianity has its own distinctive doctrinal and constitutive rules, the grammar of its religious language game, and it is only once one is operating within these that there can be a Christian interpretation of either biblical text or wider world.

Once again, this can be seen as an attempted reversal of the general understanding of religion stemming from the Enlightenment. In the latter primary importance is attributed to religious experience and it is this that is perceived to be the foundation for religious faith. In terms of the Kantian problem, faith becomes restricted to the individual, the subjective or even the aesthetic. What Lindbeck is saying is that you cannot even sensibly talk about having an experience - religious or otherwise - unless you are already within a linguistic framework or language game from where such an experience can make sense. So one has to be already living within the Christian story before any experience can be identified as specifically Christian. This is described as a cultural-linguistic approach to theology, challenging the notion that there can be any foundation for the Christian life external to its distinctive narrative or language game. An example of this would be that Roman Catholics are much more likely to have experiences of the Virgin Mary because it is already within their grammar of belief that such experiences are likely to occur.

The obvious and central problem with this approach that will be crucial for the later discussion is that it appears to make it impossible to cross the boundaries between different narratives or discourses, even those within the Christian tradition. How then is it possible to account for conversion, let alone know how to go about communicating the Christian faith to others? Any educational element is minimised and it is all about socializing people within the faith community, or preaching to the already converted. Does this do justice to what actually happens?

There are in fact a number of difficulties in Lindbeck's approach that must now be noted. The move from the Wittgensteinian insight that people operate within different language games and that it is only from within those that words and concepts acquire meaning, to the assumption that religions are in fact enclosed systems of doctrinal rules and practices appears innocuous. However, on reflection it is not immediately justifiable. Are religious traditions independent, distinctive and watertight in that way? It would appear not. As Lyotard says, the real problem of Modernity is that we move rapidly from one sphere of operation or discourse to another as we enter the different worlds of commerce, education, politics, religion, family life and so on. Are there people who live solely and exclusively within the religious language game, totally impervious to the influences and concepts of other discourses? If there are Lindbeck himself is not one of them as his encounter with Wittgenstein's philosophy amply illustrates. So why make such an extreme claim?

A further problem is that Lindbeck is unable to account for the internal pluralism of the Christian tradition itself. It is a fact of life that Christians do not always understand or interpret their faith in the same way and that there is internal conflict over key elements of the doctrines and practices of the church. The debate within parts of the Anglican church over the ordination of women or of practising homosexuals and within the Roman Catholic church over the celibacy of the priesthood and contraception are very obvious examples. Lindbeck assumes a normality and stability of a Christian doctrinal framework that fails to take account of the very different contexts and locations of faith that Wittgenstein's approach could help to describe and explain. There is a real danger of assuming or imposing just one version of the Christian tradition, of one local narrative claiming dominance over the rest.

Here, I believe, we return to the central problem of this approach. Is Christianity as a whole still a metanarrative, claiming to offer a universal explanation of human existence and thus presumably denying any validity to alternative explanations, either those of other faiths, or of scientific or political theories? Or is it just one of a number of local narratives or small stories, either in competition with or sealed off from all the other local narratives? Lindbeck seems to want the best of both worlds. So, it is both the case that there are a host of independent language games or local narratives and that Christianity is still a metanarrative making universal claims. There is surely an irreconcilable contradiction here and this can be attributed to the fact that he selectively appropriates the philosophical ideas but then ignores their wider implications in order to return to a pre-modern version of Christianity.

He has the same dilemma in trying to describe the Christian tradition itself. He presupposes a unified interpretation of Christianity, re-imposing a big story in a pre-modern fashion, but his argument is based on the Post-Modern insight that there is a plurality of discourses and language games in which there can be no one dominant narrative. At this point the warning bells should start to ring as we begin to wonder whether this whole argument is founded upon a false dichotomy. Is it the case that there can only be either a metanarrative (big story) or a series of competing and watertight local narratives (small stories)? But that is to anticipate. Another suspicion also springs to mind. If the Christian tradition is the enclosed and therefore self-sufficient discourse that Lindbeck appears to suggest then why is there a need to adopt any external philosophical ideas? Once again there is a danger of a false dichotomy: either there is a distinctive and somehow 'pure' Christianity or there is a distorted and 'impure' Christianity deflowered by contact with extra-traditional sources. Is this the way traditions really function?

A second American theologian struggling with similar issues and drawing upon very much the same sources is Stanley Hauerwas. Hauerwas is from an evangelical Methodist background and is currently Professor of Christian Ethics at the University of Notre Dame, Indiana. In his own account of his theological development he traces the beginnings of his particular doctrinal stance back to the height of the Vietnam War when he first entered his teaching career (23). He states that he found the approach of the distinguished Christian social ethicist Reinhold Niebuhr inadequate to the task of establishing a critical perspective on the Vietnam conflict. Hauerwas comes to see Niebuhr as a paradigmatic American liberal who, despite his critique of American optimistic liberalism, still sees the task of the churches as making democracy work better.

It is this close identification of Christianity with liberal democracy, itself of course the heir of Enlightenment thought, that Hauerwas now goes on to challenge. In a sense this parallels in the field of Christian social ethics the attempts of Frei and Lindbeck in the spheres of biblical study and doctrine to reverse the predominance of the Enlightenment view that it is the autonomous, rational individual who defines the interpretation of the faith. Hauerwas wants as his starting point a church community with its own internal integrity. Only from that base can one develop a Christian ethical stance.

What is being challenged here is the belief, derived from the Enlightenment, that there is some neutral or objective position, external to the Christian tradition, that could be the foundation for ethical thought. In other words, the big story that human reason is the arbiter of moral truth and can discern the criteria for ethical judgement, is put back into its place as one more local narrative. In which case, Christianity can safely revert to its own narrative as the appropriate basis for ethical reflection. The cause of liberal democracy is one more small story and should not be allowed to dictate terms to the Christian tradition.

Hauerwas argues that Christian adherence to the Enlightenment view was closely associated with the social strategies of Christendom, in other words the period when there was an identification between the church and the state. 'Such social strategies were the attempt by Christians to create societies in which it would be possible to think that Christians believed what anyone would believe on reflection' (24). Unfortunately, the result of this was to reduce Christianity to a set of beliefs that legitimated the false universalism of liberalism. Hauerwas' objective is to re-establish the significance of the church in its own right by severing the link with liberal democracy.

There is an assumption behind this that the Enlightenment vision of a peaceful order to be created through rational, political means - in this case democracy - has now been undermined. So for Christianity to continue to hang onto the coat tails of liberal democracy would be a strategic as well as a theological mistake. The point of the philosophical and political developments since the Enlightenment has been to create people incapable of killing each other in the name of God. Yet the result of this, according to Hauerwas, has been merely to replace a religious motivation for violence with a secular one:

'Indeed, I think it can be suggested that the political achievement of the Enlightenment has been to create people who believe it necessary to kill others in the interest of something called 'the nation', which is allegedly protecting and ensuring their freedom as individuals' (25).

It is significant that Hauerwas draws upon Rorty to support his argument that the philosophical presuppositions of the liberal world are undergoing radical revision. Hauerwas admits that this is not enough to justify the claim that the liberal world is coming apart, but his intention is nevertheless clear.

Post-Modernity is being used to suggest that the Enlightenment world is coming to an end and that therefore Christianity should bale out before the ship goes down.

The other strand of Hauerwas' argument that relates directly to Post-Modernity refers to the issue of belief. Again, it echoes Lindbeck's concern to show that the Christian community discourse precedes experience, not the other way round. So Christianity in the context of liberal democracy, where religious practice is not a matter of public controversy, tends to be reduced to belief. By contrast, in societies where Christianity was socially and politically condemned, it was still clear that all questions of truth and falsity are political. However, the cultural establishment of Christianity in liberal societies has forced Christians to divorce their convictions from their practices, thus damaging the intelligibility of their faith: 'By being established...it became more important that people believe rather than be incorporated into the church' (26). Furthermore, if believing is a reasonable thing that all rational people might be expected to do, then Christianity loses its cutting edge and becomes another fairly harmless cultural practice.

What is it then that Hauerwas advocates in the face of the supposed breakdown of the Enlightenment metanarrative?

'It is my thesis that questions of the truth or the falsity of Christian convictions cannot even be addressed until Christians recover the church as a political community necessary for our salvation...Our beliefs, or better our convictions, only make sense as they are embodied in a political community we call the church' (27).

As with Lindbeck, it is very much a matter of dwelling in the Christian narrative as bounded by the rules of the institutional church. Christians must cease being involved in the development of the ethics of medicine or business or sexual relationships as this still presupposes a rational, objective approach to morality external to the Christian community. There can be no autonomous morality for Christians, only the disciplined practices of the faithful within the confines of the church.

There is one further implication of Hauerwas' position that it is important to note. Given his rejection of the Enlightenment hope of open, rational and democratic discussion, there is no longer any point in using argument as a way of communicating the Christian faith to others. Hauerwas accepts that it may in fact be impossible to communicate the substance of the Christian tradition to those outside the fold by means of discussion. There is simply no basis for a discourse common and yet external to individual traditions. I think this is a most damaging conclusion, if it is justified, but it is the logic of accepting the dichotomy noted earlier. Either there is a metanarrative or there are only local narratives that are essentially separate and enclosed, defined by the rules of their own language game. For Hauerwas Christianity is a metanarrative incapable of being communicated outside the boundaries of the Christian community. He realizes that he contradicts this conclusion himself by even bothering to write books and to give lectures but: 'I simply have to acknowledge that there is no way of avoiding this awkward position' (28). In the final section of this chapter I hope to show that there is in fact a way of doing just that.

Before moving on we need to register some of the obvious doubts about Hauerwas' position. First, the idea that liberal democracy is coming to an end, or at least has been effectively undermined by Post-Modernity, is dubious given the discussion about Lyotard earlier in this chapter. Second, there seems to be a simplistic assumption that Enlightenment rationality has also now been totally ruled out of court. Once again, we have seen that this is open to question. Third, Hauerwas does appear to place the Christian community in an unnecessarily isolated position, concluding that traditions can be somehow pure and watertight. The consequence of this could be a complete withdrawal from direct political involvement. Perhaps this could be seen as exercising a prophetic ministry, but it would be prophecy from a safe distance and thus limited in its impact. Fourth, does there have to be such a clear-cut difference or conflict between the Enlightenment notion of autonomy and the Christian understanding of vocation? The point about a pluralistic and democratic society is that choice is exercised in the context of a wider community where there can still be a commitment to some common good, in addition to adherence to different traditions. It seems as though Hauerwas is disturbed by the notion of this sort of pluralism, but, as the theologian Mark Cladis comments, if Christians cannot handle this, then their faith must be very frail indeed (29).

Finally, there is still the assumption that Christianity is forced out of the public arena and into the sphere of the private in liberal democracies. In Kantian terms, religion is reduced to the realm of the subjective or aesthetic. Is this supported by the evidence? In the first chapter we saw enough examples of Christianity being involved in civic and political life to at least raise questions in our minds. Perhaps retreating into the community ghetto is more likely to cut Christians off from public life than is a continuing critical involvement.

It could be said that the major weakness of both Lindbeck and Hauerwas is that they are not consistently Post-Modern. They are selective in their use of the ideas supposedly deriving from that source and fail to take on board the full and radical implications of that position. Probably one of the most consistent attempts to develop a Post-Modern theology is that of John Milbank, an English theologian now based at Cambridge University, in his book 'Theology and Social Theory' (30). He produces a tightly argued and wide ranging approach and, at this stage, I will only attempt to cover his comments on metanarratives. Further reference to his work will come in later chapters.

At first sight it would certainly seem that Milbank's intention is to take as his starting point the Post-Modern argument about plural discourses and rationalities. In his introduction he warns that the book is to be an exercise in sceptical relativism: 'If my Christian perspective is persuasive, then this should be a persuasion intrinsic to the Christian logos itself, not the apologetic mediation of a universal human reason' (31). However, the objective is not to reduce the Christian tradition to the status of merely one local narrative, as part of the pathos of modern theology has been its false humility in the face of alternative discourses. Milbank's intention is to overcome this 'and to restore, in postmodern terms, the possibility of theology as a metadiscourse' (32).

Immediately then it is clear that Milbank, like Lindbeck and Hauerwas, sees the apparent undermining of Enlightenment universal reason by Post-Modernity as the occasion for restating the universal claims of Christianity with renewed confidence. Despite the fact that Post-Modernity relativizes and reduces all metanarratives to local narratives, Milbank intends to use it to re-establish Christianity as a metanarrative. Can this really be consistently Post-Modern?

What concerns Milbank is that theology has allowed itself to be positioned by the supposedly neutral and objective arguments of Enlightenment rationality. This is exactly the problem that we noted in the earlier discussion of Kant's arguments on the different types of reason. The Enlightenment big story about technical, moral and aesthetic reason, combined with the success of science in recent generations, has relegated theology to the realm of the subjective and the private. Christianity has been placed where it can have least impact, domesticated, or, as Milbank prefers to describe it, the sublime is now policed by the theories of a secular social science (33). However, what Milbank sets out to show through a Foucauldian archaeology of the social sciences themselves is that they are in fact a distorted form of theology. Their claim to be neutral and objective, whilst dictating to theology where it should be located, masks theological assumptions that Christianity would want to challenge. So, theology should no longer allow itself to be policed and positioned by the secular theories.

Theology has to regain a sense of itself as a social science and, in fact, the queen of the sciences, for the inhabitants of the alternative city, those on pilgrimage through this temporary world:

'Theology has frequently sought to borrow from elsewhere a fundamental account of society or history, and then to see what theological insights will cohere with it. But it has been shown that no such fundamental account, in the sense of something neutral, rational and universal, is really available. It is theology itself that will have to provide its own account of the final causes at work in human history, on the basis of its own particular and historically specific faith' (34).

In the midst of the cacophony of all the competing stories now acknowledged by Post-Modernity, Christianity will be able to show that it still has the best story of all. Milbank's criterion for the best story is of course the one that validates the Christian narrative, that is that it offers the vision of a peaceful and non-violent realm. We will return to this subject at a later stage when we review what Milbank has to say about the nihilism of secular reason.

For the moment one passing comment. It seems to me that Milbank is making out of the now well-established interpretation that there is no such thing as a neutral, value-free approach to science, either social or natural, a rather extreme argument. Because nobody else is neutral there is no reason why Christians should listen to or converse with anybody else, rather, they are perfectly justified in going off into a corner and just talking amongst themselves. Such an approach might appear childish, perverse and unnecessary to anybody operating in a business context. For instance, at most board meetings it is a matter of protocol that interests should be declared before substantive discussions begin. However, the fact that there are and always will be interests or non-neutral perspectives does not put a stop to further discussion. On the contrary, their declaration in advance is an essential component of the ensuing debate. It is possible to 'lay one's cards on the table' and still remain at the table. The question for Milbank is that of who controls the table. It seems as though unless theology is allowed to hold all the cards and dictate the game then it should not be prepared to play. Better to exit for the corridor and continue a purely private conversation.

So, in negotiating terms, Lindbeck, Hauerwas and Milbank begin by demanding the impossible - neutrality - and when it is not forthcoming they use that as the excuse to abandon the discussions. Why do that? Why not stay at the table and keep a stake in what is going on? Well, we can see what the answer is, but there is surely a real problem here. On the one hand our triumvirate presuppose the continued existence of the pluralist, liberal democracy that guarantees them their freedom of religious expression and the right to withdraw from negotiations, but, on the other, they claim to be abandoning just that way of organizing society. If everybody did the same as them liberal democracy would surely collapse and there would be a free-for-all where only the strongest or the most manipulative would survive. Violence would become the way of settling differences.

Two questions spring to mind. Is it possible for Christians - or any other group - to leave the table in this manner? Second, is it advisable or even theologically justified for them to do so? It is clear that Milbank would give an affirmative answer to both questions. Theology has to take on the mantle of a kind of Christian sociology, re-telling the story of how its own internal practices and doctrines have developed.

'The task of such a theology is not apologetic, nor even argument. Rather it is to tell again the Christian mythos, pronounce again the Christian logos and call again for Christian praxis in a manner that restores their freshness and originality. It must articulate Christian difference in such a fashion as to make it strange' (35).

One could say, rather cynically, that precisely this is to allow oneself to be positioned by a secular culture, forced to offer a pure and distinctive product that can be successfully marketed against all the other competitors in the field. We have the best story. It certainly presupposes that there is such a clear-cut and purified Christianity and that the church - in theory at least - can effectively incarnate this doctrine and practice.

I will argue in due course that Milbank is led down this blind alley by a false reading of Post-Modernity and by an unnaturally constricted view of the working of traditions. It is all very well constructing this strange and distinctive version of Christianity - and Milbank is happy to acknowledge that this is in fact a construction by and for the Christian community - but why have a story that nobody else can either understand or will be prepared to listen to? I find it hard to accept that the only legitimate role for Christians is to talk amongst themselves. Have apologetic and argument no further part to play in communicating the Christian faith?

There will be more of Milbank in later chapters, but the immediate task is to show that these extreme positions are, in part at least, a result of the way the argument has been set up. In other words, there can be only either a metanarrative a big story making universal claims, or a series of discrete, enclosed and self-sufficient local narratives, all jostling for position in the intellectual marketplace. There is another alternative, one that both takes seriously the integrity and the contextuality of traditions and enables those traditions to continue talking and listening to each other.

Christianity as a Major Narrative

The starting point of this argument is a suspicion about the rather cavalier and undifferentiated use of the term narrative and thus the idea about local narratives that is attached to it. Do these two alternatives do justice to the variety of types of narrative that humans construct and develop? It would appear not. Commenting on Lyotard's definition of metanarrative Steven Best and Douglas Kellner make the following points (36). First, we might want to distinguish between master narratives that attempt to subsume every particular and every key issue into one totalizing theory (e.g. Hegel or some forms of Marxism), from grand narratives that attempt to tell a big story such as the rise of capitalism or of the colonial subject. Second, even within those grand narratives we could differentiate between those that tell a story about the foundation of knowledge and those that try to describe and explain the emergence of a particular social phenomenon - for instance, male domination or the exploitation of the working class. Even then there are differences between stories that are chronological in nature and those that analyse historical change, discontinuities and ruptures. As Best and Kellner say: 'Lyotard tends to lump all large narratives together and thus does violence to the diversity of narratives in our culture' (37).

If this is right - and it does seem to do greater justice to the variety of narratives that are to be found - then it is far better surely to treat each narrative on its own merits rather than to categorise only to dismiss. The problem is that the complexity then becomes overwhelming to the point where the very term narrative disappears beneath a landslide of ever more subtle distinctions. I want to simplify by using the term Major Narrative. What I mean by this is that there are stories that fall between the two extremes of metanarrative and local narrative. In other words, they are still substantial enough as interpretative frameworks to make claims that transcend a specific or local context, but they stop short of making the grand or universal claims of Lyotard's metanarratives. In addition, although they cross local and contextual boundaries they explicitly acknowledge that both locality and context form an essential part of their construction. To revert to the analogy of the board meeting, they declare their interests and do not feign neutrality, but they do not then go on to restrict themselves to conversations with the local or already converted. They enter the open debate, both retaining the integrity of their interpretation and acknowledging their limited and contextual nature.

I want to argue that both Christianity and the Enlightenment tradition can be developed as Major rather than metanarratives. The advantage of this is that they can then continue to talk to each other rather than one or the other taking off into the corridor. This also offers a way of overcoming the Kantian problematic of how both philosophy and theology can position themselves without sacrificing their internal integrity in the Post-Modern situation of a plurality of rationalities. The other aspect of the debate is that this will assist in challenging that notion of pure and watertight traditions impervious to other ideas and influences. I want to propose that the concept of a Major Narrative allows for the mixing up and blurring of ideas that are inevitably a factor in the way that traditions develop. Rather than seeing traditions as solid and clearly defined practices and blocks of knowledge they need to be understood as flexible, permeable and organic entities, effectively the constructs of human thought and feeling that they are.

First, the working out of this idea within theology. Lindbeck, Hauerwas and Milbank each acknowledge the tension between the variety of local and contextual interpretations of the Christian faith and a Christian metanarrative that claims to tell, if not the whole, then certainly the essential story. However, rather than learning to live with this tension they attempt to resolve it in favour of their own particular version of a Christian metanarrative. The irony is that this is all that this can ever be - their own particular version, another local narrative. But, if instead of metanarrative plus local narratives, we interpret Christianity as Major Narrative including and composed of many sub-narratives, the tension does not have to be resolved. It becomes more possible to retain the integrity of both the local and translocal stories and to continue to require them to negotiate through critical discussion. This seems to me a better way of describing the way Christianity operates in practice.

Such an understanding is particularly important in the light of the varieties of Christianity that are developing in different parts of the world. So, for instance, in Asia, there is now a proliferation of images of Jesus (38). One way to deal with these would be to impose an 'orthodox' total and fixed portrayal of Jesus by means of a central church authority. However, as one theologian comments:

'The christological enterprise is an ongoing task. Cultures and contexts are not static entities; they constantly change and throw up warp and woof of political, social and religious strands in an ever-new fabric. As cultures evolve, as new contexts and experiences emerge, as new questions surface, so features and aspects of Jesus will continue to be discovered' (39).

I suggest that seeing Christianity as a Major and sub-narratives is better able to account for the fluid and dynamic nature of the development of Christian insights and doctrine.

What though about the Enlightenment tradition, the notion that human reason in a particular form is capable of working out all that is necessary for human emancipation or salvation? Can it too accept a more limited status and yet still make a valuable and substantial contribution? Once again, the answer I believe is that it can. For this I return to the ideas of Habermas as outlined in the last chapter. We recall that the Post-Modern criticism of Enlightenment reason is that it imposes a particular and local tradition under the guise of neutrality and objectivity. It pretends that there is no content, no value judgement grounding its approach when in fact there is. Habermas' initial response to this was to claim that his idea of communicative reason did not impose any specific content in the conduct of human discussion, but merely established a procedure for conducting that discussion. It was the procedure, not any particular content that was universal (40).

Habermas has more recently refined his position in the light of the criticism that a procedural approach is still too formalistic and can take no account of either context or local narrative. He is clear that both his concept of communicative reason and the ideas for a Discourse Ethics that flow from it are not another metanarrative in the manner of its predecessor, Enlightenment reason. If there is a universality involved it resides in the way that humans operate through language using the four criteria for effective communication as described and in the assumption that all people should have access to discussions that will affect their lives. However, if this can be seen as a Major Narrative taking into account a variety of sub-narratives then it is still possible to retain the tension between the local and the translocal that is the reality of human communication.

There is a substantial and vigorous debate still going on over this aspect of Habermas' work, too detailed to be recorded here. Yet it does need to be said that at least part of his continued refinement of his ideas is due to a feminist critique. How can the specific concerns and needs of women figure in what appears to be a very formalistic approach? The work of Seyla Benhabib has been particularly influential in developing this critique (41). However, rather than undermining the general argument, she has contributed a richer and more satisfactory articulation of this approach:

'If feminist theory has reminded universalist moralities in the Kantian tradition of the need to compensate 'for the vulnerability of living creatures who through socialization are individuated in such a way that they can never assert their identity for themselves alone'...this is a significant paradigm shift which I described...as the move away from 'legislative and substitutionalist toward interactive universalism' '(42).

In plain English, the specific and local differences of human beings and their relationships are now accounted for within the Major Narrative. It is not a matter of either universal or local, but of both local and translocal.

So there is a strong case to be made that both Christianity and the heir to the Enlightenment tradition as being developed by Habermas and colleagues fit the description of Major Narrative plus sub-narratives. As such they can meet the Post-Modern criticism that they are totalizing or metanarratives that make claims at the expense of both other people and other traditions. They can also take into account the local and particular, but without dissolving into a plethora of self-contained and incommensurable language games. But does this approach help us to understand or determine how communication between and across traditions can take place?

I believe it can, first by questioning the idea that traditions are exclusive and watertight compartments free from the influences of other traditions, and second by suggesting that there is no one guaranteed way of crossing the boundaries between traditions - each case has to be worked out individually. What Habermas' theory of communicative reason makes clear is that, through the structure of language itself, we all have a stake in the debates about both public and private life. The actual content of those debates will depend on the subjects under discussion. So Christianity does have a stake in both politics and science, for instance, but the exact nature of these can only be pursued within the specific context. I have suggested elsewhere that the concept of mediating frameworks is a way of describing the relationships between traditions (43). Thus science and Christianity would need to find a mediating framework or set of ideas that provide enough common ground for serious contact and yet enable both to retain their integrity within the ensuing discussion. Similarly for theology and sociology. Milbank would rule out any such possibility in advance of course, but this seems unjustifiably dogmatic.

These insights will be developed further in the following chapters as we begin to see some of these potential mediating frameworks emerging. For the moment we return to the questions posed at the beginning of this discussion on metanarratives. The theologians referred to, Lash, Lindbeck, Hauerwas and Milbank, are attracted by the notion that Post-Modernity has conclusively undermined the understanding of reason developed since the Enlightenment and that they perceive to have been detrimental to Christianity. This leads them to abandon discussion with other traditions and to concentrate upon the practices, disciplines and language games of the Christian community. My argument has been that this is an unnecessary over-reaction based upon a false reading of Post-Modernity. The latter, as has been illustrated through examination of Lyotard, the originator of this particular debate, is about the continuing development of plural rationalities and the relationships between them rather than a rejection of rationality or reason as such. To assume that the Enlightenment tradition has now come to an end is actually to by-pass the real questions raised by Post-Modernity. Furthermore, the latter is not to be confused with social comment of the 'end of Modernity' variety.

The theologians in question find themselves impaled upon the horns of a dilemma as a result of the position they take. Either there is a totalizing metanarrative making universal claims or there are a series of self-contained and enclosed local narratives unable to relate to each other. They attempt to resolve this by simply restating that Christianity is a metanarrative, thus pre-empting further debate about the internal pluralism of Christianity itself, let alone the possibility of serious contact between Christianity and other traditions. The irony of this position is that it presupposes the existence of the pluralist liberal democracy that they claim to be leaving behind.

An examination of the concept of metanarrative reveals that it is itself a big story requiring more detailed differentiation. I suggest the notion of Major Narrative plus sub-narratives as a more appropriate description of the way in which traditions operate and, in particular, their internal and external relationships. This releases both philosophy in the form of a refined Habermasian communicative reason and theology in apologetic mode to continue in a critical dialogue, both with each other and also with other traditions and disciplines. It also supports the view that there will be no one way of dealing with the Kantian problem of plural rationalities, but a plurality of ways as one might reasonably expect. I suggest that this is a more creative and positive direction for theology to pursue than the intellectual isolationism being advocated by those theologians who claim to have adopted Post-Modernity. They are of course entitled to choose to set themselves apart in the manner, but one must press the question of whether this really is the most appropriate means of doing justice to the integrity and insights of the Christian tradition.

5

Theology and Secular Reason

Introduction

I t is clear by now that the archvillain of the melodrama of Post-Modernity is Reason itself. In this chapter I intend to examine in greater detail why this is so. I will also evaluate the argument that Secular Reason is essentially nihilistic as found in the work of Milbank and then counter this with ideas drawn largely from Habermas. However, we must begin with a brief summary of why this is important for theology.

What are the recognised sources of authority for theology? For most at least there are three: Scripture, Tradition and Reason (1). Theology - like any discipline - is required to make judgements on what lies firmly within its boundaries and for this it needs criteria. At its most basic level, if an idea or practice that develops cannot be deemed consistent with what is already to be found in the Christian faith as contained in the Scriptures or in the Tradition, then it must be excluded. The danger of this is that it will lead to a static and inherently conservative Christianity unable to respond flexibly and imaginatively to new situations and challenges. It also assumes that there is a readily identifiable Christian tradition that will gain the consent of all Christians. Hence, in order to introduce an element of movement and of legitimate disagreement into the development of doctrine and practice it is necessary to include a third term in the equation, that of Reason. This creates a system of checks and balances where no one term can be dominant, although there will be different emphases depending upon where one stands within the whole. So, for instance, Evangelical Christians are more likely to emphasize the authority of Scripture: Anglo-Catholics that of the Tradition and Reason will be of greater significance for the liberal wing of Christianity.

The theological responses to Post-Modernity illustrated in the previous chapter are clearly an attempt to detach Reason from this process and reflect a growing dominance of the Evangelical emphasis within theology. Thus both Hauerwas and Milbank wish to jettison Reason from the theological equation because they believe its presence has led to a distorted interpretation of the faith. They are also keen to abandon Reason because they believe - mistakenly I will argue - that Post-Modern philosophy has now undermined the claims of Reason as embodied in the metanarrative of the Enlightenment. If they are correct then there will be important consequences for the future shape of theology.

One of these is that theology is reduced to an essentially static set of interpretations and another that Christianity would become exclusively a 'Religion of the Book'. This has echoes of the forms of fundamentalism examined in the opening chapter. Perhaps of equal concern is the possibility of types of reasoning still being used and yet either denied or hidden within the process and thus exercising an even more insidious dominance. Both Hauerwas and Milbank present what appear to be carefully reasoned arguments and yet seem keen to deny that argument forms part of their armoury. This could be a claim of immunity from counter-argument and, I suggest, a very dangerous ploy. A possible consequence of this would be the exclusion of any attempt at reasoned debate and disagreement both within the faith tradition and with those outside it and thus the creation of an enclosed, sectarian and fundamentalist Christianity.

The question that theology needs to face is surely this: Is a critique of Reason necessarily a total denial of or destruction of it? It will be the argument of this chapter that some contemporary theologians too readily identify a Post-Modern critique with a total destruction and thus fall into the trap of abandoning one of the three pivots of theology itself.

Reason and the Holocaust

Why has Reason fallen into disrepute? Some of the explanations for this were offered in the last chapter and I will recap briefly before moving on to more detailed argument. The belief that human society would develop into a state of liberty, equality and fraternity as a result of abandoning the superstitions of religion for the steadying hand of human reason has been seriously challenged by major events of the Twentieth

Century. Far from bringing peace, harmony and justice, the development of a Reason released from any moral or religious imperatives has led to mass destruction and the threat of ecological catastrophe. Reason has become detached from the wider framework in which it offered such promise and in the hands of unscrupulous politicians and research-blind scientists has become merely another instrument of repression. This much of the argument we have gathered by now.

However, there is a further dimension to this debate. It is one thing to say that the distortions and damage wrought by Reason are the result of contingent historical circumstances - in other words, it just happens to have worked out this way but it could have been otherwise and perhaps still could be. It is a much more profound and disturbing claim to say that these destructive developments stem from an inherent defect in Reason itself. Thus such consequences were bound to happen given what Reason is or has become. If this latter claim could be upheld then it has the most serious implications, not just for theology, but for human society at large. What are we left with as a way of organizing ourselves if Reason is essentially and necessarily damaged or demonic as this claim suggests?

Yet it is just such a claim that we now encounter in theology and that can be traced back to social theory. As the heading of this section suggests the key historical events at the centre of this argument are those of the Second World War and, more specifically, the Nazi death camps. As we touch more deeply on this theme we need to acknowledge that it appears impossible to be dispassionate or objective about, what for many, represents the depths of human depravity and evil. In fact, that is part of the problem. There is a sense in which it seems not only insensitive but positively obscene to use such circumstances as the fodder for any sort of intellectual discussion. In the face of Auschwitz the only possible human response may be a respectful and remorseful silence. Is this then what human beings have come to?

Yet of course we cannot keep silent, for we are forced to try to explain and to understand. The popular and safe explanation is that Auschwitz is a blip, an aberration, the result of a society gone massively out of control and allowing its deepest instincts and most powerful emotions to run riot on a previously unimagined scale. So it is evidence of the irrational and dark side of humanity taking over. Not so, go the counter-arguments. In fact it is exactly the opposite. Auschwitz is the ultimate consequence and logical outcome of the dominance of Reason. Far from being a blip, it is the central symbol of the society we have created by pursuing the metanarrative of the Enlightenment. How can this be so?

For an answer we turn to the work of Zygmunt Bauman, Emeritus Professor of Sociology at the University of Leeds and a highly distinctive commentator on Post-Modernity (2). To be fair to Bauman he does not hold the extreme interpretation of Reason as being inherently destructive, but his arguments do add force to the position of those theologians who seek Reason's final discrediting. Bauman suggests that the practical task of exterminating the Jews could not have been made possible without the skills and techniques of instrumental reason and bureaucracy.

'The most shattering of lessons deriving from the analysis of the 'twisted road to Auschwitz' is that - in the last resort - the choice of physical extermination as the right means to the task of Entfernung was a product of routine bureaucratic procedures; means-end calculus, budget balancing, universal rule application. To make the point sharper still - the choice was an effect of the earnest effort to find rational solutions to successive 'problems' as they arose in changing circumstances.' (3).

This was not an outbreak of random and uncalculated killing perpetrated by the odd psychopath, but an efficiently run operation carried out in an orderly and methodical manner by people who were just doing their job. It just so happened that this particular job was exterminating as many Jews as possible. Without proper organization, the necessary bureaucracy and a disciplined workforce the whole task would have been impossible. In one sense this is Modernity at its most impressive. 'The Holocaust was not an irrational outflow of the not-yet-fully eradicated residues of pre-modern barbarity. It was a legitimate resident in the house of modernity; indeed one who would not be at home in any other house' (4).

Bauman makes it clear that this is not to say that the Holocaust was determined by modern bureaucracy or that instrumental reason necessarily leads to mass extermination. But, the depressing aspect of all this is that modern rationality was not only incapable of preventing these horrific events but that it made a positive contribution to them. How then can it still be maintained that Reason can lead humanity to the Promised Land? Further, it is the bureaucratic mind-set that enables us to view society as an object of administration, as a series of problems to be solved and situations to be manipulated. Social engineering, in whatever form, only becomes a realistic possibility in the modern world. Thus Reason has to carry its share of guilt for these events:

'...it was the spirit of instrumental rationality, and its modern, bureaucratic form of institutionalization. which made the Holocaust-style solutions not only possible, but eminently 'reasonable' - and increased the probability of their choice. This increase in probability is more than fortuitously related to the ability of modern bureaucracy to co-ordinate the actions of a great number of moral individuals in the pursuit of any, also immoral ends' (5).

Here is the crux of the argument and the issue that will haunt this chapter. Reason, in the form of instrumental rationality - identifying the most efficient means of achieving a particular end - appears to be inherently amoral. So it can just as easily be turned to the task of an immoral end - such as exterminating the Jews - as it can to a moral one. It is this supposed moral neutrality that is Reason's downfall in the eyes of some moral philosophy and theology. It is because of this that it cannot produce the goods of a better society and can play so easily into the hands of human greed and evil. Its claimed neutrality is in fact a sham, at best an instance of self-deception, at its worst a disguise for an extreme form of manipulation. There is no neutral position, no 'view from nowhere' from which all reasonable human beings can adopt a critical and objective stance. The idea of a disembedded and disembodied Reason exempt from the influence of any external tradition is itself just another tradition and to deny this is to blind ourselves from the power at work behind Reason itself. This argument will be more fully developed later in the chapter.

The other major focus of discontent with the dominance of Reason in our culture is undoubtedly concern for the Environment. Although it is essentially applied Reason in the form of science and technology that bears the brunt of the environmental critique, there is no doubt that it is still the Enlightenment metanarrative of progress through Reason that is the deeper target. As much as the destruction of our fellow humans in various episodes of genocide, the potential undermining of the conditions for human life on this planet is laid at the door of a supposedly neutral Reason. Perhaps it is even more clear in this instance that ecological damage is the direct consequence of the application of rational methods. We cannot attribute the problems we now face to evil people pursuing evil ends, but rather to ordinary folk innocently striving for a better standard of living.

However, it is important for the later arguments to note that the status of both Reason and science in this particular debate are not so clear cut. There are within Environmental movements both those who reject Reason and science out of hand in a form of anti-Modernity and those who continue to utilize both in order to refine and improve upon Modernity. In other words, a critique of rationality need not necessarily lead to its complete abandonment. It seems important to recognise that acknowledging the limits of Reason can legitimately evoke a range of responses. The environmental debate illustrates that a complete retreat from Modernity is only one option and possibly the most extreme one at that. Continued critical engagement appears to be a more satisfactory base from which to further environmental concerns and to develop practical responses. Perhaps the thinkers we are now to examine might learn from this approach.

MacIntyre on the Enlightenment Tradition

For this second phase of the argument I have to introduce another major thinker, the moral philosopher Alasdair MacIntyre. MacIntyre was formerly a Fellow of University College, Oxford and is now a Professor of Philosophy at Vanderbilt University, Tennessee. Since 1981 he has written three major works on moral philosophy (6) and his thought has been an influence upon both Hauerwas and Milbank. Although he is not a Post-Modern writer according to the terms set out in Chapter 3, his work on the Enlightenment tradition forms a vital component of the theological response to Post-Modernity. He is often described as a Communitarian and, as this term will recur throughout the following chapters a brief explanation becomes necessary. The role of community in the formation of both personal identity and a moral framework is crucial for those who adopt this approach. As with Lindbeck and Hauerwas from the theological perspective, it is only once one is already within a community bound by a shared language, values and practices that judgements of any sort can be made. There is no 'view from nowhere' only a variety of views from somewhere, from within an existing tradition or context. The metanarrative of the Enlightenment is misleading to the extent that it claims that it is independent of any and every context and also undermines the actual contexts within which alone moral thought and practice can flourish to the extent that it believes itself superior to them. It is clear that such an approach is superficially attractive to a Christian notion of the importance of both community and tradition.

It is not possible to describe and evaluate the views of Milbank and Hauerwas on Secular Reason without first coming to terms with the ideas of MacIntyre, so we must examine these in greater detail. The question we need to keep in our minds is why those two theologians insist on abandoning Reason altogether, instead of being prepared to accept and work with a revised critical version of it. One of the keys to this is to be found in their interpretation of MacIntyre and the other in a false reading of Post-Modernity itself.

MacIntyre's basic position is that modern morality is in a state of chaos and confusion, so much so that we do not even recognize the seriousness of our plight, let alone have the resources to deal with it (7). The explanation for this is that we have been operating with a false and unworkable notion of Reason. The Enlightenment project has promised a version of rationality that is independent of any and every human context and tradition, in other words, the view from nowhere. Such an understanding of rationality is fundamentally flawed according to MacIntyre. There can be no such thing as Reason unless one already stands within a community or tradition. The pathos of modern morality is that all such traditions and communities have been increasingly undermined by the Enlightenment view of a neutral, objective traditionless Reason.

Immediately we see the parallels with the argument about metanarratives in the previous chapter. The Enlightenment project of a decontextualized Reason is merely another local narrative, claiming for itself a universality that cannot be justified. It is only from within the confines of a particular tradition that there can be criteria for moral judgements, just as it is only from within the Christian faith community that one can grasp the meaning of its beliefs and practices. So, the proposed solution to the current state of moral chaos is to return to MacIntyre's concept of the tradition-dependent nature of rationality. Reason and therefore any notion of morality that draws upon it, must be re-embedded within a local tradition or narrative.

However, unlike the theologians who utilize his work, MacIntyre shies away from any suggestion of moral relativism and opposes the suggestion that his theory leads to the situation where we are all uncritically sunk in the particularity of our own traditions. Reason does still have a role to play. The danger of this position is that if MacIntyre's rebuttal of moral relativism and his continued adherence to Reason should prove unconvincing - and we shall see in a moment how this could be so - and his view of morality is then combined with the caricature of Post-Modernity as a complete rejection of Reason, it opens the way for Milbank's own form of communitarian Christianity. This will become clear shortly.

We need to follow MacIntyre's argument in greater detail first. He is clear that liberalism is the strongest candidate so far for the notion that there can be a neutral ground for either Reason or morality. The fact that its arguments break down can be the best evidence we can have that such an approach is doomed to failure. 'There is instead only the practical-rationality-of-this-or-that-tradition and the justice-of-this-or-that-tradition' (8).

However, MacIntyre is acutely aware of what may appear to follow from this view that notions of rationality and justice are only internal to particular traditions. Two conclusions might be entailed. 'The first is that at any fundamental level no rational debate between, rather than within traditions can occur' (9). This is exactly the conclusion that Hauerwas appears to reach on the basis of MacIntyre's arguments. Second, given that each tradition will frame its own standpoint without any reference to external ideas it is possible that translation from one tradition to another will be precluded. Once again this could lead to the situation that Hauerwas is content to accept.

'A social universe composed exclusively of rival traditions...will be one in which there are a number of contending, incompatible but only partially and inadequately communicating, overall views of that universe, each tradition within which is unable to justify its claims over against those of its rivals except to those who already accept them. Is this indeed what follows?' (10).

MacIntyre himself is unwilling to accept these conclusions. He still wants to maintain that there is the possibility of communication between traditions on the basis of certain beliefs, images and texts that might be shared. The problem is that even these shared resources might be interpreted very differently within those traditions and be accorded a very different status. The outcome of this is that no issue between traditions is rationally decidable. 'There can be no rationality as such. Every set of standards, every tradition incorporating a set of standards, has as much and as little claim to our allegiance as any other' (11). This is the relativist challenge and it is hard to see how MacIntyre can meet it.

There is also what he calls the perspectivist challenge. In other words, if no one tradition can offer those outside it good reasons for excluding the theses of its rivals, then neither can it claim legitimacy for its own views in the face of competing claims. Everything becomes arbitrary. One can offer no reason or reasons for adopting one viewpoint or tradition rather than another, other than that one already stands within that tradition.

MacIntyre also rejects the perspectivist conclusion on the basis that it represents a false dichotomy. On one side lie the Enlightenment concepts of truth and rationality, that is that truth is guaranteed by rational methods resting on principles to be accepted by any fully reflective, rational person. On the other lies a post-Enlightenment relativism that baldly states that since the Enlightenment concept does not hold then no other alternative concept of rationality is possible. It is this that MacIntyre wishes to refute by establishing that there is an alternative account of rationality that does not go down the Enlightenment road.

In order to do this he draws upon the work of John Henry Newman and his ideas on the development of Christian doctrine (12). The argument is that traditions move through certain common and identifiable stages and that communication between them is more likely at some stages than at others. The first stage is that of an unquestioning and uncritical adherence to the authoritative sources of that tradition. In the second there are encounters with other situations that raise questions and doubts that cannot be adequately dealt with. Yet there can be a third stage 'in which response to those inadequacies has resulted in a set of reformulations, reevaluations, and new formulations and evaluations, designed to remedy inadequacies and overcome limitations' (13).

Once this third stage is attained then the members of that particular community are able to look back and contrast their current beliefs and position with their former ones. They may then conclude, in the light of those differences, that their earlier beliefs were actually false. The tradition in question will then also have developed a form of enquiry that requires the recognition of certain intellectual virtues, such as the need to acknowledge inadequacies and to be prepared to create critical reformulations. It may also be able to recognize that similar issues are being addressed from within other traditions and that there is the possibility of interaction. In other words, we can still say that there is an element of rational enquiry at work here despite the distinctive nature of different traditions.

'...to some degree, insofar as a tradition of rational enquiry is such, it will tend to recognize what is shares as such with other traditions, and in the development of such traditions common characteristics, if not universal patterns will appear' (14).

It would seem, after all this, that MacIntyre wants the best of both worlds - perhaps rightly so. He wants to acknowledge the role of context and tradition and yet to escape the relativist implications of that acknowledgement. He also wants to offer a critique of the Enlightenment liberal concept of a neutral and objective Reason that transcends and undermines all other traditions. He does this by appealing to other traditions that emphasize the character and virtues he believes are missing from contemporary moral life. Yet, it is not so easy to see where his description of the development of and interaction between traditions is so different from the liberal position he intends to criticize. Perhaps he challenges its universal claims but still, in the end, retains its spirit of rational, critical enquiry. Certainly there is still an explicit role for reasoned argument of some description in his own position.

We need to recognize that there is an ambiguity in MacIntyre's work that makes it a rather unreliable candidate for founding a theological stance. In his most recent book he offers a sketch of a postliberal university system in which different universities would be organized around distinct forms of enquiry (15). Members of such universities would both advance enquiries within their own tradition and enter into controversy with rival traditions. This would seem to embody an acceptance of liberal pluralism built upon mutual tolerance between different traditions. Yet he also insists upon the role of authority within traditions and the idea that there are guardians of a tradition who can legitimately exclude any who do not accept its basic assumptions. Thus there is a more authoritarian and socially divisive character to his suggestions. It may just be that there remain some unresolved issues in MacIntyre's work and we will need to return to some of these in due course.

However, there is a pressing question for those theologians who employ MacIntyre's thought in order to attack Enlightenment Reason. On what grounds can they justify a total rejection of Secular Reason when it is clear that, despite his critique of the Enlightenment tradition, MacIntyre still retains a notion of rationality that can operate between and within the boundaries of traditions? An examination of Milbank will answer that for us. Further, can theology then escape the dangers of relativism and perspectivism that can follow so easily from MacIntyre's arguments? The evidence of the last chapter suggests that it cannot.

Milbank on Secular Reason

In order to locate Milbank's complex discussion on Secular Reason within his wider project we need briefly to remind ourselves what that is. His position is that theology has allowed itself to be dictated to and determined by secular social theory when in fact that theory itself embodies a distorted form of theology. The objective of theology must be to cut itself free from these external influences and to re-tell its own story on its own terms. Milbank insists that, despite the Post-Modern incredulity towards all metanarratives, Christianity is still a metanarrative, capable of making and then justifying universal claims for its own position. Given this basic stance it is easy to see why Milbank has to totally discredit Secular Reason.

The theology he criticizes has been formed by a compromise in which Reason has played the mediating role. In Milbank's theology there can be no room for compromise and hence no role for Reason as the third term in the equation. To allow Reason back into the picture in any form would be to undermine Milbank's position. His argument - although given that he believes he is not offering a reasoned argument we should perhaps not call it such - only holds if he can maintain both a certain interpretation of MacIntyre and a particular understanding of Post-Modernity.

We need first to examine Milbank's use of MacIntyre. At the beginning of chapter 11 of 'Theology and Social Theory' he states that this particular chapter could be read as a temeritous attempt to radicalize the thought of MacIntyre (16). The difference between the two of them is that Milbank approaches social theory as a theologian while MacIntyre approaches it as a philosopher. So, while Milbank is prepared to accept what he describes as 'the benign postmodernism' of MacIntyre (17), he does not share the latter's belief that there are arguments of any form that can refute the more nihilistic version of Post-Modernity. What exactly is going on here?

In essence Milbank is agreeing with MacIntyre's critique of the Enlightenment tradition and its claim that there can be a neutral, external and universal standpoint from which rational and moral judgements can be made. But he does not agree with MacIntyre's attempts, as outlined in the previous section, to establish that Reason and rationality still have a part to play within the context and tradition-dependent picture. Rather than wanting to combat the dangers of relativism and perspectivism that are of such concern to MacIntyre, Milbank says 'I do not find him sufficiently relativistic or historicist' (18). In fact: 'there is for me no method, no mode of argument that charts us smoothly past the Scylla of foundationalism and the Charybdis of difference' (19). One could say that this one sentence both sums up Milbank's project and reveals the counter-project that lies at the heart of this book. Like MacIntyre I believe that there are methods and modes of argument that can chart us - if not smoothly then at least safely - between the two extremes so eloquently described by Milbank. But this requires a rehabilitation of Secular Reason.

However, in order to reach this point and to grasp its significance we must go back to an earlier stage of Milbank's 'argument'. The key question as identified in the introduction to this chapter is 'Why is Secular Reason necessarily nihilistic?' What is Milbank's justification for totally excluding any form of Reason from the theological picture he wishes to paint? His justification originates in his particular interpretation of Post-Modernity.

We find the initial clues in Milbank's comments on science. We remember that science is, in many ways, the epitome of the Enlightenment project of establishing an objective 'view from nowhere', but that, according to the Post-Modern critique must always be a 'view from somewhere'. Is Milbank prepared to accept that Reason through science, can establish an objective vantage point from which it can locate theology in some harmless enclave? It would seem not.

'...it will also be contended that natural science itself possesses no privileged access to truth and cannot purely, on its own account, build up a realist ontology. Its 'truth' is merely that of instrumental control and therefore, in the case of human interaction, is bounded by the peculiar fractiousness and innovative capacity of human behaviour' (20).

We immediately hear echoes here of Rorty's comments on Reason and science. In other words, there is no one scientific method that can guarantee direct access to the truth of an external reality. There are just ways of operating that humans have devised that are useful in some situations but that can claim no universal validity. Thus the attempt to make all other disciplines - including theology - subject to some overall 'scientific method' is fundamentally misguided because, in reality, there is no such method. Further, when it comes to the so-called sciences of human society and behaviour - the social sciences - such forms of explanation are totally inappropriate. As Milbank says: 'human interaction in all its variety can only be narrated, and not explained/understood after the manner of natural science' (21).

So this is Milbank utilizing a Post-Modern critique of Reason to establish that neither the natural nor the human sciences have a justifiable claim to locate theology on their terms or to reach any conclusions about the essence of religion.

That is the 'foundationalism' described in the earlier quotation from Milbank - the claim of Enlightenment Reason to have identified a secure base line for intellectual debate and discovery from which to judge all other disciplines and forms of life. There are no external or neutral criteria by which theology is to be evaluated. But then, if one accepts this critique in this pure form, what is the alternative? It is here that the notion of difference comes into play, with Milbank once again drawing upon Post-Modernity.

'In the 'new era' of postmodernism (which is yet in some ways an 'exacerbation' of modernity) the human has become subordinate to the infinitely many discourses which claim to constitute humanity, and universality can no longer pose as the identical, but can only be paradoxically invoked as the different' (22).

So, instead of one base line derived from Reason from which all else can be judged, there is a plurality and multiplicity of vantage points. Instead of one Grand Narrative a series of local narratives. Rather than identity there is merely difference. But then there comes a real possibility that this Post-Modern understanding will, in turn, pose itself as a metanarrative, attempting to dictate terms to all the others. Indeed, this is what Milbank believes we encounter in the work of the key Post-Modern thinkers, and he names as such Heidegger, Derrida, Deleuze, Nietzsche, Lyotard and Foucault (23).

This is where we hit the focus of the argument about the essentially nihilistic nature of Secular Reason. The problem for theology is that an acceptance of the Post-Modern position, particularly in the form of a metanarrative of difference, is that it may be no better off than under the previous regime of the Enlightenment.

It may have been located or positioned in some harmless space by the latter, but where is it in the free-for-all of Post-Modernity where there are no agreed criteria for judgement and every petty tyrant is likely to become another Hitler? Theology finds itself between a rock and a hard place: either the imposition of an external and alien tradition (Enlightenment foundationalism) or an anarchic and potentially violent open market of ideas where only the strongest will survive (the Post-Modern ontology of difference). How can theology compete and survive in this free play of different discourses and disciplines where choice is purely arbitrary and there are no criteria for judging between one and the other?

The apparent answer is deceptively simple and dangerously wrong. Theology must restate its claim to be a metanarrative, possessing privileged access to the truth. Yet it can only do this with any conviction if it seriously believes that all the other competing discourses are essentially misguided, if not downright evil. All the other discourses in Post-Modernity have to be shown to fail in some significant way if theology is to successfully re-stake its claim to be the narrative for humanity. This is precisely the line that Milbank takes.

On what basis can he make this case? The core issue on which Christianity succeeds and all other discourses fail is that of violence.

'Christianity is unique in refusing ultimate reality to all conflictual phenomena. For this reason, I shall argue, it is the true 'opposite' of Nietzschian postmodernism...By comparison, all the other myths, or narrative traditions, affirm or barely conceal an original primordial violence, which a social order merely restrains' (24).

This is Milbank's trump card. Without it he believes that theology is out in the wasteland of competing discourses, telling its story to a dwindling and increasingly disinterested audience. Put crudely, this approach to non-violence is the distinctive product that Christians take to market in the free play of Post-Modern narratives. However, there is a real problem with it. It rests still on the assumption that Secular Reason is essentially nihilistic and can lead only to conflict and violence. All other paths lead to destruction. There is no middle way. Only the Christian narrative renounces violence. Yet of course, accepting as much of the Post-Modern analysis as he does, even this is a quite deliberate and conscious social construct.

Why then is Secular Reason essentially nihilistic? The identification of the key Post-Modern thinkers with Nietzsche is the critical point of Milbank's position. We have already seen that he draws a distinction between the benign postmodernism of MacIntyre and the nihilistic postmodernism of all the others. At the beginning of chapter 10 Milbank lays his cards firmly on the table:

'For the secular postmodernists, Nietzsche has become the only true master of suspicion: the thinker of a 'baseless suspicion' which rests, unlike the suspicions of Marx, Freud and sociology on no foundationalist presuppositions. In the present chapter I am concerned with what is common to the outlook of the major Nietzschians, and I deliberately treat the writings of Nietzsche, Heidegger, Deleuze, Lyotard, Foucault and Derrida as elaborations of a single nihilistic philosophy, paying relatively little attention to their divergences of opinion' (25).

This is indeed a huge claim for Milbank to make and one that requires critical elaboration. In Chapter 3 I illustrated quite clearly that there are major and significant differences between at least some of the Post-Modern thinkers that Milbank wants to include under a single category. Above all, there are differences between them over the very status of Reason itself. At a later stage in this chapter I will provide evidence of this from the work of Rorty and Derrida in particular. For the moment I simply want to question Milbank's assumption that they can all be placed squarely behind the banner of Nietzsche. This is a convenient claim for Milbank to make, but one that does not bear much scrutiny.

It is not possible here to engage the depths of Nietzsche's philosophy, let alone that of Heidegger, but the line that Milbank takes is as follows. Nietzsche is a non-foundationalist in that he questions the existence of an objective, external system of thought that could provide the base line for human judgement. Above all, he unmasks all human pretensions to have established such a base line as a bid for power over others. Since there are no criteria, all judgements are arbitrary and cannot be justified by rational argument, therefore the only basis upon which claims can be established is that of power. The will to power, the determination of particular individuals or groups to impose their ideas and interpretations upon the rest is what actually drives human society. This is an essentially negative and nihilistic view of human existence. There is no deeper meaning or significance to human life as all attempts to establish such are reduced to the power plays of particular groups. Even Christianity - in Nietzsche's opinion - can be reduced to the will to power of a particular group within society. Thus anarchy and ultimately violence reign at the heart of human society.

Now, while it may well be legitimate to attribute these views to Nietzsche, it seems to me far from obvious that they can equally be attributed to Lyotard, Rorty, Foucault, Baudrillard and Derrida in the way that Milbank would have us do. By doing this he is forcing all of these thinkers into an extreme position on the issues of Post-Modernity as I have described them in chapter 3. I do not accept that their complex and different ideas can justifiably be reduced to that of the Nietzschian will to power. In which case, it is also doubtful whether their work can simply be summed up and dismissed as nihilistic; in other words, suggesting that they reduce all meaning to its most arbitrary and therefore violent level.

The most likely candidate for a Nietzschian interpretation is Foucault, for whom Nietzsche was an acknowledged influence, and who does deal explicitly with the subject of power. However, as we have seen in the discussion of Foucault on power, that is about as far as the similarity goes. Foucault is concerned with where power is located and with how it operates within different discourses, but he does not make the nihilistic judgements that Milbank believes must follow.

Where does this leave Milbank's 'arguments'? I suggest that they rest upon shaky assumptions. First he uses MacIntyre in order to support the undermining of the Enlightenment metanarrative, but then abandons him to move into the dangerously relativistic and perspectivist territory that MacIntyre himself wants to avoid. He also declines to pursue MacIntyre's attempts to define and describe a continuing role for Reason - perhaps because he correctly recognizes that this would lead him back too close to the liberal Enlightenment position. Rather, Milbank selects to portray the Post-Modern alternative to Enlightenment foundationalism in exclusively nihilistic terms by reading Lyotard, Foucault, Derrida et al through the eyes of Nietzsche. Only in this way can he justify reclaiming the high ground of Grand or metanarrative for Christianity. Secular Reason is forever condemned as being essentially nihilistic and leading inevitably to violence and conflict. We recall that this is much more extreme than saying that Reason happens to have fallen prey to particular historical circumstances that have led to its distortion and manipulation. I suggest that on the basis of what we have already learnt about the Post-Modern thinkers and in the light of more detailed arguments that will follow, we might conclude that Milbank's position rests upon a number of forced and dubious interpretations.

Before we move on, there is a very straightforward way of describing this whole debate. Milbank can only make his case by setting up the polarity that he defines as the Scylla of foundationalism and the Charybdis of difference and then denying that there is a middle path between them. However, there is a logical error in this. If there is no longer one criterion for judgement (Enlightenment foundationalism) then two other possibilities remain. Either there can be no criteria (nihilism) or there can be many or a number of criteria (pluralism). What Milbank does is to reduce pluralism to nihilism by his characterization of the Post-Modern writers as Nietzschians. Yet it is not simply the case that the critique of the Enlightenment metanarrative of Reason leads only to nihilism, anarchy and to the acceptance that all judgements are arbitrary. It is just as likely, as we saw in the discussion of Lyotard in the previous chapter to lead to a plurality and multiplicity of criteria. Theology then can either try to work out its position in relation to the other narratives available or retreat behind closed doors still claiming privileged access to the truth. I believe that the first of these is the appropriate way forward.

A critique of MacIntyre

In the second half of this chapter I intend to initiate a rehabilitation of Reason. It has to be said that this is far from being an uncritical adherence to a particular interpretation of it, or simply a return to the Enlightenment tradition. However, I believe that it is possible both to take serious account of contemporary questions and doubts about the role and nature of Reason and to retain enough of its significance to avoid its total abandonment as advocated by Milbank and Hauerwas. This will mean that theology cannot straightforwardly dismiss this aspect of the Enlightenment tradition but must continue a reflective and critical engagement with it.

Both Christianity and the unfinished project of the Enlightenment are contemporary major narratives that need to remain in contact with each other if social and intellectual life is to avoid even further fragmentation.

This rehabilitation will fall into three parts. First, a return to the work of MacIntyre to show that his supposed demolition of the Enlightenment is not so conclusive as some theologians are wont to assume. Second, reference to a key debate over Reason itself from within Post-Modernity - that between Rorty and Derrida. This will illustrate, amongst other things, that Milbank's attempt to attach all Post-Modern philosophy to a Nietzschian nihilism does not succeed. Finally, the reconstruction of a convincing and substantial role for Reason in a very practical context as suggested by Habermas. I propose that this route will enable us to steer successfully between the Scylla of foundationalism and the Charybdis of difference.

So, let us retrace the argument to MacIntyre since he has been such an influential figure in the development of a philosophical alternative to both the Enlightenment and to Post-Modernity. It may be recalled from the previous chapter that one of the weaknesses of the sectarian position being proposed by Hauerwas and Milbank is that it presupposes the continued existence of the liberal democracy it claims to undermine. This parallels a criticism that can equally well be aimed at MacIntyre. It could be argued that, despite his stringent attacks on the Enlightenment, in practice his own methods and values still owe a great deal to that very tradition.

Consider for instance the comments of Richard J. Bernstein, an American philosopher, on MacIntyre's 'After Virtue' (26). Bernstein places MacIntyre's attack on the Enlightenment in the context of the current 'rage against Reason' and points out that there is an element of 'overkill' in each of these critiques. There are parts of the Enlightenment project, for instance, its protests against injustice and the exclusion of whole groups of humans from the 'good life' that some of its critics might well want to retain. What is particularly interesting about MacIntyre is that he appears to agree with the Enlightenment principle, derived from Kant, that all of humanity should be included in the new forms of community life that he is concerned to advocate. In fact, he is slightly embarrassed that Aristotle, whom MacIntyre uses as his model for moral virtue in the text, excludes non-Greeks, barbarians, slaves and women from the moral process. This approach MacIntyre does not share, although he does still want to attack what he calls the abstract universalization of the Enlightenment.

However, as Bernstein notes (27), there is a rather different form of universalization that MacIntyre himself does advocate, that which says that every person has a right to belong to a local community or a local tradition where moral and political life will flourish. It seems to me that this poses a question for all forms of Communitarianism, including the Christian versions of Hauerwas and Milbank. It is all very well to say that morality, politics or even Christianity can only flourish or make sense within the confines of a specific community, but then what about those who fall outside those boundaries? Do they not matter, or should they too have access to communities of their own? In which case, how is such a society to be held together? This is surely one of the major questions with which the Enlightenment tradition has been trying to grapple and to which communitarians such as MacIntyre have yet to provide a convincing answer. The scenario they paint is that of a society of disparate communities, protected by rights, each pursuing its own understanding of the virtues or the good life. Either one tries to create a homogeneous communitarian society by means of coercion or one accepts the liberal pluralism that the Enlightenment itself claims to defend and sustain.

As Bernstein says, it makes no sense in the end to state that the 'Enlightenment project was not only mistaken, but should never have commenced in the first place' (28).

This '...is to fail to recognize how much MacIntyre himself appropriates from this tradition in his critical reconstruction of the virtues: his implicit appeal to a concrete determinate universality; his defence of the principle of freedom where every participant can share in the type of communal life required for living a good life; his emphasis on the shared vision of a moral life by the participants in such communities; his demand that we treat all other human beings with respect and recognize every agent's capacity to act rationally' (29). The question we need to pose to Hauerwas and Milbank on the basis of their appropriation of MacIntyre is that of where they stand on these key issues.

There is a further difficulty with MacIntyre's position that needs to be noted and - once again - this echoes a reservation expressed in the previous chapter about the nature of metanarratives. Where exactly are these 'communities' that MacIntyre and the other communitarians commend so strongly? Who defines them and how are their boundaries established and maintained? Is not the idea of community as elusive and confused as that of a metanarrative? According to MacIntyre, both the Enlightenment and the liberal democracy that has flowed from it were bound to fail because they are based on a false philosophical presupposition. Liberalism rests upon an incoherent account of rational agents that views them as persons constituted independently of their social context and answerable to historical, transcendent norms of reasoning. The alternative is that forms of practical rationality can only arise from within a specific community or tradition. However, do such radically distinct communities actually exist?

I suggested in the previous chapter that such an idea is difficult to defend, particularly in the world as it is experienced now. Rather than belonging to one metanarrative, community or tradition in such a clear and exclusive way, it seems far more likely that most of us inhabit, or are influenced by, a range of major narratives or communities. Not all of these will necessarily be mutually compatible and we may or may not be aware of the tensions and the conflicts inside ourselves that result from this form of pluralism. If this is right then it will be no easy matter to isolate and identify a practical rationality that derives from one of the traditions or communities.

Perhaps this is one reason why Milbank wants to abandon the idea of Reason altogether, despite MacIntyre's position, it would commit him to the pluralist alternative that would counter his Christian metanarrative. I would argue that Christianity, in its various forms, already includes notions of rationality and that it is both impossible and unnecessary to try to isolate and detach them in the way that Milbank suggests.

The problem with MacIntyre's notion of radically distinct communities is, as John Haldane says, one of clear identification:

'What exactly...are the criteria of identity for cultures and societies? Where do we stop and others begin? Certainly, geography and time may separate communities but this empirical fact is, in itself, philosophically trivial. What has to be shown is that there are points of separation beyond these spatio-temporal ones which constitute incommensurable differences' (30).

This raises further problems about translation and understanding between cultures and communities that it is very difficult to resolve. How can one know that there are such strict differences between two cultures and communities unless one can understand both - in which case it obviously is possible to translate and measure between them? Either there is some base or common ground between these different entities that makes communication possible or one can never know anything about another culture and therefore cannot make judgements of any sort about it. The latter seems to me a patently absurd position that nobody acts upon in practice. We are constantly crossing these boundaries, both inside and outside ourselves and in fact need to do so. The problem with the Enlightenment tradition is that it appears to claim that there is one guaranteed way of doing this that will work on every occasion - using Reason or rationality - but this elevates both then to a superior and universal status. This can be challenged by the idea that there is no one guaranteed means of communication across cultures and communities, but in fact a range of methods that have to be worked out and identified in each particular instance. Thus communication between science and Christianity is not going to be identical to that between Christianity and Buddhism or between Buddhism and science. Even then there is the question of the communication between different strands of each of those traditions. No one criterion certainly, but not no criteria either, rather a range of criteria to be sorted out case by case.

This may sound complicated, but I would argue that something like this is going to be closer to the truth than MacIntyre's communitarianism that seems unable to avoid the charge of relativism, or than Milbank's vision of an arbitrary and exclusive Christianity. If we are dealing with major narratives that are, to a certain extent, both porous and flexible, then it will be possible to establish mediating frameworks that form the bases for communication across traditions, disciplines and communities. Grand Narratives or metanarratives are too fixed and enclosed to allow for this possibility and quickly revert to forms of fundamentalism. Once again I am attempting to steer between the Scylla of foundationalism and the Charybdis of difference.

The need for a solution such as the one just described becomes clearer if we examine MacIntyre's own attempt to avoid the relativism that would preclude the possibility of communication between traditions. It will be recalled from the earlier exposition of his work that MacIntyre attempts to deal with this by identifying discrete stages in the development of traditions. It is in the third of these stages that communication is deemed to be possible. Within this stage an encounter with an alien tradition has suggested resources or ideas that might meet a perceived inadequacy within the original tradition. Yet, according to MacIntyre, there must be enough remaining of the original to justify talking of continuity rather than a takeover. This is where the problem comes. One must be able to discredit one's own tradition still using the standards of rationality belonging to it. However, learning that another tradition is rationally superior to one's own presupposes a process of conversion to the new standard of rationality belonging to the alien tradition. It appears that either one has learnt nothing after all or else the old tradition really has been ousted and replaced by the new. It is hard to see how one can get beyond this if MacIntyre's case that there are only ever context-dependent rationalities is to be upheld. Why can there not be both context-dependent rationalities and also mediating frameworks that allow for the cross-tradition and cross-cultural communication that MacIntyre himself and indeed I want to retain? It is such a version of rationality that I want to establish and defend.

Rorty and Derrida on Reason

The second move in the rehabilitation process is to examine in slightly greater detail the ideas of two of the key Post-Modern thinkers on the subjects of Reason and rationality. As suggested in chapter 3 the work of Richard Rorty is of significance in this respect, particularly given his interest in science. However, there is now a debate between Rorty and Derrida and a number of secondary commentators over Rorty's interpretation of Derrida and the extent to which he takes a similar line on Reason and rationality (31). Reference to this will make it clear that there are significant differences between the two and that it is dubious to argue that there is one clear-cut Post-Modern line on Reason. Thinking of Milbank and Hauerwas, the irony is that the critique of the Enlightenment tradition they attribute to Post-Modernity is actually much closer to Rorty's position than to Derrida's. Yet Rorty is a firm advocate of the liberal democracy that both theologians are so keen to abandon. As we shall see, Derrida now seems to be much closer to the Habermasian position that I will return to in the final section. One sometimes wonders whether theologians give due attention to the primary texts of the Post-Modern thinkers.

What is Rorty's stance on rationality? His particular concern is to debunk the idea that the natural sciences possess and pursue a method, or form of rationality that is somehow superior to all other disciplines. He says that we need to stop seeing the scientist as some sort of priest and to gain a more realistic perspective on the work on which the scientific community is engaged. In order to do this it is necessary to distinguish between two different senses of the term 'rationality'. In the first to be rational is to be methodical; to have criteria for success laid down in advance. Scientific theories appear to have clear criteria of success so that they are able to predict and thereby enable humans to control some portion of the world. So, if to be rational means to be able to lay down criteria in advance, then natural science could be seen as the paradigm of rationality.

However, this would mean that the human sciences are never going to be able to qualify as rational activities, unless we acknowledge that there is a second form of rationality. There is, and this could be described as being 'sane' or 'reasonable' rather than being methodical. It names a set of moral virtues, amongst them tolerance; respect for the opinions of those around one; willingness to listen and a reliance on persuasion rather than upon force (32). So being rational is about behaving in a civilized manner as defined within liberal democracy. Any idea that rationality is about seeking objective truth, correspondence to reality, methods and criteria should just be abandoned in favour of the second definition. In which case the dominance of the Enlightenment tradition through the influence of natural science in particular can safely be brought to an end. It is after all just another story that we tell about the world and therefore can no longer claim precedence over any other stories. We end up with a whole series of local narratives realising that there can be no privileged discourse or metanarrative. Milbank would presumably want to interpret this as nihilistic while agreeing with its debunking of Reason and science.

Now, the interesting question is whether this view coincides with that of Derrida. If it does not then it raises serious doubts about Milbank's assumption that he can classify all the Post-Modern thinkers as essentially nihilistic. Acknowledging that we are entering a minefield here, it does become evident fairly quickly that Derrida's project is much closer to the Enlightenment than that of Rorty.

In an interview given in 1986 (33) Derrida says some very revealing and important things about his relationship to the Enlightenment tradition and his own approach to Reason. Responding first of all to the charge that his philosophy is a form of irrationalism he expresses surprise that such a suggestion might be made:

'In the history of philosophy no one ever suspected a philosopher of irrationalism when he asked a question about reason. If there is here and there in France a critique of reason e.g. by me myself, then that doesn't at all mean a rejection of reason, a tendency towards irrationalism, but, on the contrary, to a large extent a responsibility and a consciousness of the responsibility of the philosopher before reason' (34).

This is exactly the point I was making at the beginning of this chapter. As Derrida goes on to say, if one asks about the principle of the origin of Reason one is indeed going beyond that principle itself, but not in opposition to it, rather in order to open up the possibility of questioning it. A critique is far from being a destruction, either partial or complete. Derrida describes irrationalism as a 'symmetrical shrivelling of reason', more akin perhaps to the projects of Milbank and Hauerwas, however: 'the questions about reason that interest me seem to me to be necessary even in the name of a new Aufklärung - thus, no irrationalism, and above all no methodical irrationalism' (35).

A further question then arises about the exact nature of Derrida's notion of deconstruction. We saw in chapter 3 that one possible interpretation of this was that of a complete destruction or disruption of meaning in which anything could mean anything. However, Derrida himself once again makes it clear that this is not what deconstruction is about. In fact it still has a direct relationship with rationality: 'I maintain that deconstruction isn't irrational. But it also doesn't aim at producing a new Reason or order of Reason. For all of that, it's a symptom of the change in the order of rationality within which we live' (36). Derrida goes on to disclaim the identification of deconstruction with either antistructuralism or poststructuralism. Deconstruction is not a technique or a method in the manner of a scientific critique, but an approach to texts that aims to bring out different possibilities of meaning and to show that they cannot easily be subsumed under one heading or even reconciled. In a real sense we are back with the original equation here. There is not one meaning only, but that is not the same as saying that there is no meaning. Rather, there is always a range of possible meanings. Thus there is no one foundation, but neither is there the total anarchic free-play of difference, rather a middle ground where meaning is indeed flexible and negotiable, but always within certain limits.

I cannot see how this can justifiably be described as nihilistic. That would imply a total lack of concern for truth or the despair that all such concern can only ever mask a will for power. Once again, Derrida is quite explicit that a questioning of truth is not the same as an abandonment of it to arbitrary or coercive forces. There is indeed a kind of frustration that we experience as we struggle towards truth, particularly if we acknowledge the ambiguities of meaning that Derrida himself brings to the surface. But that is, in a way, just being realistic about the way things are and not falling into the foundationalist trap. It is not like disappearing into a black hole where it is pointless trying to make any judgements at all, so it surely cannot be identified with the popular caricature of Post-Modernity.

This would appear to leave Milbank's interpretation of Derrida in a somewhat precarious position. It may even be that his view of Heidegger - a significant influence upon Derrida's work - can be brought into question. Is Heidegger a nihilist, proclaiming the end of meaning in his critique of metaphysics? Derrida thinks not: 'When Heidegger speaks of the overcoming of metaphysics he says very complicated things about it. Overcoming is not the end. One doesn't jump out of metaphysics one fine day, in order to go over to something else' (37). This particular comment will prove significant at a later stage in this book. The basic point is the same though: the critiques of Reason, Truth and metaphysics are neither the end nor the destruction of those ideas, but the continuation of them in a revised form. In which case, Milbank's categorization of them as nihilistic begins to look increasingly simplistic.

If further evidence of this were required Derrida himself provides it as he responds to the suggestion that deconstruction leads to a form of ethical nihilism:

'I would like to emphasize that deconstruction is far from being the amoral or ethical nihilism it is often presented as. Deconstruction is an affirmative thought of a possible ethics, of an engagement beyond the technology of the calculable. Concern for responsibility stands at the centre of the deconstructive experience' (38).

Even on the subject of difference, the polarity that Milbank invokes in trying to re-establish Christianity as a metanarrative, is itself different from the way that Derrida describes it: 'What I call difference, dissemination, divisibility, is not essentially fragmentary. It's a dissolution of the relationship to the other, to the heterogeneous, without the hope and without the wish for totalization. It's another experience of difference' (39). I presume that Milbank could counter this by saying that it is all argument when argument has now to be abandoned because it has been irrevocably compromised by the distortions of Reason. But then there is no need to adopt such an extreme position, nor to take Christianity out into the wilderness where it can have no further contact with other disciplines or ideas. Milbank himself may choose to ignore what the Post-Modern writers themselves say on the subject of Reason and rationality and to impose his own interpretation upon them, but then that seems to me an exercise in interpretative violence. He will also have to accept that he may end up talking only to himself.

I think we have seen enough to establish that Derrida takes a much more positive approach to Reason and rationality than we might have expected from the Post-Modern label that is attached to him. That label is actually a hindrance in trying to understand his work. Even the philosopher with whom we are to conclude this chapter, Habermas, has fallen into the trap of categorizing Derrida's writings in this way. In fact, on this issue of rehabilitating Secular Reason these two have more in common than first meets the eye (40). Derrida's explicit concern for truth and Reason and indeed for a new Enlightenment are very much echoed in Habermas' own project. The final stage of the rehabilitation is to move onto this work and to show that Reason can still have a positive role to play both for society at large and for theology in particular.

Habermas and the rehabilitation of Reason

To sum up the argument so far. Despite the attempts of certain theologians to establish that Reason has been totally discredited and can be consigned to the dustbin of history, it has become clear that the reality is more complex. Even some of those who are credited with the debunking of the Enlightenment tradition, notably MacIntyre and Derrida, want to retain a role for Reason and rationality. Their respective critiques aim to refine and revise not to destroy or discredit. Unfortunately, a particular brand of theology has a vested interest in portraying a more extreme picture. But the consequence of this is likely to be the withdrawal of Christianity from critical engagement with the wider world and, in particular, from dialogue with an Enlightenment tradition that survives in a more limited and yet still significant form. The task now is to sketch the outlines of a reconstituted Reason and to show how it can make a more positive contribution to social and cultural life and indeed to theology itself.

For this we return to the work of Habermas. It was shown in chapter 3 that he has made a bold and imaginative attempt to establish an alternative to the Instrumental Reason that has been the target of the critics of the Enlightenment. He is in agreement with the latter to the extent that he recognizes the distortions and the damage created by this one-sided view of Reason. Habermas' proposal for a communicative reason, although subject to the predictable barrage of criticism, still stands as the major alternative and challenge to the Post-Modern route. I do not intend to repeat the description of this as this has been offered in chapter 3. Rather, I want to build upon these earlier ideas and show how Habermas has done the same. The importance of this will be to argue that Habermas's notion of communicative reason has enabled the development of ideas in two practical fields, that of morality and that of the law.

In his book 'Moral Consciousness and Communicative Action' (41), Habermas begins to suggest how the theory of communicative reason might have a direct bearing on the study and practice of morality. We recall that one of the major criticisms of the Enlightenment tradition is that it establishes a form of Reason that is essentially amoral. It can lead to any consequences or courses of action as it does not offer any moral content to the reasoning process. The counter- reaction of MacIntyre was to say that this was an unworkable formulation and that morality can only emerge from within particular communities or traditions. There can be no context-transcending Reason or morality.

Habermas acknowledges the problem but opts to deal with it in a different way. He draws a distinction between morality and ethics. Ethics refers to the codes of behaviour that develop within traditions and communities, but morality operates on a broader, trans-local framework and must still retain an element of universality. This approach also presupposes a division between content and process. Individual context-dependent ethical codes will clearly contain content in the sense of embodying particular values. The actual nature of the 'good life' will vary from tradition to tradition. Morality, by contrast, is about process and procedure, a way of going about things that can be agreed despite different sets of values. So this is essentially a procedural concept of morality that does not presuppose specific ethical judgements. In that sense it is the heir of the Enlightenment tradition. However, unlike the latter, it carries a commitment to the open communication that Habermas believes is embedded in language itself. This procedural concept of morality is a natural extension of the notion of communicative reason.

The basic principle on which this is founded Habermas describes as follows: 'Only those norms can claim to be valid that meet (or could meet) with the approval of all affected in their capacity as participants in a practical discourse' (42). In other words, the universality is expressed in the principle that all those who are likely to be affected by a particular set of ethical norms should have had the opportunity to participate in their development by contributing to an open and democratic discourse. Hence this is known as the theory of Discourse Ethics. If people are excluded from this process then the norms that are established cannot be deemed valid. It is Habermas' contention that this principle of Discourse Ethics holds good across the boundaries of all traditions and communities.

It will be clear that other rather stringent conditions are entailed by this principle. First, a mutual and reciprocal recognition by all those involved that each person is an autonomous, rational subject whose claims will be acknowledged if supported by valid arguments. Second, there must be no social or political constraints preventing people from taking an equal part in the discussion. Third, there must be the possibility of challenging traditional norms and of opening up all ethical matters for rational discourse. One problem of course is that there invariably are constraints on open discourse and inequalities caused by disparities of power, wealth or authority. Nevertheless, this offers a set of criteria by which to evaluate the practical discourses that do occur.

Another potential criticism of this approach is that it is too formal and abstract to be of any use or guidance in the real world. However, Habermas is careful to maintain that the fact that people could reach a consensus on a particular norm does not, in itself, legitimate that norm. It will also have to be seen by those involved to be acceptable in terms of content. This discussion would counterbalance the more formal side of the process. Discourse Ethics requires that actual discussion will take place and makes it clear that morality is not about the deliberation of the individual conscience but requires full and equal participation by all. In that sense it is a democratization of morality.

Following on from this is the criticism that has been levelled against all procedural concepts of morality, that is that they are unable to take account of local and changing circumstances. In many ways this is a repeat of MacIntyre's critique of Enlightenment Reason. That which is universal is, in the end, so distant from the realities of daily life, as to be impossible to relate to it. Between the general and the particular is fixed an unbridgeable gulf. Hence the communitarian approach to ethics is to ground it exclusively in the local and the particular and to decry any attempts to create a more general moral framework. Habermas counters this objection by introducing into the theory of Discourse Ethics a distinction between justification and application (43).

There is an inescapable duality attached to the notion of a valid norm. On the one hand it should be capable of commanding the rational consent of all those affected by its observance but, on the other, its observance should be appropriate in all situations where it is applicable. However, these two requirements cannot be satisfied at the same time because it is impossible for those engaged in a practical discourse to be able to take account of all the situations in which a potential norm might be applicable. Human agents can only do the best that they can in particular circumstances and try to anticipate other situations where the norm might apply.

This requires that they accept that the norm might have to be adapted in the light of unforeseen circumstances and that therefore their present conclusions are necessarily provisional and contingent. Thus the question of the justification of a norm can be seen to be different from that of its application. The latter calls for a new discursive procedure employing the notion of appropriateness. Should this norm continue to be followed in this new situation in the light of its relevant features? The belief that Discourse Ethics can remain impartial requires both the justification through a practical discourse open to all and the application of the norm in particular circumstances in the light of its appropriateness. In this way Habermas takes account of both the universal and the local, both the general and the particular.

The process that Habermas is describing here is very familiar to theology and returns us to the issue with which we began the chapter. How is theology to adapt to local and changing circumstances? On the one hand it has its formal principles and doctrines, but the problem with these is that they are distant from the everyday dilemmas and decisions that Christians face. One can accept that one is expected to love God and to love one's neighbour, but how is that to be put into practice? What does it mean I should do here and now? On the other hand, if it is all a matter of reacting and adapting to new situations how can there be any coherent identity or continuity in the Christian life? Is monogamy the norm here but polygamy acceptable in another cultural context?

Presumably Christians need to engage in both the open discourse that develops valid norms and debates about the application of those in particular circumstances. The danger is always that of setting up a specific local version of Christianity as being the valid version or interpretation for all time - a danger that both Hauerwas and Milbank appear to fall prey to. The way surely to guard against this is to employ something like Habermas' communicative rationality that is committed to involving all Christians in the debates while still accepting that there is a role for local interpretations. Take Reason out of the picture and we end up with an arbitrary version of Christianity.

The other requirement for Christians is that they retain ways of establishing open debate both amongst themselves and with those of other traditions. This cannot be done unless there is common ground between and across those boundaries. Once Reason is extracted from this process it is difficult to see how this could take place. Hauerwas and Milbank seem content that Christians just talk to themselves, but this cuts across any notion of mission to the wider world let alone the notion that God might be encountered beyond the confines of the church. Habermas has an answer to the question of intercultural communication...' concepts such as truth, rationality and justification play the same role in every language community, even if they are interpreted differently and applied in accordance with different criteria' (44). Thus it will be possible to cross the boundaries without either abandoning the integrity of one's own tradition or compromising that of another. Reason - in communicative form - is the third and mediating term in the conversation.

In his most recent major work Habermas has turned his attention to another potential application for the theory of communicative reason, that of the law (45). As was suggested earlier in this chapter the proposed demise of Reason is a concern not just for philosophers, but has implications for the way that social life is organized and held together. Given that most societies now contain a plurality of social groupings and sets of beliefs, practices and values, how is any form of social integration possible? It is here that law and the legal system must now play a key role. Habermas argues that, in earlier stages of social development, religious beliefs would have provided the framework within which a high degree of social consensus would have been possible - the glue holding society together. So, there was some overall narrative that most people at least would have felt comfortable with and to which they would probably have given their uncritical adherence. In Modernity however such unifying structures have become fragmented thus creating the need to develop new ways of reaching agreement. It is through the law as constituting binding norms of behaviour, that such agreement is now sought.

Yet, societies as well as individuals experience a tension between the values and practices of their own traditions and social groupings and the need to establish a wider framework within which such differences can be held together. If the independence of the many local narratives is not to deteriorate into a state of social and political anarchy there needs to be a legal system that both respects differences and yet itself commands respect and general assent. The alternative would be the nihilism and chaos that Milbank associates with Post-Modernity. Contrary to Milbank though I would say that it is essential for society to steer between the disintegrating foundationalism of a metanarrative and the incipient political chaos of social difference. Individual groups may choose to duck this issue and go their own way regardless - always the danger of the communitarian approach - but most will surely want to adopt a more responsible attitude.

Habermas suggests putting the theory of communicative reason to good use in this context. How is it possible to construct a legal system that can command the respect and agreement of all the different social groupings? This can only happen to the extent that all those affected by such a system have an equal role in constructing it and can therefore own both the process and the results of it. As in Discourse Ethics, open discussion and argument leading to negotiated agreement free from external constraints is essential to this process. Mutual understanding worked towards and hopefully achieved in this way has to replace any external authority as the legitimation of the law. It is only to the extent that members of a society perceive the process of the construction of the law to be rational in that particular Habermasian sense that they will be prepared to submit themselves to it.

Issues of morality and justice also seem to impinge and Habermas of course acknowledges this. The actual content of legal norms must be acceptable to people in addition to their recognition that the process by which those norms were agreed was open and democratic. There is always likely to be disagreement over the content in a pluralist society. So what is required is a system of rights that grants to everyone free and equal access to this process of establishing the law. This will parallel the right to individual determination that is taken for granted in a liberal democracy. Public and private autonomy need to go hand in hand. The latter Habermas places under the heading of Solidarity - the requirement that one will respect and cater for the needs of others as individuals. Public autonomy is a matter of Justice - the right of all to be equally involved in the creation of the legal framework that will hold society together (46).

It is clear that Habermas rejects the communitarian solution to the dilemmas of liberal democracy. In other words, it will not be possible to return to a unifying concept of the 'good life' that all will share. In a pluralist society such a strategy would have to be imposed by force. Yet the alternative of a plurality of value systems and traditions need not lead to anarchy if consensus can be achieved at the level of constitutional principles and procedures. Differences do not have to lead to social disintegration and will not do so unless every single group claims that its belief structure is a metanarrative. Communicative reason - the commitment to engage in the process of unconstrained communication as embodied in the nature of language itself - thus has a direct and vital social application.

Obviously, this can be no more than a brief summary of what is a complex and developing argument, but our particular aim was to challenge the notion that Secular Reason is essentially nihilistic. I would suggest that, on the evidence presented in this chapter, it is clear that both some of the Post-Modern philosophers and critics of the Enlightenment tradition such as MacIntyre hold the view that Reason - in a particular form - has indeed led to problems and distortions. However, they question and challenge Reason in order to refine and to reconstruct it, aware that without its mediating role human life will be on the verge of descending into even greater chaos. I also suggest that Habermas has perhaps done more than anybody else so far to tackle this task of reconstructing a form of Reason that is better suited to the non-foundationalist and pluralist culture in which we now live. His ideas will require further elaboration and will engender much criticism, but here at least is a creative and convincing starting point for the rehabilitation of Reason. The idea that it can now safely be abandoned in favour of the individual sets of values and practices of a whole host of competing and conflicting traditions and communities is surely a case of taking to the lifeboats while the ship continues to sail off into the sunset.

Theology needs to come to terms with this new situation. It cannot simply go on appealing to Reason as found in the Enlightenment tradition as it needs to take account of the work of critics such as MacIntyre and Derrida. Neither however can it afford merely to abandon it in the manner of Hauerwas and Milbank for the reasons I have spelt out. Rather it must take note of the revision that is going on in the work of Habermas and others and keep the lines of communication open. If it fails to do this then it will alienate itself from its surrounding culture and create fundamentalist pockets within the Christian tradition itself. Theology still requires a reformulated and rehabilitated Reason to be the third and mediating term in both its internal and external discussions.

6

Post-Modernity and the Self

Introduction

What stake does theology have in discussions about the self and human agency? I would argue that it has a very considerable one despite the fact that it can be suggested that it is only in recent generations that there has been the development of an explicit Christian anthropology (1). Until then at least the Christian understanding of what it is to be human had centred on two basic ideas, first that humans are made in the image of God and second that all humans participate in original sin as described in the biblical account of the Fall (2). This lack of a deeper interest in the self mirrors the situation within Western culture generally. The self as an object of detailed examination and discovery is a relatively recent phenomenon and reflects a growing concern with human subjectivity that stems from the Enlightenment although some would trace it further back (3). The idea that humans are autonomous rational agents, self- directed and self determining beings, capable of standing clear of the influence of all religious and social structures is a central tenet of Modernity. It is an integral part of the package that Post-Modernity now appears to undermine.

In some respects this is an area that theology has entered with not much of a contribution to offer. The two central doctrines just mentioned do not tell us all that much and even appear to be in conflict. Being created in the image of God leads to and supports the notion that all humans are of equal value in the sight of God and should thus be attributed equal dignity and respect. It can also be interpreted as meaning that we are all capable of becoming like God in some significant respect and are basically good. On the other hand, the doctrine of original sin appears to suggest the opposite;

that all humans are fundamentally flawed and do not have it within themselves to achieve goodness, let alone perfection. One way of dealing with this apparent conflict or tension is to say that there is a difference between what we are essentially meant to be and what we are in practice: a difference between the ontological and the existential (4).

While this debate says something of general interest about human nature, it has never been entirely clear how it relates to the insights and ideas about the self that have been developed since the Enlightenment. It can place them in one of two camps, the positive or the negative, the optimistic or the pessimistic, but that is about all. The major area of difficulty is undoubtedly the Enlightenment assumption of human autonomy and the supposed power of humans to determine their fate independently of religious tradition and discipline. The question is whether this necessarily conflicts with a Christian understanding by suggesting that humans are capable of seeking and achieving their own perfection. In that extreme form the answer is that it probably does as there is no acknowledgement of sin and no place for an external reconciliatory being. However, if linked to ideas about human growth and development, it could be argued that it is consistent with the doctrine of Imago Dei. Becoming autonomous beings could mean growing towards the God-ness in each of us. It all depends whether one emphasizes the optimistic or the pessimistic strands of Christian belief on human nature.

If theologians conclude that human autonomy conflicts with Christian doctrine, then a Post-Modern view of the self that appears to undermine that Enlightenment assumption would hold an obvious appeal. Humans' expectations of themselves would be seen to be unfounded and the need for an external source of strength or guidance would be re-established. However, is there a coherent or defensible Post-Modern understanding of the self that could function in that way? That is the question that must be answered in this chapter. If there is not such an understanding then are there alternatives that could contribute to or provide common ground with the Christian doctrines? I will suggest that there are.

In order to structure the discussion I will focus on the issue of human agency. How much control over our lives do we in fact exercise? Are humans self determining or are the limits and constraints upon this so great as to make autonomy no more than an illusion? A key area where these questions have surfaced in recent years is in feminism and attention to this debate will also form part of this chapter.

However, before we dig deeper, a practical illustration of how this could affect religion in general and Christianity in particular. As suggested in the opening chapter, one way of describing Post-Modernity is to say that it is characterized by a pick-and-mix approach to religion. In other words, individuals decide for themselves what they will believe by selecting from the various religious packages now on offer. So shared practice and belonging to a community or tradition are replaced by deliberate choice from a range of products. Within this it will clearly be possible for people to create their own personal cocktail of beliefs and practices without any regard for the boundaries set by religious institutions. Without criteria of some description anarchy will reign. All religious institutions will perceive this as threatening and argue that it distorts the true nature of religious belief.

However, such an approach does now seem to be upon us. A particularly vivid example of this is the way that Information Technology enables individuals to pick-and-mix. The World Wide Web is currently witnessing a proliferation of religious sites ranging from one run by the Vatican to a website devoted to the old Norse religion featuring Thor and other assorted gods (5). The point is that anybody on the Internet can gain unlimited access to any and every form of religious belief. The only control will be that exercised by the limits of each individual's curiosity. Where this will lead is, as yet, unknown. It could conceivably create greater tolerance, mutual understanding and even unity between religions, but just as likely exacerbate the fragmentation that is already under way.

What price human agency in this free-for-all? Are humans capable of coming up with a sensible and reasonable choice faced with this bewildering diversity? Can religious institutions provide criteria and guidance that will safeguard some form of community and tradition? It would seem that there is a real danger of people being manipulated and controlled through an uncritical accessing of the more dubious religious products - although the established institutions themselves can hardly be immune from that same charge. Perhaps the freedom to choose is merely an illusion and that without the safeguard of a community of believers we are free only to select our own worst nightmares. Many Christians would want to point out that faith is not so much about choosing as about being chosen or called, often against the grain of one's own natural inclinations. How will such an understanding survive or be communicated via the medium of the Internet?

There are inevitably more questions than answers. Yet we can see that the issue of the scope and limits of human agency have a direct practical bearing on the future of religion itself. We must now press further into the philosophical discussions about Post-Modernity and the self.

The Disembedded Self

We begin with the Enlightenment view of what it is to be human. As recorded above, it can be summed up by the phrase 'rational autonomous agent', implying that an individual can have direct knowledge of themselves that leads to a reasoned and independent self control. This is part of the Grand Narrative of Modernity. Reason is a capacity that all share by virtue of being human and that all can exercise as they make both moral and technical decisions about their lives. In parallel with the view from nowhere we now have the person from nowhere and to whom the vagaries of gender, class, creed or ethnic origin make no difference. Hence a disembedded self, divorced from the contextual influences of community or tradition. This is a person in general who will judge and then make decisions according to universal rational criteria. So we should all make essentially the same decisions given the same circumstances.

The more one describes what now seems such an odd notion the more incredible it becomes. But this has been a vitally important component of the Enlightenment package that it is easy to ridicule in its extreme form. We must recognize that the universal self is also a way of acknowledging the full and equal worth of every human being and thus, in some respects, the secular heir to the Christian doctrine that humans are made in the image of God. The notion of the disembedded self, the autonomous rational agent, was one of the foundations of the development of liberal democracy. As Bernstein reminded us in response to MacIntyre's total rejection of the Enlightenment tradition, it is disingenuous now to abandon all the cornerstones of contemporary culture. It was a necessary development of its time that we may now see as inadequate, but without which little progress would have been made.

So, why is the disembedded self now seen to be inadequate? The main reason is because it is too general to encapsulate the varieties of humanity that do exist and because it is clear that it represents a far from universal tradition. It is itself a local narrative, even though it has claimed to be a meta-narrative. It is the story told by white Anglo-Saxon men from within a capitalist liberal democracy. The situation now is that we acknowledge that there is a plurality and multiplicity of local narratives expressing the different self identities of those of other ethnic origins, religious beliefs, sexual orientations and, of course, of another gender. The picture is that portrayed in the previous two chapters, of the breakdown of a big story that claimed too much for itself in favour of a host of different stories told by those who were excluded by the original metanarrative. However, this is only the beginning of the current critique of the autonomous rational agent.

The De-centred Self

The undermining of the Enlightenment notion of the rational autonomous self is not simply a result of the recent rise of previously disenfranchised minority or interest groups. It also stems from a rethinking of the internal aspects of human nature. The assumption of a coherent, identifiable and stable self-identity has been radically challenged by the insight that we are all much more complex and fragmented than the neat view would suggest. Rather than being centred or founded on one clear personal narrative that tells the whole story, each of us is de-centred and thus constructed from a confused and disparate set of narratives that are open to reconstruction and indeed manipulation. Who I am is not a question to which I can give a straightforward and once-for-all answer. Tomorrow I may be somebody different.

This begins to sound extreme, but we recall that Bauman describes the self in Post-Modernity as either a vagabond or a tourist and there is enough truth in this to capture the contemporary imagination. Why a vagabond?

'The vagabond is a pilgrim without a destination; a nomad without an itinerary. The vagabond journeys through an unstructured space; like a wanderer in the desert, who only knows of such trails as are marked with his own footprints, and blown off again by the wind the moment he passes, the vagabond structures the site he happens to occupy at the moment, only to dismantle the structure again as he leaves. Each successive spacing is local and temporary - episodic' (6).

The sense of this is clear: no final destination; a structure to be created and then re-created at will; life is essentially episodic. But how then does the vagabond relate to the external world? Apparently in the manner of a tourist, passing through different worlds and self-consciously consuming them as she goes, without any particular feelings for those who live there. 'The world is the tourist's oyster. The world is there to be lived pleasurably - and thus given meaning' (7). What is missing from this, according to Bauman, is any sense of moral responsibility, the formula for living is 'physically close but spiritually remote'. Touch, taste and see but don't get involved. Simply move on to the next experience. So there are no permanently shared experiences, no universal answers to the question of what it is to be human. Can this lead to anything other than a state of total disintegration and disorientation, there being no stable entity that can be called the self?

As I said, this interpretation does sound extreme even if it is partially recognizable. For those privileged enough to travel at will around the globe and without the ties of a job or family perhaps it can really feel like that. While acknowledging that neither jobs nor families necessarily last that long either these days, I would suggest that they do still provide some element of psychic anchoring within the wider maelstrom. However, is this all simply a passing phenomenon of Post-Modernity, or is there some longer term movement in operation here?

I believe it is important to adopt a longer term view and to be cautious about the notion that we have suddenly moved into a new era where human existence is so radically disordered and different. It would perhaps be more accurate to say that what we are now seeing and experiencing is the further development of a process that began some generations ago, maybe with the beginnings of Modernity itself. The story would be that, in Pre-Modernity, personal identity was fixed, solid and stable. Everybody knew their place in a pre-given social structure and identity was not susceptible to change or to renegotiation. Identity crises were still a thing of the future.

With the onset of Modernity all this begins to change. Greater social mobility and the increasing requirement upon each individual to play a range of differing roles - at home, at work and in one's social life - begin to undermine the stability. Personal identity becomes more mobile, multiple, self-reflexive and open to innovation. Yet there are still quite definite constraints upon this. Even though one is forced to face questions and to make decisions about who one is going to be...

'...there is still a structure of interaction with socially defined and available roles, norms, customs, and expectations, among which one must choose, appropriate and reproduce in order to gain identity in a complex process of mutual recognition' (8).

So the question still has to be answered through a process of negotiation with those around.

There is a subtle shift going on here, away from the Enlightenment concept of personal identity as something essential, substantial, unitary, fixed and unchanging. Certainly for the existentialist philosophers Sartre, Camus and the early Heidegger, self and identity become a project, a matter of the self conscious creation of the authentic individual (9). Without the external guidelines of social structure or tradition we each have to choose or resolve who it is we are going to be or to become. We have to take that responsibility upon ourselves and the result may be either a feeling of being trapped by external circumstances, unable to exercise that freedom because of other responsibilities, or else of being overwhelmed and alienated by the sheer diversity of possibilities. What does it mean to be authentic in this context?

Post-Modernity is, on one level, a further development of this movement. The very idea of being able to establish an authentic identity is itself now brought into question. The challenge comes from two different angles. First, there are the external pressures of a rapidly changing society in which increased bureaucracy, media influence and the dominance of consumerism all serve to fragment any sense of a coherent self identity. Each of us is bombarded with series of externally imposed self-images - the 'perfect family', the diet conscious female, the 'new man'- that present a kaleidoscope of possibilities. Then there are the interpretations of the internal self offered by psychoanalysis and philosophy - that subjective identity is a myth, a construct of language and society. There is no objectivity to the coherent and unified self.

'It is thus claimed that in postmodern culture, the subject has disintegrated into a flux of euphoric intensities, fragmented and disconnected, and that the decentred postmodern self no longer experiences anxiety...and no longer possesses the depth, substantiality and coherence that was the ideal and occasional achievement of the modern self' (10).

This picture of the Post-Modern self is strongly related to the more cultural aspects of Post-Modernity that do not form the focus of this book. It is the particular philosophical aspects or background to the argument that will concern us here. The key question is clearly that of the limits and scope of human agency. If there is no longer any coherent personal identity but rather the scattered and confused fragments of experience of the vagabond or tourist, increasingly subjected to the manipulative forces of the media, advertising and bureaucracy, what freedom or autonomy remains? It would seem that we have moved from Pre-Modernity where the self was externally determined by the weight of tradition and social expectation, through the growing self determination and conscious self construction of Modernity, to a Post-Modernity where the self is, once again, prey to external forces. Divide the self and conquer it seems to be the message. Can such a view be supported by the evidence of the philosophical arguments? We shall answer this shortly, but we must first see how contemporary theology has responded to this debate.

Theology and the Post-Modern Self

As hinted at earlier in this chapter a particular version of theology could well have a vested interest in appropriating the Post-Modern view of the self. The argument would be as follows. The Enlightenment notion of the autonomous rational agent, freely evaluating and choosing between different moral or religious stances, has served to undermine the credibility and authority of Christianity. Rather than being chosen, humans choose for themselves on the basis of their powers of reasoning. Unfortunately, too many have chosen to abandon the Christian faith. However, if this concept of autonomous rational choice is shown to be an illusion after all, particularly if this so-called freedom turns out to be merely a mask for the power of manipulation, then Christianity might be able to reassert its claim to have the key to true freedom - the insight into what humans have the capacity to become. If self creation and self determination are revealed as arbitrary and ultimately destructive, then the Christian vision of a self created and determined by God could once again be back in the frame. My argument will be that, although this view is superficially attractive, it is in fact simplistic and misleading.

In a recent book entitled 'Interpreting God and the Post-Modern Self' (11) Anthony Thiselton, Professor of Christian Theology at the University of Nottingham presents exactly this sort of view. Apparently accepting what he interprets as the Post-Modern critique of the Enlightenment concept of personal identity, he states that 'Postmodernism implies a shattering of innocent confidence in the capacity of the self to control its own destiny' (12). In other words, all attempts to shape both the individual and society based on the Enlightenment belief in self determination were bound to end in failure. Trust in such strategies has now been destroyed to be replaced by anger, alienation and anxiety. 'The postmodern self faces life and society with suspicion rather than trust' (13).

It is clear that Thiselton, like Milbank, is determined to read Post-Modernity through Nietzschian spectacles. His argument is that Post-Modernity, following in Nietzsche's footsteps, views all claims to truth as devices that legitimate certain power interests. So, truth is merely a mask for power and, as a result, a culture of distrust and suspicion is created. This has a damaging impact upon the notion of human agency. 'The postmodern self perceives itself as having lost control as active agent, and as having been transformed into a passive victim of competing groups. Everyone seems to be at the mercy of someone else's vested interests for power' (14).

Apart from the fact that such an idea is ultimately incoherent and contradictory - presumably no such statement can even be made because it too would represent another power play and not a claim to truth - Thiselton makes the mistake of attributing this position to Foucault. This will be challenged in the next section. However, this leads Thiselton to reiterate the classic Christian description as outlined at the beginning of this chapter. On the one hand, Christianity recognizes that there will always be those - even within the religious arena - who try to manipulate truth for their own benefit. On the other, respect for each other requires that we see all as unique agents or active personal subjects. So humanity is both 'fallen' and yet made in the image of God. This is fine as far as it goes, but it does just repeat the original doctrines without offering any insights into the nature and scope of human agency as revealed by contemporary ideas. The challenge to Christianity of the notion of the autonomous rational agent is conveniently side-stepped on the basis of a caricature of the Post-Modern critique.

It seems to me that there are two weaknesses in Thiselton's exposition. First, he is over-reliant upon a nihilistic interpretation of the Post-Modern philosophers in a way that owes more to Nietzsche than to the thinkers themselves. Second, in order to reassert the traditional Christian position on human nature, he takes an essentially negative view of both Modernity and Post-Modernity. Is there nothing that Christianity can learn from modern thought, except that human nature is flawed and always susceptible to both internal and external manipulation? Like MacIntyre, he is too ready to dismiss the progress that has been made as a result of the Enlightenment view. This allows him to ignore what further developments of this might contribute to a Christian understanding.

For a more positive theological appropriation of Foucault and Post-Modernity one need only turn to the work of the Canadian scholar Charles Davis (15). Like myself, Davis challenges the identification of Post-Modernity with a Nietzschian nihilism. According to his approach nihilism only emerges where there is an idolatrous closure of interpretation - the belief that one has finally reached the truth and need look no further. He believes - as I do - that Post-Modern thinkers such as Derrida and Foucault, far from closing down further interpretation, leave questions and spaces for further interrogation. When we actually examine what Foucault says about the self and human agency we will see that he puts question marks against all premature attempts to define self identity, thus leaving open the possibility of the further exploration, or even transcendence, that might be of interest to the Christian. In Foucault's rejection of a deeper and essential self, Davis is inclined to see the challenge to all idolatrous interpretations that theology too would want to launch.

Once more we face the question of whether a critique of the Enlightenment - either its view of Reason, or of the autonomous rational agent - can simply and automatically be equated with a destruction of the same. To question, challenge and even to deconstruct is not necessarily to destroy. Thiselton wants Post- Modernity to be seen as reducing the notion of human agency to that of the passive victim of power play in order to reintroduce a traditional Christian view. However, if he is mistaken, as I am suggesting, then Christianity cannot avoid the challenge of the Enlightenment idea of human autonomy. Post-Modern understandings of the self are not user-friendly in that straightforward manner as we shall now realise in an examination of Foucault's work.

Foucault on the self

In the introduction to Foucault in chapter 3 I suggested that there is a risk in theology adopting a simplistic interpretation of his work. In particular, there is a danger of reading into it a concern about power as domination and manipulation that is potentially misleading. One consequence of this is to conclude that Foucault's notion of the self destroys any scope for autonomous human agency. So all human actions and decision represent merely the power plays and interests of other groups. There is, in effect, no human freedom of action. I will now argue in greater detail that this is to misunderstand and to misrepresent his intention. It is not so much that Foucault denies human agency as that he brackets that issue out of the consideration in order to attend to other aspects that are his direct concern. Like Davis, I believe that Foucault leaves the question of the self open, thus creating a rather different set of ambiguities and problems.

We need first to review Foucault's approach to Reason and to the Enlightenment generally. It is crucial to clarify this in order to support the argument that his critique of the Enlightenment need not be seen as an attempt to denigrate or to destroy it. While acknowledging that Foucault is a somewhat elusive thinker and that it can be argued that his work passes through a process of change and development, there is general agreement that his most substantial work on the self dates from his later period (16). So it is legitimate to focus upon the writings that originate from that time.

In an interview with Paul Rabinow published in March 1982 (17),

Foucault offers some significant thoughts on the subject of Post-Modernity. In particular he agrees with Habermas that if one just abandons the work of the Enlightenment there is a risk of lapsing into irrationality (18). He then makes it clear exactly what his own project throughout his academic career has been:

'I think that the central issue of philosophy and critical thought since the eighteenth century has always been, still is, and will I hope remain the question: What is this Reason that we use? What are its historical effects? What are its limits and what are its dangers? How can we exist as rational beings, fortunately committed to practising a rationality that is unfortunately crisscrossed by intrinsic dangers' (19).

Not only should we remain close to the questions about Reason, but we should guard against the mistake of saying that Reason is the enemy that should be eliminated. It is also important to assert that critical questioning of rationality does not lead to irrationality. This is surely that same point that Derrida tries to make. So then, the function of intellectuals and of critical thought '...is precisely to accept this sort of spiral, this sort of revolving door of rationality that refers us to its necessity, to its indispensability, and at the same time, to its intrinsic dangers' (20).

It seems to me that this clearest of statements throws considerable doubt upon Thiselton's assumption that Foucault is simply pursuing a Nietzschian path. If that were the case then every exercise of Reason would automatically be dismissed as another instance of the will to power. Foucault does not do this, but rather appears to be drawing our attention to the permanent ambiguities of Reason while simultaneously acknowledging its essential role. This balanced approach surely has much to commend it. It also leaves open the question of where and how humans do exercise some freedom of thought and action. What we must attend to now are the questions that Foucault was actually concerned to explore, in contrast to those that some theologians would find more convenient.

It is in Foucault's later work that we find the discussions of the self that are most significant. In particular, the three volumes of 'The History of Sexuality' represent his most sustained attempt to investigate the different ways in which humans have constituted themselves as subjects (21). This may sound a strange way of expressing it, but it is important to grasp that it is exactly this that forms the focus of this writing. What Foucault is saying is that there is no such thing as the universal or essential self, in the sense that no one way of understanding ourselves as subjects has existed across the boundaries of time and culture. What it is deemed to be human, what a human subject is perceived as, has changed over time. Foucault's interest is in examining these different understandings and the circumstances in which they have arisen.

We need to be very clear that this examination assumes a human capacity for self creation and is not based on the assumption that humans are shaped by the external forces of institutions or other social orders. This runs parallel with the more positive interpretation of the Enlightenment on which we have already commented. Foucault himself sees this as a shift of emphasis in his own work.

'If one wants to analyze the genealogy of the subject in Western civilization one has to take into account not only techniques of domination but also techniques of the self. One has to show the interaction between these two types of self. When I was studying asylums, prisons and so on, I perhaps insisted too much upon the techniques of domination...I would like, in the years to come, to study power relations starting from techniques of the self' (22).

What exactly does he mean by 'techniques of the self'? Essentially the various ways in which humans create and constitute themselves as subjects; the operations they carry out on their bodies, their thoughts and their conduct in order to attain certain states of being. So the objective may be to attain a state of happiness, or of purity, wisdom or perfection. The subject is no longer seen as being externally determined by impersonal forces, but in part at least, a self creation in the light of certain further objectives. For instance, Foucault gives considerable attention to both the Greek and Roman cultures where certain clearly defined areas of experience - diet, family relations and sexuality - became the target for self-conscious moderation and self control. One's life is seen as a work of art, to be shaped and fashioned according to particular cultural values. The austerity that is more often associated with the rise of Christianity already in fact had its place within these earlier cultures. Care of the self, including self control, becomes a personal task for those belonging to those times.

According to Foucault, Christianity brings with it a significant shift. Whereas the Greeks and Romans saw desire and pleasure as perfectly acceptable, provided they were contained and ordered, in the Christian view they become evil in themselves. Thus the human subject needs to renounce and do all it can to debase such natural instincts as it strives for a different sort of moral perfection. Foucault refrains from making any explicit value judgement on these respective approaches, his role as a historian is to describe and examine what is actually there. However, one suspects that he favours the Greek and Roman approach to self creation, positively affirming the good of pleasure and desire.

In these later investigations we certainly hear echoes of the more popular picture of the Post-Modern self. So there is no essential or universal self to be discovered or unearthed; no secret inner being that psychoanalysis, for instance, can successfully penetrate. Rather there is the constant task of self creation and self production, becoming whatever it is we wish to be and - presumably - being able to change that if we so desire. Like much of the other Post-Modern writing we have encountered this acknowledges a multiplicity and plurality of possibilities: the undermining of one Big Story that we might tell about ourselves in favour of a wide range of local or personal narratives. The question is whether this necessarily leads to the anarchic and nihilistic free-for-all where there are no criteria nor guidelines for this process. I will return to this in the concluding part of the chapter.

What is the exact nature of the freedom that Foucault appears to be offering? It is clearly not that which might result from acknowledging and dealing with one's own deeper feelings or emotions. The psychoanalytical story is itself seen as merely one more approach that humans have devised in order to deal with themselves. It is not a matter of realising one's true self through therapy or counselling and then making the necessary adjustments. For Foucault there is no true self to be understood: the very notion is itself another cultural creation. Yet the alternative is not to admit that all that we are is the product of our social or cultural environment, although these are still part of the picture.

'The subject is still discursively and socially conditioned for Foucault, and still theorized as situated within power relations: the difference is that now he sees that individuals also have the power to define their own identity, to master their body and desires, and to forge a practice of freedom through techniques of the self' (23).

The understanding of human agency that Foucault offers is thus a dialectic between an active and creative subject and a social field where there will always be certain influences and constraints. We are mistresses and masters of our own fate - but always within limits. It is important to see that there is a continuity here with his earlier work. Power is still an issue, but seen as a productive and creative force as much as a negative one. Power is the capacity to bring about change but is to be located within individuals as well as within institutions. Domination is when one person or group attempts to impose their ways of being on other individuals against their will, or to the exclusion of other ways of being. The most common form of this has been through the influence of a metanarrative of what it is to be human. To the extent that the Enlightenment has tried to do this it is to be criticized and resisted because the effect has been to marginalize, displace and disenfranchize certain groups of people. Hence freedom and agency require open access to other ways of creating and shaping ourselves.

However, we need to acknowledge that there are particular weaknesses or perhaps unanswered questions in Foucault's approach. First, there is an inherent individualism that is characteristic of his work. The emphasis is very much upon what the lone individual might do for themselves in terms of self creation. Perhaps this reflects his suspicion of institutions and traditions and the undue influence that both can exercise. Yet, for many, both may also be a positive factor in the process of self production. We do not operate in a vacuum and others do offer us resources in a non-coercive manner. Foucault perhaps underestimates this. The second area of concern is that he leaves decisions about what to be or who to become hanging in thin air. If we are to choose rather than allowing an institution or some external force to decide for us, then how are we to determine to follow path A rather than path B? Some criteria will be called for and they will have to be derived from somewhere, even though we recognize that they may emerge from within a particular culture, tradition or set of practices. How are we to go about this when we are faced with such a multiplicity of choices? If we are not merely to be manipulated by the media for instance, how do we develop, sustain and exercise any sort of critical faculty? It seems that Foucault never gave explicit attention to this question but, as we shall now see, there are social and political consequences of this gap that must concern us. It is all very well to say, as Davis does, that Foucault's critique of the universal self opens up a space for other possibilities, but what is going to fill that space and how are we to deal with that? To help answer that question we move on to examine ways in which feminism has responded to this issue.

Feminism and Post-Modernity

The scope for debate here is vast and we need to be aware that our specific concern - how to develop an appropriate notion of human agency - forms only one part of a larger whole. The relationship between feminism and Post-Modernity has been creative but uneasy. There is the usual limitation of generalizing on this as there are different strands and versions of feminism as there are of Post-Modernity. However, the question left open by Foucault appears to be pivotal. First though the common ground between the two areas of thought.

It would seem that feminism and Post-Modernity are natural allies lining up against a common enemy. Both challenge the idea of a universal, rational autonomous self as found in the Enlightenment metanarrative. While the Post-Modern thinkers do this from a philosophical angle, feminism's concerns are often more practical and political. Thus the Enlightenment metanarrative is after all just another local narrative - one devised, told and written by men and about men, and to the exclusion of a female perspective and interests. However, that is about as far as the alliance can safely go, for differences emerge as soon as one asks what an alternative to the Enlightenment understanding of the self might look like.

We have already seen that one of the problems with Foucault is his unwillingness to articulate criteria for self creation. Yet without such criteria it is very difficult to argue that one form of human being or becoming is better than any other. Clearly, this is something that most feminists at least will want to do. They do not want to replace the masculine local narrative by just any old alternative or admit that there is no means of choosing a better way of being. They want some form of specific feminine narrative in the belief that this will be more adequate to describe how women are. This is where life gets complicated, at least it does unless there is a mediating framework, or a major narrative on what it is to be female. There appear to be two extremes: either the Enlightenment metanarrative of an essential autonomous self, or the proliferation of Post-Modern local narratives - including a feminist one - but with no method of choosing between them. If a feminist critique is to be sustained it looks as though it requires a major narrative about what it is to be a woman. This will not claim to be establishing an essential or universal female self, but will be substantial enough to provide the basis for an alternative to the masculine models. Post-Modernity, certainly in the shape of Foucault, does not seem able to offer this or even to show how it might be possible.

Feminists have identified another problem with Foucault's approach (24). Self creation sounds very liberating and exciting, but where is the self who is going to do this self creating? Is it not necessary to assume that there is a self already in existence, in which case where has this come from and how is creation or transformation going to be effected? If this pre-existing self is merely the product of external or even internal forces beyond the individual's control, then we are back where we started with no real scope for human agency. Foucault does not appear to be prepared to accept this form of determinism, but neither does he convincingly show how this is to be avoided in practice. Feminists require more than simply Foucault's unanswered question here: they require an answer.

So, we can begin to see that the Post-Modern notion of a de-centred and fragmented self, consisting solely of random and historically contingent aspects and formed out of the discourses of the surrounding social and cultural environment, does not provide the basis for a feminist alternative. In fact it leaves each of us as isolated individuals with never enough common ground to form into bodies or groups of resistance. Those in support of the status quo would thus be in a position to divide and conquer. For women - as for other marginalized people - there has to be enough common ground to justify forming political alliances and an effective opposition. Yet, if the claim is then made that there is an essential or universal female self, we are back with the another version of the Enlightenment metanarrative. Feminism needs a major narrative. As Assiter says:

'...unless one does identify the category of woman (and other such categories), it is difficult to see how one can avoid a return to the particularism and individualism against which feminism originally set its face. If there is nothing but individuals, with no common characteristics, then one cannot speak of structural social features, such as discrimination against individuals as participants in social groupings. Correspondingly, the idea of a political community of women based on these shared characteristics, breaks down' (25).

As she says, what applies to womens' groups is equally true for all other marginalized people. The interesting point is to remind ourselves that Lyotard, Derrida and Foucault each championed the needs and rights of such groups through direct political action at some stage in their careers. One can assume, on the basis of this and other evidence that we have examined, that this exhibits some degree of consistency with a continued adherence to Enlightenment hopes and aspirations.

It is important to register that the dilemma or tension we have just identified cuts right through feminist debate. One of the internal problems of feminism has been that, in its early stages, it appeared to be representing only one section of the female population - white, Western and well-educated. As other womens' groups were formed the question inevitably arose of how to more effectively present the experiences, feelings and needs of those who did not belong to this elite. Was this apparent fragmentation of the movement the precise illustration of the truth of the Post-Modern view? In other words, there is a plurality and multiplicity of differences amongst women themselves. The problem that remains is that of finding the basis for significant common ground without turning that into another metanarrative.

This debate has centred on the notions of gender and sexuality. Is it possible or justifiable to draw a distinction between the two? One proposal might be that sexuality refers to a minimal notion of the body and to a set of necessary biological factors. If this could be sustained then there would be at least some account of what is 'essential' to being either male or female. Gender then would refer to the culturally determined characteristics or articulations of an individual's sexuality: the aspect of a self that is open to change and to the influence of contingent historical circumstances. So gender is socially and culturally produced and the explanation for differences within the respective sexes. Some feminists have objected to this distinction on the grounds that it creates too exclusive a separation of the body from other personal characteristics: it suggests that the body is largely passive and that gender can be independently created or manipulated. However, it would seem that such claims are not essential to the distinction and that therefore a mediating framework of this nature can be upheld. In which case it is possible for feminism to steer between the Scylla of Enlightenment foundationalism and the Charybdis of Post-Modern difference - to use Milbank's phrase once more. There needs to be enough common ground to provide women with the means of both meaningful analysis and political organization, but also the acknowledgement of difference that allows for movement and change.

The sex-gender distinction does not fit easily with Foucault's approach. It would appear that, according to his interpretation, sexuality is not an essential personal characteristic, but is itself the subject of external forces. If not simply the result of the exercise of either power or domination, it is still a development of different discourses or cultures. Sexuality is part of self creation and thus presumably always open to negotiation. Yet, if sexuality is to be either the site of or a basis for feminine resistance, it needs to be more fundamental than Foucault is prepared to accept. Perhaps we can say that the sex-gender distinction forms part of the answer to the question but that Foucault has not progressed beyond the question.

This brings us back to one of the earlier ways of describing the same debate. A universal or essential self - either male or female - is necessarily disembedded. In other words, it is deemed not to be determined nor influenced by the surrounding context or culture. At the other extreme, a totally embedded self would seem to be so determined by context and culture as to have nothing in common with other selves from other contexts. Neither of these extremes seems to do justice to the way people are and yet both contain an element of truth. The challenge surely is to describe and maintain some sort of balance between them. So, both women and men have certain needs and desires that flow from their sexuality and that will form part of the given within which they operate. However, there will also be distinct, context-dependent aspects of the self that will always have to be taken into account. Any notion of human agency or autonomy must at least be able to acknowledge this tension, without trying to resolve it. We are, each of us, both embedded and disembedded, or, as Seyla Benhabib would prefer to describe it, we are all situated selves. We are both within particular contexts and yet capable of going beyond them (26). To abandon that tension is actually to undermine any coherent account of human agency and to risk admitting that we are totally determined, either by our biological nature or by our cultural context. Such a 'solution' is surely better avoided.

Christianity and Autonomy

Although we have now seen how feminism at least can begin to answer Foucault's open question about the self, it is not perhaps obvious to glimpse how Christianity can begin to develop a similarly balanced approach. It would seem to have a vested interest in accepting the Post-Modern critique of the Enlightenment notion of the universal autonomous agent. However, it would face exactly the same philosophical and political problems as feminism if it were to totally embrace the concept of a de-centred and fragmented self. It would have no way of valuing or of validating the insights of its own tradition and would undermine any sense of community. Yet, if it simply reverts to its own doctrines - Imago Dei and the Fall - and claims that they are metanarratives, then it excludes itself from the ongoing debate about the self and ignores the challenges of other groups. Since the most notable of these are probably womens' groups and most churches have now taken on board at least some of their criticisms and ideas, I do not see how Christians can escape engaging in the wider debate and taking note of other contemporary ideas. It is therefore to some of those that I want to turn in the final section of this chapter.

I do not think there is much doubt that one of the most fruitful sets of concepts to emerge from this field are those based on the assumption that humans go through certain identifiable developmental stages. I say 'sets of concepts' because the basic idea now takes on a variety of forms. I do not intend to describe them in any great detail here since this has been done elsewhere (27), but merely to point to them as a significant contribution to the debate.

The concept is often associated originally with Piaget's work on cognitive development - the ways in which our understanding and knowledge of the world is likely to change and develop at different ages. Jung's name is linked with the beginning of a more explicitly psychological dimension to the theory, but this has now been carried further by Erickson and Levinson (28). Theologians have since taken up the developmental theme, initially in the work of Tillich, but more recently in that of James Fowler and his notion of Faith Development (29). The argument is still that it is possible to identify characteristic stages that people go through as they grow older and that this can be correlated with different and developing understandings of faith. So, for instance, people can move beyond the understanding of Christianity as unquestioning adherence to a written moral code to a point where they judge for themselves on the basis of response to circumstances as well as in the light of the tradition. Going by the spirit of the law rather than the letter of the law. It is interesting to note that Habermas has drawn upon the same research as Fowler in his attempts to construct a non-foundational basis for moral theory (30).

There are a number of question marks hanging over this approach. The first concerns the actual nature of the empirical research that underpins it and is based on a feminist critique of both the sampling and the findings (31). There are also limitations in applying the model too strictly and trying to categorize people according to age and stages. The more complex the model becomes the more dubious the categorizations, so one must beware of making exaggerated claims. However, I believe that a developmental model of some sort is valuable because it does acknowledge scope for human agency within Christianity. Faith is not a static state of being unable to respond and adapt to challenges and new experiences, but a pathway or pilgrimage of the self within the context of a particular tradition. Autonomy as such may not be the goal of that journey, but the development of autonomy can form part of the process. The model seems to provide one contemporary way of describing both the tension between what humans are meant to become and what they are and the more modern dilemma surrounding the influences of biology and culture and human agency. There are both certain givens or limits and the capacity for growth and transformation. An adapted version of this could form a mediating framework for this area (32).

However, there is a further resource that I believe is helpful in this context, a way of looking at human decision making described by Giddens in this country and then taken further by Ulrich Beck and Scott Lash (33). Each of these has developed a slightly different way of understanding the notion of reflexivity. Again, there is not the space here to go into great detail, but I do want to explain how and why this set of ideas is important. If we take Giddens as the starting point, his suggestion is that in Pre-Modernity most life decisions facing people were fairly clearly determined in advance. One's life was laid out according to family, class, religion and nationality. With the onset of Modernity this began to change. The options were no longer so clearly determined and people were increasingly faced with genuine questions and dilemmas about what to do and who and what to become. In the current later stages of Modernity this process has now gone even further. Certainly in the capitalist world, each of us can be faced with almost daily choices over a whole range of issues, some of them trivial but some of great significance. For instance, there are questions of relationships, of employment, of location, even of life and death that were perhaps not so open in previous generations. Reflexivity is the way of describing how most of us now use the resources of knowledge available to us as we struggle to make those decisions. So, for instance, given that we now know that one in three marriages ends in divorce, do we decide to get married or not? Do we take this particular job knowing that the firm may relocate to another part of the globe ? Beck has captured this particularly vividly:

'In the individualized society the individual must therefore learn, on pain of permanent disadvantage, to conceive of himself or herself as the centre of action, as the planning office with respect to his/her own biography, abilities, orientations, relationships and so on' (34).

There is an ongoing debate between Giddens, Beck and Lash over the different interpretations of reflexivity and the notion is also now being utilized by economists attempting to identify flaws in market based theories (35). However, there are two points that I want to highlight in the context of our discussion about human agency. First, it may be too limiting to see reflexivity as simply a cognitive or an intellectual exercise. In other words, it could well involve more than just our knowledge of ourselves and our world and could include also the dimension of our feelings and imagination. After all, we make decisions in a variety of ways and at a number of levels. One might say that reflexivity is the opening up of spaces for questions at any level of our being where the new and unexpected is likely to break through. Thus humans have the capacity to change independently of the influences around them, but this is more than simply an intellectual matter. Second, as Lash points out (36), if one were constantly faced with uncertainty and life-shaping decisions, it could lead to chronic emotional paralysis and a complete breakdown of activity. It seems more realistic to say that most of us can cope with limited change at any one time and that we each need at least one aspect of our lives to remain constant while all else is in flux. So there will be limits to reflexivity.

Once again though, the value of this notion is that it both acknowledges the frightening pace of change and the external influences that threaten to dominate our decisions and the continuing human capacity to reflect upon and thus to retain some control over these events and our lives. There is a level of human agency and autonomy within the wider framework of cultural, economic and political structures. The question for Christianity is surely this: 'What contribution can it make to this process?'

It may be that, along with other forms of faith, Christianity provides people with resources to help to cope with themselves in this further stage of Modernity. A reflexivity that goes beyond the intellectual and includes the affective, imaginative and spiritual, would surely draw upon such resources. It would also acknowledge the extent to which many are situated within communities and traditions and thus counterbalance the individualism that seems inherent in the idea of the vagabond or tourist. We do indeed face a whole host of confusing and often conflicting decisions, but we do not have to make them alone. We may choose to do that but that is a different matter.

I want to conclude by outlining what Giddens has described as the dilemmas of the self, because I think they usefully summarize the situation we are now facing (37). According to Giddens there are three such dilemmas. The first he terms fragmentation versus unification. Fragmentation occurs because people face such a range of different settings in which they have to operate but where they still have to be able to present themselves effectively. Hence the Post-Modern description of the de-centred self - a self lacking any clear or coherent focus. Yet we would be mistaken to assume that this diversity of context inevitably leads to a fragmentation of the self. As Giddens says: 'It can just as well, at least in many circumstances, promote an integration of self' (38). For one thing, as we encounter a wider variety of other people and learn to adapt effectively, we may achieve a firmer and more cohesive self identity.

However, we do need to acknowledge that there can also be pathological reactions to this complexity and variety:

130

'...the type of person who constructs his identity around a set of fixed commitments, which act as a filter through which numerous different social environments are reacted to or interpreted. Such a person is a rigid traditionalist, in a compulsive sense, and refuses any relativism of context' (39).

This seems to me to describe quite well the Christian who wants to continue to claim that their faith is the metanarrative. One could of course go to the other extreme and simply slip uncritically from one situation to another, conforming to whatever context one happens to be in. This would be the Post-Modern free-for- all, pick-and-mix mentality, abandoning both judgement and personal integrity. The challenge, as ever, is to steer between those two extremes, acting with some freedom, flexibility and autonomy but also with some clear criteria.

The second dilemma is closely related to the first and is described as authority versus certainty. How is one to make the myriad of life decisions? One way is to submit oneself to an external authority - a religious tradition, a closed community or even a political party. The other extreme reaction is to fail to make any decisions at all, effectively paralysed by the sheer range of choices available. The middle route is surely to act with some limited autonomy, aware of the guidelines and resources of those external authorities but making deliberate and self-conscious choices nevertheless. Deciding to accept the external authority of a religious tradition is still a decision and a choice and one cannot disguise the fact that one could have chosen otherwise. Knowing that, how does one justify that choice to oneself, let alone to others? Now we know that we choose we cannot avoid the responsibility of owning that choice. I suspect that the Christian understanding of vocation - or being chosen - will have to be altered in the light of reflexivity.

Finally of course, and this is a third dilemma, we have to be clear to what extent our choices are really our own, or whether we are simply falling prey to advertising or other forms of external manipulation. If the choices are simply between competing but standardized products, then are we not fooling ourselves in imagining we are exercising real autonomy? Even religion can now be presented as a series of convenient or tailor-made packages, so how do we know that this is a sensible or justifiable choice to make? I will return to this crucial question in the next chapter. The point is that there must be criteria for such choices and although such criteria can be purely a private matter, if we take a Habermasian line, let alone a Christian one, they are more likely to be developed and therefore justified in an inter-subjective and public context. Returning to the initial example of religion on the

Internet, the real problem is not the access to the range of possibilities, but the likelihood of people making a decision alone and thus outside the context within which religions were meant to operate. As lone individuals we are surely much more susceptible to external manipulation. Religion was never designed to be a purely private affair.

The conclusion has to be that Christianity cannot simply turn its back on the Enlightenment notion of human autonomy and that it must examine the ideas of Post-Modernity on the self more carefully. Some concept of human agency remains a necessity for both theology and philosophy and social theory. It is the ongoing discussion about the nature and the limits of that agency that should concern Christians as they attempt to come to terms with contemporary developments in this areas. Within Christian doctrine there is the possibility of retaining the tension between an optimistic and pessimistic view of humanity but this needs to be supplemented by insights from more recent thought such as feminism, developmental theory and the ideas on reflexivity. It would seem that choice is unavoidable, even in the field of religion. Rather than denying this by retreating to Christianity as a metanarrative, would it not be better to acknowledge this reality and to face up to the questions of how such choices are to be made?

7

Theology and Difference

Introduction

In this penultimate chapter the focus is on the central Post-Modern theme of difference and its potential significance for theology. Interest centres not so much upon a specific area of belief or doctrine as upon the nature of theology itself. This may sound strange to readers in the United Kingdom for whom theology is readily equated with an academic discipline determined and dominated by universities. However, in other parts of the world, not least the U.S.A. and Latin America, there has been what one might describe as a loosening up of the understanding of theology in response to more practically orientated requirements. An awareness of these recent developments must form part of the background to this investigation.

In the first part of the chapter I will review contemporary changes and challenges to traditional theology drawing on the work of two American theologians. This will illustrate what we might call the internal pluralization of theology. I will then move on to contrast this to the response to the encounter with other faiths that has emerged from the Post-Modern interpretation of John Milbank. In this case the argument focusses upon difference as identified in the external pluralization of religions. In the third section the work of Derrida as the key Post-Modern thinker contributing to this debate will be examined in greater detail in order to illustrate that theology must be more subtle in its interpretation of difference. Finally I will offer some substantial suggestions as to what theology might look like in years to come in the light of the previous considerations. This is deliberately designed to be controversial, but is I believe necessary, if there is to be an alternative to the contemporary neo-orthodox reaction of Milbank and colleagues.

The American theologian David Tracy has offered an illuminating insight into the nature of theology that can preface the ensuing debate. Much will depend on the exact audience for a particular theology. Tracy identifies three such potential audiences: academia; the churches and the world (1). His suggestion is that each of these will have different requirements and normal modes of operation and that we need to recognize, for instance, that theology written in the context of the academy, may appear different to that produced within the confines of the churches. While Tracy provides a helpful distinction here I do think it is possible to overstate the case. There is a real danger of creating the attitude that there is a second or third class theology. Thus real theology is only that produced within the academic environment, even though that may be distant from and incomprehensible to ordinary worshipping Christians. Likewise, the practitioners within the churches struggling at the coal face to create a practical theology that relates to their specific context, may believe their approach to be superior to the abstract theorizing of the academics. We can see immediately that there are differences within theology itself that are neither readily resolved nor reconciled. The old distinction between theory and practice only serves to exacerbate these divisions.

I do not intend to offer easy solutions or to nail my colours exclusively to a particular mast. I believe that a theology worth its salt would have something to offer to different audiences as, ultimately, these cannot be watertight compartments. One could argue that church theology is bound to be narrow and restrictive as it serves the needs of the committed and their respective institutions. One could equally argue that a theology for the world is always in danger of compromise or of selling out to secular ideas or concerns. One could also say that academic theology is in danger of becoming an inward looking circus where the performers have to create ever more spectacular displays in order to gain preferment and secure their research funding. Each of these descriptions contains an element of truth, but then we have to recognize that there is no neutral or perfect base from which to do theology. There are just different starting points and contexts, each with differing but important requirements.

Shifts in Contemporary Theology

In their introduction to the volume 'Reconstructing Christian Theology', Rebecca Chopp and Mark Lewis Taylor, two American theologians refer to a number of discursive shifts that they believe can be identified within contemporary theology (2). In other words, theological discourse, the ways in which theologians talk, write and reflect, has undergone significant changes in recent years. They further describe this as a move away from the idea of the melting pot where all differences are somehow subsumed and submerged beneath a general consensus, to that of a collage where those differences are acknowledged and allowed to stand. On one level of course this may be peculiar to the American context where there is such an explicit range and diversity of cultural backgrounds and ethnic differences. However, there is a powerful argument that the same picture can be painted in other countries where there is also often a considerable cultural and ethnic mix.

What is being challenged here is presumably a Grand Narrative that all these diverse elements can be readily and easily combined to form a new society or culture with its own distinctive characteristics. In which case the differences have to be acknowledged and somehow contained within a different sort of structure. Here is the classic dilemma of Post-Modernity and, according to Chopp and Taylor, it is now evident within theology.

'Theology in the United States...has undergone a shift from using a melting pot model, in which theology as officially understood sought a dominant or common human experience, to a model that values the collage of different faces, voices, styles, questions and constructs. Black theologies, Asian-American theologies, feminist theologies, womanist theologies, theologies from gay men and lesbian women, and theologies offered from the perspective of the disabled are all presented on the scene today' (3).

These are no longer viewed as special or minority interests but as making a vital contribution to a dynamic and developing theological diversity. The contrast with dominant British theology is acute. Apart from a lively feminist theology most academic departments have continued with business as usual, even the responses to Post-Modernity being used as a justification for a new neo-orthodoxy. Perhaps they have not yet caught up with the wider cultural diversity that is now evident within the life of British churches.

Beyond feminist theology there have only been isolated and limited attempts to develop a more contextual approach and these remain either unknown to or unacknowledged by most academic institutions. I offer as examples the work of Laurie Green in Birmingham; the Urban Theology Unit based in Sheffield and my own attempt to describe a local theology in a deeply rural setting (4). By and large mainstream theology still dominates both the academic and the vocational training institutions.

What then are these discursive shifts that Chopp and Taylor claim to have identified? The first is what might be described as a developing Post-Modern sensibility. The idea that there could be a systematic theology whose task it is to elaborate a clear, logical, univocal system of thought that could address all the important questions, has been abandoned in the face of the diversity and heterogeneity associated with Post-Modernity. So theology no longer has a Grand Narrative about itself, but recognizes what I would describe as a plurality of major narratives. We note here that Milbank's response to Post-Modernity has been much more limited in scope, effectively only extracting Enlightenment reason from the theological equation, but still leaving the remaining non-rational project as a Grand or metanarrative. Theological pluralism appears anathema to him.

A more consistent approach to Post-Modernity, I would suggest, is that described by Chopp and Taylor:

'Is theology about sure foundations that never waiver and provide a closure against the winds of change (modernity), or is theology about envisioning new spaces for personal and social flourishing? Postmodernity, as a challenge to theology, consists of finding ways to address a culture with a penchant for the fragmentary, the open, the ambiguous and the different' (5).

The second discursive shift is to a postcolonial sensibility. Once again, this is based upon a critique of a Grand Narrative, that of First World cultural and economic imperialism. The latter is now resisted and challenged as a source of oppression and injustice, serving only the economic interests of the already industrialized nations. However, as we have already noted there is an ambiguity here. Remove the imposed political structures of liberal democracy and what will take its place? Sometimes the cure is more deadly than the disease as the vacuum is rapidly filled by another layer of exploitative capitalism no longer kept in check by a residual democracy. This is the political equivalent of the potentially nihilistic and anarchic consequences of Post-Modernity feared by Milbank and a major reason why a Habermasian approach to ethics, law and democracy is so essential.

The final discursive shift, and the one that will be examined in greater detail shortly, is a turn towards an interest in other world religions. Chopp and Taylor are clear that this is occurring in a spirit of mutual critique and dialogue. They include within this category not only the other major world religions, Judaism, Buddhism, Hinduism, Islam and so on, but also the lesser known beliefs of indigenous peoples that the old Grand Narrative of Modernity had dismissed as primitive. There is a whole range of issues here that we will pursue shortly, but what emerges clearly from this review of Chopp and Taylor is that theology, as they understand it, is increasingly responding to that which is other, or different, or non-identical with itself. That other may be from within the Christian tradition or from within the surrounding culture or from beyond both. Response to difference is a determining factor in the way that theology itself is now being shaped.

What will be the defining contours of this reconstructed theology? First, it will be contextual, rooted in and emerging from the specific and local situations in which Christians find themselves. Second, it will use the resources of its own tradition, the symbols, stories and doctrines, to create the spaces and opportunities for informed and faithful reflection upon the issues people are facing (6). Third, it will be explicitly intersubjective, carried out within the context of those who share those issues, and thus it will not be dependent upon the lone theological expert who travels in from afar. Listening to what is happening and offering space for the voices that are normally silenced, plus critical analysis are all part of the process (7). What one should not expect is the emergence of a linear and single Christian doctrine, applicable at all times and in all places.

This is obviously a fundamental challenge to theology's traditional self understanding. Perhaps this is why there is such resistance to this approach in more conservative theological circles. The fear is presumably of a Post-Modern free-for-all where all boundaries are broken down and religious anarchy reigns. This seems to be founded upon a lack of trust and confidence in Christians at grass roots level by those in the academic and church hierarchies. They may perceive such developments as a threat to their status or control. But what is at stake here: a search for truth or merely the power of the few over the many? We may be witnessing an increasing democratization within religion itself and thus the need for a new theological self understanding. Feminist theology has already begun to travel down this path and it seems likely that others will soon follow. The question we must now address is why Milbank in his particular appropriation of Post-Modernity finds these approaches so unacceptable.

Milbank on Difference

Before we examine Milbank's arguments on the relationship between Christianity and other faiths we need to be clear about his grounds for rejecting the contextual theology advocated by Chopp and Taylor. Why is this response to Post-Modernity mistaken? Milbank's main objection is to the political and Liberation theologies and the fact that they employ a

Marxist version of social analysis (8). He would presumably extend this to any form of theology that employed ideas, presuppositions or analytical frameworks from non-Christian sources. We recall that his basic argument is that the Enlightenment Grand Narrative of Secular Reason has falsely positioned theology, when what theology should really be doing is to establish its own distinctive social theory and critique. Milbank's is a highly sophisticated version of the argument that Christians should not allow the world to set the agenda.

Now that Post-Modernity has undermined Secular Reason - according to Milbank - even a Christian socialist such as himself should avoid any Marxist or other secular social theory. 'It should, in fact, be peculiarly the responsibility of Christian socialists at present, to demonstrate how socialism is grounded in Christianity, because it is impossible for anyone to accept any longer that socialism is simply the inevitable creed of all sane, rational, human beings' (9).

There is no point any Christian appealing to reason or common sense to justify a particular political stance as Post-Modernity has undermined the claims of reason itself. That of course is Milbank's claim and one that we have already had cause to challenge. However, it leaves him with the tricky problem of how to justify his particular brand of socialism.

It is worthwhile glancing at how he aims to do this because, I believe, it illustrates the weakness of his position. Effectively he tries to make a virtue out of necessity. If there is no trustworthy Secular Reason and thus no external court of appeal to justify one's political stance, then one's decisions appear to be arbitrary. This is a good thing Milbank would have us believe, because it allows for the greater freedom and flexibility and indeed access to God's guidance that a more reasoned approach would deny. To justify this he utilizes the work of Blondel, a rather obscure theologian whose details need not concern us here. However, one quotation summarizes Milbank's position.

'For Blondel, our thought depends entirely upon contingent, theoretically unjustifiable assumptions, and on equally unjustifiable additions to the received tradition, and yet it is precisely this historicist confinement of our thought which renders it irreducible to any immanent process, and always dependent upon its participation in a transcendent plenitude of realized action, of thought as word and deed...we really do invent a God we cannot control, so that we are all, as Blondel says...giving birth to the divine image in our conjecturing practice' (10).

The problem with Secular Reason and its derivatives in social and political analysis is that they pretend to offer an account of the way things are that would confine divine activity to a straitjacket. Better to be arbitrary, irrational and random and to know it, so that the uncontrollable God can burst through more easily. I find this a counsel of despair and cold comfort indeed for those individuals and groups who continue to suffer at the hands of arbitrary and irrational regimes. Once again Milbank presents us with two extreme alternatives: a Marxist social determinism or a Christian socialist freedom. What however about a form of social analysis that did or does not make such deterministic claims to describe things 'the way they are', but accepted the contingent and historical nature of social enquiry? It is just such an approach that I will return to later in the chapter.

It seems to me ironic that Milbank's objection to Liberation theology and other contextual theologies is that they utilize non-Christian sources within the theological process, but that his own rejection of Secular Reason is based on what is clearly a non-theological approach - that of Post-Modernity. He uses philosophy to establish that philosophy should be given no place within theology. I can see no need for this, nor does it seem consistent. It is surely a rejection of that which is different or other from theology, assuming of course that the latter does possess some clear and distinctive self identity. It is as if theology itself is somehow immune from the Post-Modern critique and can remain as a/the only modern Grand Narrative. I believe that Chopp and Taylor are more consistent in acknowledging that theology is now a Post-Modern collage of different voices, styles, questions and constructs.

So then, what of Milbank's approach to the relationship between Christianity and other religions? The main source for this is an essay that he contributed to a collected volume entitled 'Christian Uniqueness Reconsidered' (11). This book was itself a response to another collection of essays edited by John Hick and Paul Knitter, and we need to be aware that Milbank is participating in a multi-sided discussion (12). Nevertheless this particular essay stands in its own right. What are the grounds for Milbank's objection to the religious pluralism advocated by the writers in the other volume? Basically that despite their supposed support for the non-Christian religions, they are in fact guilty of imposing the Grand Narrative of Western universalism upon these other traditions. This is a subtle argument that requires more detailed explanation.

First, there is a distinction between those writers on the subject who have now accepted the Post-Modern critique and agree that there is no Archimedean point of theoretical reason from which one can survey all religious traditions and authors such as Hick who seem intent on downgrading the 'unique' aspects of particular religions and subsuming them under a new Grand Narrative. In other words, Hick's approach is to create a definition that claims to describe all the major world religions, that being that they are all Reality centred. Any Post-Modern thinker would automatically be suspicious of this as it seems to deny genuine differences.

However, Milbank is no happier with the first category of writers, as he believes they are still clinging on to a residual pluralism that must itself presuppose 'a timeless logos enjoying time-transcending encounters with an unchanging reality' (13). So although they have apparently abandoned theoretical reason as a basis for dialogue with other religions, they turn instead to a practical (ethical or political) reason in order to establish a starting point for inter-religious discussion. As we would expect, Milbank is not prepared to countenance the use of reason in any form because - in his view - all versions of it are variants upon the ideal of universal Secular Reason that Post-Modernity has discredited. Secular Reason is not neutral, but merely one tradition amongst many, and enshrines the values, power and interests of Western culture. Thus it falls prey to the charge of cultural imperialism. Remove it from its role as arbiter between the different religions and you destroy the pluralist basis for inter-religious dialogue.

This is certainly a highly significant argument, because, if Milbank is correct, it must be immensely damaging to all attempts to find common ground between, or to establish the peaceful co-existence of the different religions. He might deny that the latter is necessarily true, but I believe that this is a real danger in his position. What he is saying is that the very terms of discourse that are normally identified as the basis for negotiation between the various religions are already culturally loaded and thus unusable. Thus Hick and colleagues have got it wrong.

'The moment of contemporary recognition of other cultures and religions optimistically celebrated by this volume, is itself - as the rhetoric of its celebration makes apparent - none other than the moment of total obliteration of other cultures by Western norms and categories, with their freight of Christian influence' (14).

So, where does the discussion go from here? Milbank does not suggest what might be possible, but is keen only to further substantiate his view that difference and otherness are such as to preclude what have become the accepted paths to follow in pursuing the encounter between religions. For instance, any idea of comparative religion should be abandoned, to be replaced by the contrasting of cultures. That is the best that we can aim for as any suggestion that we can discover other roads to our definitively religious goals has to be an ethnocentric illusion. There is no way that we can suddenly jump out of our particular religious or cultural skins, created as they are by the narratives of our tradition, and enter into an alien or different culture and then make judgements about their meaning. Comparative religion presupposes that one is comparing like with like, but that is precisely what we cannot know. There is no single known object independent of our own narrative, biographies or traditions that could be that 'like with like'. So there is no way that one could make the judgement that all the different religions are really pointing towards the same reality. This argument of course only holds if there really are such sharp and clear-cut differences between different cultures and traditions. As we have seen in our earlier discussion of MacIntyre, this is at least open to question.

Another problem with Milbank's position is that it is almost impossible in practice not to make some sort of assumption about what 'religion really is' and then to start applying it across the different religions. We assume that religion is an area of universal human concern that we can consider and discuss, but Milbank believes that this is misguided because the varieties of religion may actually have disappeared as their cultures change or disintegrate. However, Milbank himself here makes an apparently universal judgement about religion.

'If religions concern 'what there is', then it is evident that a person's relation to such an imagined ontology will be for the most part practical and nonreflective. It follows that any adequate description of a religion must attend to practice at least as much as to theory' (15).

But is this not a blatant exercise of the comparative religion that Milbank himself condemns? Either it is possible to speak with some conviction about other religions despite one's own religious adherence, or it is not. If it is not, then Milbank should not dare to comment upon the importance of practice for religions, let alone say that they concern 'what there is'. If it is possible to do so then there must be some basis, some terms of discourse for the encounter, even though these are non-neutral because derived from a particular tradition. In which case, inter-religious dialogue is still a possibility.

We shall examine in due course how, and perhaps why, Milbank sinks into this confusion, but we must give one more example first. He is clearly uneasy with the dialoguing advocates of an inter-religious approach who appear to claim that they can somehow transcend the particularities of their original tradition. In Milbank's view the major religions are already universal in their scope and claims and thus cannot be reduced or relativized in this way. So there is a difference between local religions and pieties that have not had to confront the problem of different religions, and the major religions that have had to confront religious differences and have presumably successfully subsumed them. This means that the latter are far less susceptible to conversion or accommodation 'precisely because they already embody a more abstract, universal and deterritorialized cultural framework' (16). Thus dialogue can mean only one of two things for the major religions. Either one side actually converts the other by the force of its discourse, or it creates a new, particular and elite religion, possibly that of the 'superior, jet-hopping, dialoguing selves'.

It seems to me that the whole tenor of Milbank's discussion here is incredibly deterministic. I do not see how one can predict in advance the likely outcome of the encounter between the major religions. Milbank's position is based on an assumption about their abstract, universal and deterritorialized cultural frameworks. Yet one might have thought it was just such an assumption about the nature of other religions that his espousal of the theory of religious difference rules out of court. Milbank is making a universal judgement about the universalizing tendencies of the major religions. If there is no basis for the encounter between different religions, no terms of reference for inter-religious dialogue, how can he consistently claim to make such judgements?

The reality is that once reason is extracted from the equation, the only alternative base for such judgements is the arbitrary imposition of one's own ideas or tradition. Milbank, following Blondel, believes that this is fine and indeed justifiable. You do just board the enemy vessel and take it by force of arms. Sadly, this is the very logic of Western capitalism that Milbank insists he is challenging. Survival of the fittest, or the strongest discourse, or the most compelling narrative is the only option. I cannot believe that this should be the future for the encounter between the world religions, yet it seems to be the logic of Milbank's position.

How then does he end up in this unenviable location? Fundamentally it is because he believes that there is no way of steering between the Scylla of Enlightenment foundationalism and the Charybdis of Post-Modern difference. The crucial factor in this instance being his interpretation of difference. I intend to show in the next section that another interpretation is both possible and preferable and can be derived from the work of Derrida himself. But that is to anticipate.

The clues emerge from Milbank's criticisms of one of the contributors to the other volume, Raimundo Pannikar. The latter apparently maintains that pluralism is still the appropriate approach to the encounter of religions because reality itself is plural. From within the Christian tradition he uses the doctrine of the Trinity to support this argument. However, Milbank finds this unsatisfactory because he believes that the multiplicity of unco-ordinated local struggles will be unable to resist the tide of liberal moder-nity. Why does be believe this? Because the differences between these local approaches are incommensurable:

'...localities themselves can never, on the basis of their locality, contest an imperial sway, and...the incommensurable differences between locali-ties...can only be mediated by the instrumentalist neutrality of the market and the bureaucracy' (17).

Thus, presumably, any local or contextual theology as indeed any local religion, is always going to be vulnerable to the capitalist principle of divide and conquer. Once again that is surely a huge assumption and borders on determinism. It can be challenged from two angles. First, the Habermasian argument for a mediating communicative reason as outlined in earlier chap-ters. Second, it embodies an extreme interpretation of difference that pre-supposes that differences must be incommensurable. But why are such dif-ferences automatically and inherently incommensurable? I can see no justi-fication for that assumption. One can only suppose that it comes as a result of Milbank's reading of Post-Modernity and that this leads him into a con-fused and idiosyncratic conclusion. Each religion is bound to reclassify the other incommensurable accounts of different religions according to its own perspective - so the argument would go. Even a philosophy respecting dif-ference must pursue this path to the point where it has to decide whether the difference must involve conflict or can mean reconciliation. So differ-ences are encountered, overcome and held at bay, but there is no valuation of the Other as such. That is just impossible. Where does this leave the encounter between Christianity and other religions?

'With an extreme degree of paradox, one must claim that it is only through insisting on the finality of the Christian reading of 'what there is' that one can both fulfil respect for the other and complete and secure this otherness as pure neighbourly difference. Then, at last, a conversation is established which is itself the goal of true desire, and not a debate about truth, in the manner of dialogue' (18).

Inevitably though this means that Christianity is intent on subverting the other discourses and conducting the conversation exclusively on its own terms. As Milbank says, under these conditions it would be more honest to replace 'dialogue' with 'mutual suspicion' and it is clear that the expectation of such conversations is 'to constantly receive Christ again, from the unique spiritual responses of other cultures' (19). One might ask somewhat cynically when is a conversation not a conversation? It would seem when it is conducted by a Christian in the manner advocated by Milbank. Monologue is perhaps a better description.

I do not believe that this approach offers a realistic or acceptable way forward. Milbank sets up the differences between religions in such a way that it is impossible to communicate between them, let alone to achieve peaceful co-existence or any form of reconciliation. The discussion has to be on Christian terms or not at all. If the three main options for relating Christianity to other religions are indeed exclusivism, inclusivism and pluralism (20), then it is hard to see how Milbank can be in any other than the first category. Might there however be a fourth alternative, building upon the Habermasian approach commended in earlier chapters?

There is not the space to develop a position at length, but I think that an outline does begin to appear. The point about communicative reason is that, despite the fact that it cannot and does not claim the neutrality of the discredited Enlightenment Secular Reason, it does have a trans-local validity while not damaging or distorting individual traditions or cultures. So it does provide a potential means of access between traditions while leaving issues of truth open. This is surely critical for the encounter between religions. The question of truth cannot finally be avoided, either by a Milbankian dogmatism or a lazy pluralism. It is not possible to uphold all claims, particularly if some of them conflict. So, by what criteria are such judgements in this area of human activity to be made?

There are a number of possibilities. First, the criteria might be derived exclusively from one tradition, as in Milbank's case. Second, they may derive from a tradition external to any religion, so for instance that of Enlightenment Reason. Neither of those now appear acceptable. The third option is that criteria can be developed from within the ongoing encounters of the different traditions. The cry will then go up that this means creating a new religion thus destroying the uniqueness and denying the universal claims of the major religions. Well, perhaps this just has to be so and perhaps this is what Post-Modernity or the radicalization of Modernity means for religion. This is part of the democratization of religion. The powers, hierarchies and institutions of established religion may not like it, but they may not be able to do anything about it. In which case, it is surely far better to try to establish some criteria rather than having none at all. Far better that people have some means by which they can make judgements about what constitutes a valid religion than that they sink into the anarchic, nihilistic and arbitrary free-for-all of an extreme Post-Modernity. I will offer some suggestions as to such criteria in the final section of this chapter. First we need to return to the work of Derrida to pursue the discussion of difference itself.

Derrida on Difference

To preface this part of the discussion a little more on the use of the term *incommensurability*. We have already had reason to question Milbank's understanding of this as he appears to assume that it means there is an unbridgeable gulf between different religions, cultures and traditions. Such an interpretation is by no means obvious and further examination will reveal a number of other options. I am drawing here upon the work of Richard Bernstein, an American social theorist and philosopher who, perhaps more than anybody, draws together the differing strands of Post-Modernity and Habermasian Critical Theory (21). Bernstein reminds us that the use of the term *incommensurability* in recent debates stems from Thomas Kuhn's groundbreaking work on the structure of scientific change and, in particular, his notion of paradigm shifts as an explanation of how such changes come about. The key point to remember is that one paradigm is only replaced by another when it can no longer provide a satisfactory explanatory framework for the evidence that is emerging. The original paradigm and the new one may then be considered incommensurable.

However, this seems to be something rather less drastic than Milbank has in mind. As Bernstein says:

'Kuhn never intended to deny that paradigm-theories can be compared - indeed rationally compared and evaluated. In insisting on incommensurability his main point was to indicate the ways in which paradigm-theories can and cannot be compared' (22).

Although this may have been Kuhn's intention, his idea does run the risk of appearing to suggest that there are indeed frameworks of explanation, or even languages and traditions that hold us prisoner and prevent further communication. 'The myth of the framework' - as it is sometimes called - does seem to haunt the very notion of incommensurability and potentially lead to an extreme relativism. The different is so different as to preclude anything other than some mystical conversion as a means of communication across the respective boundaries.

We may recognize here that MacIntyre has added fuel to this debate and that he is probably a major source for Milbank's ideas on this. MacIntyre has tried to show how rival traditions may be incommensurable, with each tradition developing its own standards of rationality. Yet he is still left in a position where one particular tradition can believe itself to be rationally superior to all its rivals. Hence he can be accused of a form of cultural imperialism. We recall that Milbank produces his own version of this, abandoning MacIntyre's adherence to any notion of reason or rationality and holding onto Christianity as a metanarrative. But the problem that remains is that identified in the last section: if one presupposes in advance an unbridgeable gulf between different traditions, cultures and religions, then it is impossible and certainly inconsistent to make any further comment beyond one's own tradition. If there really is no possibility of translation then there is nothing further to be said. Yet even that conclusion seems to rest upon some knowledge of the other tradition.

I agree with Bernstein when he reaches the following conclusion. It may indeed be the case that there is no universal, neutral historical framework into which all languages and traditions can be adequately translated and which would enable a rational evaluation of the respective validity claims. This is where Post-Modernity has correctly identified the Achilles heel of Enlightenment Reason. However, this does not mean that the supposed incommensurability of languages and traditions must entail a self-defeating or self-referentially inconsistent form of relativism or perspectivism in the manner of Milbank. Rather, languages and traditions can be compared and rationally evaluated in multiple ways through the cultivation of hermeneutical sensitivity and imagination. The key word here is 'multiple'. There is not one way - as the Enlightenment might have claimed - but rather a whole host of ways, and the task is always to work out which way is appropriate in a particular conversation. Hence the need for criteria and for a number of different and appropriate mediating frameworks.

So, incommensurable languages and traditions are not to be thought of as self-contained windowless monads that necessarily share nothing in common. There will always be the possibility of points of overlap and to deny this is to succumb to the myth of the framework. Communication is a possibility, although we have to acknowledge that it is always susceptible to breakdown and failure. But then, as Bernstein says, it becomes a moral task, if not a moral imperative, to try to establish and maintain this communication:

'Learning to live with (among) rival pluralistic incommensurable traditions...is always precarious and fragile. There are no algorithms for grasping what is held in common and what is different...The search for commonalities and differences is always a task and an obligation' (23).

This, it seems to me, is the appropriate approach for both the internal religious pluralism heralded by the contextual theologies and the external pluralism of the relationship and encounter between different religions.

The really interesting point that Bernstein goes on to make is that the same conclusions can be reached through a reading of Derrida's work. If this is so, then it certainly questions Milbank's attempt to support his position by an appeal to Post-Modern philosophy. The argument is almost exactly parallel to that on incommensurability, but still requires some explication.

It is undoubtedly the case that one of Derrida's main preoccupations has been with the subject of otherness or alterity. It was made clear in Chapter 3 that his own personal circumstances - the fact that he came from the margins of French intellectual and political life - play a part in this interest. However, the exact interpretation of Derrida's work poses distinct problems, and it is clear that there are some sharp and significant differences of opinion within scholarly circles. Like Bernstein and Norris I have attempted to play close attention to what Derrida says about himself rather than to adopt the easy caricatures of other secondary commentators. That said, I wish to reiterate the view stated in Chapter 3 that Derrida does not advocate the free play of interpretation or the anarchic destruction of all boundaries, where anything can mean anything. His aim rather is to point out and then to sustain the tensions that exist within all meaning and interpretation. One decides on a particular meaning in full light of the fact that other interpretations are always possible. Such a decision is indeed a form of closure, but decisions are inescapable and inevitable. The point is to be aware of the other possibilities and to know - if possible - why one has chosen this way rather than that.

The result of this approach is that Derrida is seen as a champion of otherness, whether this means the other meanings available, or the voices and needs of other groups which have been neglected in the normal course of events. Hence the interest in his work by marginalized groups within society and, potentially, those attempting to develop contextual theologies. The question is, does Derrida's understanding of otherness create the impassable barriers between people, traditions and cultures that Milbank, and to a lesser extent MacIntyre, espouse?

It would seem not, and Bernstein offers as evidence Derrida's comments on the Other as individual in support of this. Although the Other is indeed an alter ego, unless it can be recognized as an ego, any sense of alterity would collapse. It may sound perverse, yet is surely logically correct to say that it is only on the basis of some common ground that otherness can be recognized at all.

'...the other as alter ego signifies the other as other, irreducible to my ego, precisely because it is an ego...This is why, if you will, he is a face, can speak to me, understand me, and eventually command me' (24).

The crucial point would seem to be that Derrida is, once again, trying to sustain the tension within the personal encounter. It is not a matter of reconciling all differences and oppositions, nor of creating such a division that there can be no recognition in the first place. It is a both/and not an either/or. 'In short, there is both sameness and radical alterity, symmetry and asymmetry, identity and difference in my relation with 'the Other' and above all in the ethical relation.' (25)

The conclusion then parallels that of the discussion on incommensurability. Yes, there is always difference and otherness, and it is when these go unrecognized or are suppressed that individuals and groups suffer at the hands of those in power. However, this does not mean that there is nothing in common between the I and its genuine 'Other'. If that were the case we would be back with Milbank's self-defeating relativism and perspectivism. So there must always be, at least in principle, ways of understanding the Other, although it must be acknowledged that this process can always go wrong. We cannot often know in advance exactly what these ways will be as they will vary from situation to situation, but, as Bernstein says:

'...we can say that to think of 'the Other' as an absolute Other, where this is taken to mean that there is no way whatsoever for relating the I to 'the Other' is unintelligible and incoherent' (26).

Neither traditions, cultures or individuals are windowless monads or exclusive frameworks, impenetrable to one another. There is a reciprocity in relationships, if only as an ethical demand. To abandon this is almost to destroy the foundation of human social existence. How can one say, except as an act of gross cultural imperialism, that the Other is so other as to be beyond understanding and communication? If the Other is so far beyond our understanding then we cannot really be said to know them as 'the Other'.

One final comment from Bernstein, following Derrida, because it seems to me to have much to say to the subject of the encounter between Christianity and other faiths.

'The search for commonalities and precise points of difference is always a task and an obligation...Without a mutual recognition of this Aufgabe, without self-conscious sensitivity of the need always to do justice to 'the

Other's' singularity, without a heightened awareness of the inescapable risks that can never be completely mastered, we are in danger of obliterating the radical plurality of the human condition' (27).

I now want to summarize the argument of the first three sections before moving on to an ambitious attempt to describe how theology can respond appropriately to this interpretation of Post-Modern philosophy. It seems to me that Milbank's objections to the internal pluralization of theology created by the growing number of contextual theologies, and the external pluralization represented by the open encounter between Christianity and other religions, is based on a dubious interpretation of Post-Modern thought. This becomes clear when we examine Derrida's work in some detail. Derrida does not attempt to resolve the ambiguities and tensions within meaning or relationships into a permanent or irrevocable difference. If he did, there would indeed be the anarchic multiplicity of possibilities that Milbank fears, and all decisions would be arbitrary. Only in that context could there be a justification for arbitrarily resolving the differences and ambiguities in favour of a particular tradition - in this case Christianity - in the way that Milbank and others recommend. However, we have seen that such an extreme approach is neither necessary nor desirable. The different or the Other cannot be so different that communication, comparison, or any meaningful relation is automatically ruled out in advance. The task then is surely this: in each single instance of an encounter between traditions, cultures or religions, to try to identify both common ground and difference. All attempts to legislate in advance how this might work out can be seen as a form of determinism.

So, the practical tasks for theology will now look something like this. It must both acknowledge the contribution of the developing contextual theologies and exercise a wider critical judgement through the identification and application of appropriate internal criteria. Hence the contextual theologies must be subject to a wider process of discernment and discrimination. However, this in turn must give due recognition to otherness and difference and be aware of the power exercised by central church authorities and academic institutions. A parallel process is necessary in the encounter between Christianity and other religions. There must be that acknowledgment of difference and a continuing search for common ground, but alongside that the identification of appropriate external criteria for judging what constitutes a genuine and acceptable religion. I recognize the difficulties of this, but I can see no way in which this challenge can be avoided. The question of what is true cannot be shelved nor dissolved into an amorphous relativity. In the final section I will offer some tentative proposals for these processes.

Some Futures for Theology

It might be assumed that, given my criticisms of some of the theological appropriations of Post-Modern philosophy, I believe that theology will be able to carry on with business as usual. I cannot see this being possible, certainly in the long run. My argument, particularly in relation to Milbank, is that he has used Post-Modern thought in order to return theology to what is, effectively, a pre-Enlightenment and pre-Modern position. Thus theology can continue to make universal claims and to present itself as a metanarrative because Post-Modern philosophy has dissolved the old Enlightenment order into a state of anarchy and chaos. Here anything goes, and there are no longer any acceptable criteria for rational judgement, so one chooses the Christian narrative because it is as good an option as any other, and/or because it tells a better story. I believe that this is based on a misreading of Post-Modern philosophy and, as I have tried to show in the previous chapters, the concerns of Foucault, Lyotard and Derrida can be seen as a continuation of the Enlightenment rather than as its destruction. To criticize something can be to honour and to try to improve it as much as to destroy it. This being the case, theology would be making a major mistake to dismiss the Enlightenment challenge as if it had never happened. Far better to take note of the Post-Modern critique and its implications for the Enlightenment project and then respond to both in a positive and creative manner. I have argued that this will benefit from taking into account the work of Habermas, Giddens and, more latterly Bernstein.

So, where does theology go from here? I deliberately talk about the futures of theology because I cannot see that in this situation of both internal and external pluralization, any one clear path will develop. In responding to a plural reality one might reasonably expect there to be a number of possible paths. One of those will surely be the continued emergence of contextual theologies as described by Chopp and Taylor. This seems to be an appropriate and inevitable response to the critique of Grand Narratives launched by Post-Modernity. Just as theology can no longer claim to be a Grand Narrative to the outside world, so it will no longer be able to tell a big or unifying story about itself. There will indeed be, as there already are, a number of what I describe as major internal narratives.

However, this does create a problem, or perhaps a new challenge for theology. How can there be continuity or coherence within the Christian churches and tradition if there is this splintering of theology itself? Does this not spell the end and the disintegration of Christianity as we know it? It could be the fear of this that encourages the likes of Milbank and Hauerwas to try to re-establish Christianity as a metanarrative. The problem is a real one but, I wonder whether it is not a situation that, in a sense, Christianity and all the major religions have always had to face. How to maintain unity in diversity is hardly a new question. The apparently new answer suggested by Post-Modern philosophy is that there can be no one single solution. Any such attempt, for instance that of Milbank to appeal to the strength of the Christian narrative in creating a peaceful order, is bound to appear arbitrary because most Christians can see that there are other possibilities. If there can be no one answer though are we not back in a state of anarchy?

By no means. It is in response to this question that I have tried to develop the idea of mediating frameworks (28). If theology is plural as it encounters different groups both within and outside the churches, then it can also construct sets of questions and ideas in response to these differing situations. These will, of course, always be subject to revision and negotiation, but they will provide a way to structure each encounter. So, for instance, I have suggested that it is possible to draw upon such a framework, derived largely from Liberation Theology, where Christianity encounters those on the margins of society and whose voices are not normally heard (29).

I am aware that Liberation Theology has had a bad press in recent years, both in the United Kingdom and in conservative circles in the United States. Perhaps part of the reason for this is that too much has been claimed for its particular method of working. It will not and cannot expect to be the appropriate model in all situations and circumstances. There have been attempts, misguided I would argue, to transpose it without remainder into very different political and cultural contexts. I cannot see why one should expect it to transfer in a straightforward manner from Latin America to the urban environments of Sheffield or Chicago. However, the model does have some purchase in these different contexts. The task is to work this out in proper detail. Certainly, the value of listening to the local stories, which may not be biblically based or easily translated into those terms: the need for critical social analysis, but one based on advanced capitalist economies not developing ones, and the exercise of reflection in conjunction with practical engagement, seem to me to hold good in the context of working on the margins.

The challenge clearly is to discover and to draw up different mediating frameworks for different situations. As Bernstein says, the search for commonalities and differences is a constant one and requires interpretative skills, flexibility and imagination. Hence the need for a rather different mediating framework where Christianity encounters the higher echelons of the business and commercial world. This does not however mean an uncritical collusion with the values of that world, but rather an attempt to establish a base for critical dialogue. Some may say that there can be no such thing and that any exercise of this nature constitutes a sell-out. I think this is naive and defeatest. If Christianity expects those outside its boundaries to take serious note of its criticisms, then Christianity, in turn, cannot claim for itself immunity from critique. Such is the nature of genuine encounter and relationship. Perhaps contemporary models of personal and professional development emerging from the business world might form the basis for a mediating framework in this context.

That, I would suggest, is a possible way forward for contextual theologies. However, there is an equally pressing and difficult problem that faces the relationships and encounters between different religions. Referring back to the example in the previous chapter of easy access to a whole range of religions via the Internet, we are faced with the need to establish criteria for what might be acceptable as religion. This may sound both unlikely and over-ambitious as a project, but others are already attempting something similar and I believe that such attempts will continue. So, for instance, the American theologian John B. Cobb Jnr, writing in the same volume as Milbank, but on the subject of a pluralistic theology of religions, states that there are two modes of evaluation of individual religious traditions, those being internal and external.

'If a religious tradition claims to provide a way of life that leads to a just, peaceable, and stable social order, then we can ask whether, when its precepts have been most faithfully followed, the result has been a just, peaceable and stable social order. If a religious tradition claims to provide a way to attain personal serenity and compassion toward all, then we can ask whether, when its precepts are most fully followed, the result has been personal serenity and compassion toward all' (30).

This all sounds eminently reasonable, but the greater complications occur, as Cobb acknowledges, when it comes to establishing external criteria. We appear to be faced with two extreme alternatives: either there is some essence of religion from which to derive a set of universal criteria, or we are in the situation of conceptual relativism. Post-Modernity now renders the first of those untenable, leaving the second, which is, in effect, the Milbank position. However, Cobb, like myself, believes that a third way is possible:

'The actual course of dialogue does not support either theory. One enters dialogue both as a believer convinced of the claims of one religious tradition and as a human being open to the possibility that one has something to learn from representatives of another religious tradition...In many instances, precisely as a believer one is open to learn from others, believing that the fullness of wisdom goes beyond what any tradition already possesses.' (31)

In other words, there is always more to be learnt, but this openness does not deny nor negate what one has already experienced, but rather builds upon it. This is as far as Cobb is prepared to go, but is it possible to say more and to actually suggest some concrete criteria? One particularly interesting and significant piece of work in this area is that carried out by the American philosopher of religion Ken Wilbur (32). Using a developmental schema he identifies three major stages that religions pass through: the pre-rational; the rational and the transrational. This may appear at first sight to be just another Enlightenment categorization of religion, but Wilbur's work is far more complex and sophisticated than that and stems directly from a substantial engagement with the major world religions.

There is not the space here to enter into the arguments in any detail, but I want to offer some thoughts of my own that draw upon Wilbur's work. It seems to me that it is correct to seek both internal and external criteria for the judgement of religions, but I would rather describe this as operating on two axes, a horizontal and a vertical one. On the internal or horizontal axis three areas should be taken into account, in addition to the 'by their fruits ye shall know them' approach of Cobb. First, is it possible to establish an analysis or awareness of power - the possibilities of domination or distorted communication - within the particular religion? Contextual theologies have highlighted the importance of this question. Second, is there a realistic grasp of the global cultural context of religion? So, for instance, reference to the Modernity - Post-Modernity debate, to the nature of cultural and political pluralism and to the questions of self identity now emerging through the growth of reflexivity. Finally, can there be an analysis of the changing nature of social relationships? Thus, there could be an acknowledgement of changes in the understanding of community; the relationship between the private and the public, the personal and the political and the range of concerns brought to the surface by feminism. It seems to me that any religion that cannot or will not come to terms with these three areas of change and uncertainty will face a bleak and isolated future.

On the vertical axis the basic question is one identified by Wilbur. Does this religion represent progression or regression? Is it a return to some sort of pre-rational state or set of beliefs, or has it moved on to a grasp of the transrational? I think this is of particular value in evaluating the myriad versions of spirituality now emerging. So, for instance, how much of the contemporary New Age movement and the various forms of ecological spirituality are really about the supposed return of humanity to the state of an undifferentiated unity with the natural world? To the extent that they are they represent a regression. To achieve the transrational, or higher levels of consciousness, is likely to require a realistic engagement with the political and philosophical questions on the horizontal axis. The rational level needs to be encountered, acknowledged, critiqued and then transcended rather than being ignored or denied. Religion cannot be pre-Enlightenment, but only post-Enlightenment in the sense of a critical absorbing and then passing beyond the earlier stages. Hence the potential importance of the work of Habermas and Derrida for this project.

As I said at the beginning of this chapter, I realise that this may appear highly speculative and may sound unfamiliar to orthodox believers, but I do believe that work of this nature is already underway and contains potential for further development. However, there is one final strand of thought that I suggest is illuminating for theology and highlights the tasks that face it in response to Post-Modern thinking. This derives from recent philosophy of science and a relatively new school of thought known as Dialectical Critical Realism (33). Perhaps the main exponent of this is the philosopher Roy Bhaskar, currently based in Oxford. I am introducing this into the discussion not in order to set another hare running, but because it feeds directly into the present debate.

One of the commentators on Dialectical Critical Realism has drawn up a list of themes and issues that I believe directly parallels my concerns for the future of theology (34). I will work through these briefly in order to support this contention.

Dialectical Critical Realism and the writing of Bhaskar in particular aims to steer a middle ground between irrationalism and positivism in the scientific field. As such it continues the thought of the Enlightenment while taking seriously the critique of Enlightenment foundationalism associated with Post-Modernity. I find myself identifying strongly with this project. The major argument of this book is that it is possible and desirable to steer a middle way between the irrationalism represented by an anarchic free-for-all, and the positivism of neo-orthodox theologians such as Hauerwas and Milbank. I would hope this is clear by this stage. I find it encouraging that there is, within the philosophy of science, a very similar attempt and I believe that theology should take note of this example. One might say that an appropriate description of my project is to establish a Dialectical Critical Theology.

A second area of common interest centres on the argument that non-realists are all realists about something and that non-realism is an attempt to gain immunity from critique or refutation. The parallel here is that the theologians mentioned above present a Christianity that is supposedly so unique, distinct and different that it too then becomes immune from external criticism. It is only from within the tradition that judgements of any sort can be made. All other and alien traditions are interpreted as some distorted form of Christianity. As I have pointed out, I believe that this is a very dangerous tactic. It gains apparent safety or immunity from external critique at the cost of both dialogue and relationship. Dialectical Critical Realism, by contrast, makes substantial public claims that are open to refutation. I believe that theology must do likewise and thus be prepared to remain open to external criticism.

Bhaskar and colleagues argue that there is no such thing as no philosophy, only a choice between good and bad philosophy. I think this is particularly important as we review much of theology's response to Post-Modern philosophy. The latter is appropriated, for instance by Milbank, in order to justify a retreat from philosophy and indeed other disciplines such as sociology, into a safe Christian enclave and the 'better' narratives of its own tradition. Any form of argument or use of reason is explicitly abandoned. I have argued that this is in fact inconsistent and unnecessary. It is a case of bad philosophy in the sense that it rests upon a dubious interpretation of the key Post-Modern thinkers. Bhaskar believes that the role of the philosopher in relation to science is that of the underlabourer, analysing concepts that are already given, but that are confused. I would argue that there is a similar role for philosophy in relation to theology and that this book has been an attempt to do some underlabouring.

Dialectical Critical Realism maintains that our knowledge of the world is always fallible. There can be no final theory that explains everything, nor can there be any identifiable eternal truth. However, there can still be transcendental argument, meaning that humans do have indirect access to a deeper reality. It could be argued that theology should develop a similar self understanding. After all, is Christianity a closure of interpretation in that it claims to have discovered the definitive meaning of human existence? Is it the theory to end all theories or do Christians accept that there is still more to be learnt? If it does make universal and absolute claims it is very difficult to see how this will continue to carry conviction or how such claims could be justified. Perhaps one could view Christianity - and indeed other religions - as religious thought experiments, closing the interpretation of certain aspects of reality in order to observe changes in other areas. Such is the experimental method of science. Fundamentalism could then be seen as attempts to achieve permanent and premature closure of interpretation.

Another possible parallel concerns Bhaskar's comments on what he calls epistemic relativism (35). This is the theory that all our beliefs are socially produced, transient and fallible. Milbank appears to hold this position to the extent that he accepts the Post-Modern view that our beliefs are socially produced. Yet, this need not lead to judgemental relativism - the position that all beliefs are equally valid as there are no rational grounds for choosing between them. Milbank rejects the idea that there can be such rational grounds for judgement and that there are any possible external criteria of judgement, thus leaving Christianity trapped within its own framework. Bhaskar argues that this form of relativism is not justified within science. I would argue that it is not acceptable within the theological field either.

The final parallel is as follows. There is a long running debate within science between empiricists and rationalists. The former try to build scientific theory from the base of human experience alone, whereas, for the latter, pure thought is deemed to be the appropriate starting point. This reminds me of the current debate within theology between the contextualists and the neo-orthodox. The first group tries to respond to concrete human situations and to thereby create a grass roots movement grounded in experience. The second begin with the doctrines and practices of the received tradition and the enclosed Christian community and then tries to work outwards. Dialectical Critical Realism attempts to bridge this gap by acknowledging elements of both context and theory. The weakness of contextualists is that they tend to ignore other explanations of events while that of the traditionalists is that they remain too closely tied to the past and cannot deal with existential questions. Perhaps a Dialectical Critical Theology could also steer between these two extremes.

I believe that there is much fruitful work yet to be done in this whole area and that theology will begin to see reflections of itself in Dialectical Critical Realism. However, these are only meant to be pointers to the future. For the moment the task has been to suggest that theology can respond to Post-Modern philosophy in a creative way and does not need to end up in the blind alley of a new positivism or neo-orthodoxy, retreating behind the barricades of its own community narratives. That which is different or other is not so different that it makes no difference. The self identity of theology is not so certain and secure that it can claim immunity from other influences, disciplines and traditions.

8

A Non-Foundational Transcendence

The Polarities of Post-Modernity

Throughout the foregoing discussion of Post-Modern philosophy a discernible pattern has emerged. Invariably, the various aspects concerned split into two opposing, extreme and apparently irreconcilable positions or polarities. My approach has been to try to show that there is substantial middle ground and that it is here that theology should be engaging with the debate. On one side of the divide are all the ideas associated with Modernity, the Enlightenment and the foundationalism characteristic of Western philosophy over the last 250 years. So, for instance, we encounter the notion of a Grand Narrative of human reason; of a clear and self-determining human identity free of religion and tradition generally; of the common ground for a universal ethics and the understanding of science as an objective activity that offers direct access to an external reality. On the other side are the undermining arguments characteristically associated with Post-Modernity. Thus the breakdown of all Grand Narratives into a multiplicity of local or regional narratives; the de-centred self or vagabond/tourist wandering without order or purpose through a confusing world and prey to all manner of external influences; the consequent fragmentation of social and family life and a growing state of ethical anarchy; a relativistic and pluralist understanding of both reason and science as merely the convenient constructs of a capitalist liberal democracy. The temptation for theology is to assume that this spells the end of the enemy Enlightenment and then to take refuge in the chaotic kaleidoscope of Post-Modern thought. So even if Post-Modernity is not exactly an ally it appears to be less threatening to Christianity than the Modernity it replaces.

I have argued against succumbing to this temptation on two grounds. First, a closer examination of the work of the key Post-Modern philosophers reveals a more complex and nuanced picture. Certainly, in the cases of Lyotard, Foucault and Derrida, it is becoming increasingly clear that there is significant continuity with and continued concern for Enlightenment themes. Put simply, the critique of reason is not a straightforward rejection or denial of it, and it is dubious to place these three thinkers behind a Nietzschean nihilist banner. Second, a study of the work of Habermas, Giddens, Bernstein and Bhaskar makes it clear that the extreme or strong version of Post-Modernity contains serious flaws and contradictions that can be countered by a more balanced Post-Enlightenment philosophy and sociology. Based on their work I have offered glimpses of a middle ground: the promise of a communicative reason; the idea of the major narrative; theories of human development and of cognitive and aesthetic reflexivity; a discourse ethics and the contribution of Dialectical Critical Realism. I argue that these allow theology to progress in its own self understanding without losing faith with its own tradition. Here we see Christians exercising a form of critical consciousness as they question and challenge both the resources of their own faith tradition and those of the other cultural resources available to them.

The key image that captures the whole discussion is that of Milbank when he states that there is no safe way of steering between the Scylla of Enlightenment foundationalism and the Charybdis of Post-Modern difference. I do not claim to have shown the one secure, incontrovertible and universal passage through these straits, but I do believe that it is possible to see that the rocks on either side are not quite as dangerous to theology as Milbank imagines and that there are a number of possible routes through in any case. The remaining questions, it seems to me, are these. Is it still possible or desirable to talk of God in the midst of all this? What are we to say of spirituality in this context? In searching for an answer to both these questions I want to explore the idea of a non-foundational transcendence, drawing from philosophy on the work of Habermas and Derrida and from within theology on some recent feminist writing.

Habermas and Derrida on Transcendence

There will be those who question the need to bring philosophy into the equation at all. Is there not one of those ultimate and irreconcilable differences between the exercise of human thought for its own sake and reflection upon a truth originating from outside the human imagination? Reason and revelation do not belong together and any attempt to combine the two merely results in an unsatisfactory compromise. This has certainly been one way of viewing the relationship, but it is by no means the only one possible. The crucial issue is surely that of human autonomy. Are humans capable of penetrating the truth of existence through their own thought processes and reasoning? If so, then what role is left for religion? Once again, it seems to me, we are faced with a polarity: either reason or religion. While there are undoubtedly those who would maintain an irreconcilable difference between the two, there are also those of us who do not have such an exalted expectation of either approach and are prepared to try to learn from both sources. As a Christian I would argue that God can use any source to communicate, and that will include normal human thought processes. As a philosopher I would argue that reasoning alone is limited in what it can achieve and must leave the field open for other possibilities. So there is both an acknowledgement of genuine human autonomy and agency, but also an understanding that this is always going to be limited in its scope and power.

Working on that assumption, what might one expect contemporary philosophy to contribute to theological self understanding? Gone are the days when proofs of the existence of God enter the picture. However, it may still be that something a little less direct is still possible. What I mean is this. Human thought in the form of both science and philosophy can take us just so far on the journey and then leave us staring out into space wondering if there is more to be discovered. Religious belief through imagination, direct experience and communal practice may take us further on that journey - not necessarily contradicting what has gone before, nor simply filling in the gaps in our knowledge, but taking us beyond. That is what I take Wilbur to mean when he talks about the transrational.

Clearly the descriptions here become difficult and speculative. However, the interesting thing is to discover neutral or even hostile philosophers such as Habermas and Derrida now producing similar ideas. So, for instance, Habermas, in a number of recent essays has emphasized that religious discourse may continue to convey an existentially orientating and inspirational semantic charge, a sense of contact with the 'extraordinary' or the 'unconditioned', which cannot be entirely appropriated or discursively redeemed by philosophy (1). Despite the collapse of metaphysics and the undermining of foundationalism by Post-Modernity there remains at least a residual awareness of something more. This also emerges in his discussions on ethics.

Habermas is clear that although philosophy can demonstrate the possibility of the moral point of view, it cannot of itself provide an answer to the question 'Why be moral?'. He seems to be acknowledging that this lies beyond the scope of philosophy itself. It is worth quoting in full one of Habermas' comments on the role of art and religion.

'In the wake of metaphysics, philosophy surrenders its extraordinary status. Explosive experiences of the extraordinary have migrated into an art that has become autonomous. Of course, even after this deflation, ordinary life, now fully profane, by no means becomes immune to the shattering and subversive intrusion of extraordinary events. Viewed from without, religion, which has largely been deprived of its worldview functions, is still indispensable in ordinary life for normalizing intercourse with the extraordinary' (2).

It is for this reason, according to Habermas, that religious practice continues to co-exist with post-metaphysical thinking. Religion has a function that philosophy cannot fulfil. Habermas thus sees a continuing human need for a transcendence that goes beyond the awareness of the universal validity claims of language that are his major concerns. Without transcendence sources of ethical energy and moral inspiration, even the life of the most democratic state will sink into an oppressive and purposeless routine. Every culture needs a 'thorn in its side' to keep alive a critical moral sense.

'Even that moment of unconditionality which is stubbornly expressed by the transcending validity claims of everyday communication is not sufficient. Another kind of transcendence is disclosed in the undefused force which is disclosed by the critical appropriation of identity-forming religious traditions' (3).

This is presumably Habermas' way of saying that philosophy does not exhaust the possibilities and that it may even require the sort of transcendence supplied by religion in order to do justice to its practical insights. Even more revealing is the fact that Derrida also now appears to be opening up a similar range of possibilities. In one lengthy article he approaches the subject of negative theology with considerable insight and sympathy and, like Habermas, allows for a space where theology might continue to operate (4). There is of course no easy way of summarizing Derrida's thought here, but a number of points can be noted.

We understand that negative theology is taken to refer to the apophatic tradition of spirituality. Its other pole, the kataphatic tradition, relies upon what can be said about God through language, symbol, metaphor and so on. The apophatic tradition maintains rather that all such forms of expression are inadequate to the task and thus to be avoided. However, Derrida is aware that, even here, there is an underlying ambiguity.

'In the most apophatic moment, when one says 'God is not', 'God is neither this nor that'...even then it is still a matter of saying the entity, such as it is, in its truth...It is a matter of holding the promise of saying the truth at any price, of testifying, of rendering oneself to the truth of the name, to the thing itself, such as it must be named by the name, that is, beyond the name' (5).

Thus in even saying that something cannot be said, one is still having to say something and so is living on the edge of self-contradiction. In order to express that something lies beyond expression one is still having to use language in attempting to communicate. This means that negative theology lives in a state of unresolved tension between silence and speech, between mystery and meaning. This could be seen as placing a question mark against all other forms of theology. What should one make of their attempts to give voice to that which lies beyond language? It is perhaps for this reason that the apophatic tradition finds itself at the borders of Christianity, living in an uneasy tension with traditional dogma and practice and being seen as a challenge to ecclesiastical authority.

'An immediate but intuitionless mysticism, a sort of abstract kenosis, frees the language from all authority, all narrative, all dogma, all belief - and at the limit from all faith. At the limit, this mysticism remains, after the fact, independent of all history of Christianity, absolutely independent, detached even, perhaps absolved, from the idea of sin, freed even, perhaps redeemed, from the idea of redemption' (6).

One can see immediately why this set of ideas appeals to Derrida. Negative theology exists on the borders, on the margins of meaning and expression itself. Those engaged in it are always likely to find themselves in trouble with the religious authorities, living on the very edge of heresy. The significance of this for our purposes is that Derrida is pushing back the boundaries and indicating a space where theology can operate beyond the limits of both philosophy and language. In some sense, like Habermas, he is pointing towards an understanding of transcendence. Yet this is not a transcendence to be identified with a metaphysical grounding or a discredited foundationalism, but that acknowledges that more that cannot even be said. Or can it?

I think it is best to leave Derrida on a deliberately enigmatic note. It would be foolish to read too much into the comments of either Habermas or Derrida. They are not claiming to be theologians, yet it does appear that they are pointing towards a non-foundational transcendence. Perhaps it is possible for philosophy to identify that space where theology can operate; the question is whether theology can appropriate that for itself. For that we must turn to theology.

Feminism and Transcendence

I want to convey my final thoughts by means of a brief commentary on a recent and radical book of feminist theology (7). Daphne Hampson has now left the fold of the Christian tradition, unable to continue to reconcile what she believes as a feminist with her understanding of Christianity. The significance of this for our purposes is that her main argument rests on her assumption about differences between women and men, and the implications of this for the nature of God. Hampson is eager to retain some notion of transcendence and indeed still believes in God and the value of some form of spirituality. However, because of her feminist convictions she will no longer describe any of these in conventional Christian terms. It will become clear that I am largely in sympathy with many of her positive comments but that I do not share Hampson's view that they necessarily lead to her negative evaluation of Christianity. One could argue that this is simply evidence of the gendered difference that Hampson addresses, but I believe that there is more to it than this.

Hampson's starting point is that it is inappropriate and indeed impossible now, to turn back the clock to a pre-Enlightenment stage of human self understanding. The idea of human autonomy - the need for each of us to exercise our own powers of reasoning and discrimination independently of religion and tradition - cannot now be overturned. Although the thinking behind this stems originally from a male dominated arena, in recent generations women too have begun to make gains as a result of it, notably through the language of equality and rights. I will come to her discussion of the exact nature of this autonomy shortly. For the moment I want to register general agreement with this position. Throughout this book I have been arguing that theology cannot now ignore nor reject the Enlightenment, even on the basis of Post-Modern philosophy. I believe that Hampson is correct to say that human autonomy - despite its limitations and drawbacks - will not now be surrendered to a pre-Enlightenment tradition.

However, the second stage of her argument is, by no means, so convincing. She believes that because Christianity is a religion of revelation it must understand God as other from the world, and the implication of this is that there will be a heteronomous relationship between God and humanity. This particular view of transcendence is a threat to the hard-won autonomy of Enlightenment women and men.

'Were there to be a God, of the kind which God had always been held to be, absolute and transcendent, the relationship to God would represent an ultimate heteronomy on the part of human beings. For such a God - if God were to be God to the human - would necessarily have to be obeyed' (8).

As one might expect, Hampson gives this argument a very powerful feminist slant. It is not simply that God has been 'other' to man. It is also that, within Western culture, woman has represented that which is 'other' to men. Given that God has been pictured as male, men then place themselves in the 'female' position in relation to God, being humble, passive and obedient. Thus there is a hierarchy with God at the summit, men below and women basically nowhere. So Christianity is essentially a patriarchal religion. 'Woman has thus been cast as the primordial 'other' in relation both to the male God and to men' (9).

If this is the case, then feminism is more than a new critique of Christianity that will one day painfully but inevitably be drawn into its thinking. It is the destruction of that faith in its recognizable form. Once woman ceases to fulfil the role of the 'other', then there will no longer be a symbolic 'other'. The space or location that the Christian God has hitherto occupied will cease to exist.

'Thus the loss of a primordial 'other' consequent upon the rise of feminism, represents the greatest unsettling of religion in four thousand years. If 'no bishop, no king' then we may say 'no patriarchy, no God': or at least no God as God has been envisaged within Western society' (10).

Quite what will replace this is not so clear. Hampson talks about a bipolarity giving way to a heterogeneity, in which there is no longer that which is One or those who can be 'other' to that One. This sounds like another version of the Post-Modern argument. If she is saying abandon unity for plurality then that is a very interesting suggestion that could be consistent with some of the ideas I have been advocating. However, if she is saying that any notion of that which is 'other' will then mysteriously disappear, I do find that very difficult to understand or to accept.

I believe that this is critical for our discussion about the nature of God and the future of spirituality. Another set of polarities brought to the surface by Post-Modernity is that of Identity - Non-Identity. Thus I assume that when Hampson talks about God as One, she means God as Identity;

an understanding of a God who is monolithic, essentially male, absolute and all-powerful, leaving no questions and no remainder. This God is like the monarch of a hierarchical and patriarchal society. Once this has been dissolved by the 'other' that is woman, so the Non-Identity as plural, female, relational and inter-dependent, then what remains will be unrecognizable to the Christian tradition. There will no longer be God as either Identity or Non-Identity, but something in between.

The problem with this is not the feminist critique in itself, but simply that woman is not the only 'other', and that even if this particular form of otherness were to be dealt with in the way that Hampson suggests, more would still remain. I suppose I am arguing that the Identity - Non-Identity polarity is fundamental to the human condition and cannot be dissolved by the onset of feminism. If this is true, then Hampson is naive to expect to dissolve that tension into some new and amorphous concept, just as Milbank is mistaken in trying to dissolve it in favour of a Christian meta-narrative founded on irreconcilable difference. The objective should be to sustain that tension between Identity and Non-Identity, or between if you like Enlightenment foundationalism and Post-Modern difference.

This may sound difficult to grasp, but I can explain further. On a practical level, who is 'other' to myself? Obviously, if I happen to be male then it will be anybody female. But it could surely also be anybody else - male or female - of another tribe, culture, colour, creed, Football Supporters Club or whatever. In other words, there is a host of potential significant differences between myself and an 'other'. Let us also remember that it is the causes of those excluded and marginalized 'others' that have been taken up both by thinkers such as Derrida and Foucault and by recent contextual theologies. Presumably Hampson would acknowledge all of this, but would want to go on to argue that gender difference is somehow foundational. It is the most significant, or even primordial difference, the one that provides the key to all the rest. So, deal with gender difference first and then the rest will slowly begin to melt away.

I cannot see the justification for such a claim. It appears to be making a Grand Narrative out of the feminist story. I can see it as a major narrative running alongside a number of other major narratives related to race, creed, access to economic and cultural resources and so on, but that is a very different scenario. Hampson is surely in danger of denying the importance of other differences. There are other forms of Non-Identity and otherness that will persist, even were this particular one to disappear or to be resolved.

A further observation here. I also feel that Hampson has an image of a human person as whole, complete, at peace with themselves and identical with all that they are meant to be or could become. In other words, there is nothing that is 'other' within ourselves. If this is so, then it is a picture I find difficult to accept. I believe it is more accurate to say that there is both external and internal otherness. So, there are parts of ourselves we are not aware of; aspects that may suddenly and frighteningly emerge as we encounter new situations. There is not a complete or whole identity in that sense, even though there is hopefully a large measure of continuity and coherence of personal being. There is not a Grand Narrative of myself, but a number of major narratives and probably minor ones as well. Some of these will be explicit, some implicit. One of the functions of personal development, counselling or therapy, is surely to help individuals identify, come to terms with, and perhaps deal more effectively with, the implicit narratives that are often so powerful simply because they have remained hidden. I would thus argue that the Identity - Non-Identity tension or polarity is to be found within each one of us. One can describe this as a plurality of narratives of personal identity without having to dissolve that tension.

I will return to this in the conclusion because I believe it provides a key to the questions about God and spirituality. However, another glance at Hampson will reveal the danger of theology simply siding with difference and non-identity. As part of her argument she offers detailed evidence and description of the feminine characteristics that theology now needs to acknowledge. So, for instance, there is the suggestion that women see others 'in relation' whereas men are more likely to see others 'in opposition' (11). Autonomy for women may be better described as 'inter-dependent autonomy' whereas for men it is based upon an individualistic, substantive and non-relational notion of the self (12). Women are better at centering themselves, listening and giving attention to others and cooperating, whereas men are externally focussed and more competitive. Thus while, for men, self assertion may be equated with pride and sin, for women, self-deprecation is their true failing, and appropriate empowerment is necessary to counter this. It is not the content of this that I want to take issue with so much as the claims that are then made by Hampson. At first sight she appears to be correctly cautious.

'To argue thus is of course not necessarily to hold that women have different intrinsic possibilities qua women (which would be an 'essentialist' position). It is a discussion of practices which have been learnt within the particular contexts in which peoples' lives have been set' (13).

I agree with that, but, it is surely the case that, earlier in the argument,

Hampson does take an essentialist stance. She does claim that it is universally true that men treat women as 'other' and that they then perceive themselves as 'other' in relation to God within Christianity. It seems to me that she is trying to have it both ways. If the feminine characteristics she advocates are indeed learned or acquired behaviour and not essentially feminine, then why is men's response to 'otherness' within Western culture and Christianity also not learned or acquired behaviour that can therefore be changed and adapted? In which case, why say that Christianity is essentially, inherently and irrevocably patriarchal and thus beyond redemption as far as feminism is concerned? We are faced with the question of which differences are universal and thus inevitable, and which are contingent and merely the product of a particular culture. We saw in Chapter 6 that feminism has to draw a line somewhere in order to provide a base for political action. I suggest that the sex-gender distinction is still a better candidate for this than Hampson's blanket use of 'otherness'. If the nature of 'otherness' can indeed be reformed - as Hampson's later comments would surely imply - then why is Christianity irredeemably patriarchal?

One of the sad and potentially divisive aspects of this debate is that women are now left only talking for women and men only talking for men. I believe that the characteristics Hampson highlights as being feminine are found across the gender divide and need to be advocated as such. I also see the growth of equality leading to increasing numbers of women adopting the 'male' characteristics of which she is so critical. Yet the debate about what is really required for everybody now is silenced because men feel that only women can comment on what is appropriate for other women. Meanwhile men's 'normal' values or modes of operation are constantly under attack although women then hesitate to say what they would like to see instead. There seems to be a general deterioration in communication and a decreasing lack of confidence in articulating both differences and common ground. Simply describing certain characteristics as either 'male' or 'female' seems positively unhelpful.

The danger to which I am drawing attention here is that of turning identifiable differences into universal categories and static characteristics. What is contingent and thus susceptible to alteration is portrayed as necessary and thus unchanging and unchangeable. Difference and non-identity are turned into an ontology - a theory about being itself. As I said earlier, I believe this is a mistake. So, for instance, it is always tempting to describe Identity as positive and Non-Identity as negative and then to make one of these the key category for interpreting existence. We recall that Bhaskar wants to steer a middle way between positivism and irrationalism in science, thus refusing to identify being wholly or exclusively with either extreme. Turn the positive into the key category and you immediately exclude and repress that which does not fit in. However, replace it with the negative and you instead undermine any sense of order, coherence or continuity. The objective should surely be to retain the balance and tension between the two. Both Identity and Non-Identity contain elements of truth and each requires the other to guard against distortion. With that in mind I turn to some concluding remarks.

God, Transcendence and Spirituality

Like Hampson I want to retain an understanding of transcendence. She offers a limited but helpful definition to which I suspect many people could probably subscribe. She says simply that humans have an awareness that there is another dimension to reality (14). 'God' then is the word she uses to describe that other dimension (15). The concept of God thus serves a transcendental function because it points humans beyond themselves. Spirituality then focusses upon particular ways of being that are in tune with relating to this dimension, that are derived from feminism, and that Hampson identifies as attention, honesty and ordering (16). Her 'new' religion appears to point to a resource or power that people can draw upon as they strive for healing and for more effective personal and political relationships. 'We shall need a much more dynamic understanding of God: as energy, light, power, love and healing. These things themselves should be understood to be what God is: something to which we have access' (17).

All of this is fairly unobjectionable, although it would probably not satisfy the conventional Christian - nor is it designed to. But does it really say enough? If religion is merely the vague awareness that there is more to life than immediately meets the eye, then why bother retaining the word God? What does it add or contribute to the general understanding? Perhaps Hampson will, in due course, renounce theology as she has done Christianity, as superfluous to requirements. But then, for a professional theologian that could be difficult. One can acknowledge the value of the characteristics she identifies as spirituality as general life skills, but then is that all it is? Perhaps this 'thin' description of religion, God and spirituality is all that we are going to be left with in a Post-Enlightenment feminist age, but I am not convinced that it provides much to inspire or to motivate people in the face of the deepest human challenges. But then, I have a different corner to defend.

I want to argue for a renewed philosophical theology and a revised and revived Christian apologetic in response to the genuine challenges of Post-Modern thought. Both are currently out of favour and out of fashion, but that in itself proves little. Both require a rather more substantial description of God and transcendence than Hampson has to offer, and for this I want to return to the earlier comments on Identity and Non-Identity. My belief is that we must retain both of these as the best means we have of describing the limits and boundaries of human existence. Our lives shift and shuffle backwards and forwards between these two extremes. But, attempt to remove either one of them and the result is either totalitarianism or anarchy. This is true personally, socially, intellectually and spiritually.

We can apply this to the concept of God. For instance, if God is described as 'wholly other', distant, complete and probably patriarchal, then 'he' is so removed from humanity and creation as to be either irrelevant or else as to demand total obedience as some form of cosmic tyrant. On the other hand, identify God totally with humanity or creation, as is the tendency in some ecological theology and even perhaps in Hampson's interpretation, and then you close down the spaces and locations for transcendence and undermine the motivation to strive for further stages of development (the transrational). However, retain the tension between Identity and Non-Identity, with neither claiming to capture the whole story, and each can act as a corrective to the other. I would argue that, from within the Christian tradition, such a strategy keeps faith with enough Christian thought and practice to retain its integrity.

This would also provide continuity with the two key strands of Christian spirituality mentioned earlier in the chapter, the kataphatic and the apophatic. The tension between what can be said and what must remain unspoken is also retained. Derrida's comments on the ambiguity of a negative theology are particularly relevant here. The spiritual practices advocated by Hampson would contribute to this, but in conjunction with the criteria outlined in the last chapter. It cannot just be the case that 'anything goes' or that every format be accepted as an appropriate spirituality.

Finally, the crucial area of human autonomy and personal development that has been central to this whole debate. If we continue to recognize that there is an internal tension between Identity and Non-Identity, that which we are and that which we are not or might be, then there is clearly space for growth, development and change. We are on the journey as pilgrims - not as vagabonds - but we know that we are not there yet and that the destination is not quite so clear. We also realise that none of us exists as lone, self sufficient and self resourcing operators, but rather as members of various networks of relationships. Thus human becoming and flourishing require those inter-active and relational skills highlighted by feminism and, I would argue, to be found within the Christian tradition in any case. They also allow scope for reasoning of the communicative kind described by Habermas. It is this that enables us to cross barriers, to transcend cultures and traditions and to enter into genuine relationships with others. So difference and non-identity are fully acknowledged, but not taken to the point where they preclude real communication. Retain both Identity and Non-Identity and it is clear that humans are capable both of cooperative and creative relationships with others and can achieve a sense of community, belonging and common purpose, and yet are incomplete, distorted, manipulative and will resort to coercion when differences are denied or rejected. This is to be realistic about human nature.

The function of transcendence is to keep us alert to the fact that the Identity - Non-Identity polarity is an inescapable dimension of existence. Perhaps the most significant contribution that Post-Modern philosophy has made to theology has been to highlight the importance of retaining this tension in our thought and understanding. It is in this respect that it is an ally to the Christian enterprise.

References

Chapter One

1   Martin Wroe, Faith, hope - but not too much clarity, (The Observer Sunday 26th December 1993), p19.
2   Ibid., p19.
3   Ibid., p19.
4   Grace Davie, Religion in Britain since 1945: Believing without Belonging (Blackwell Publishers 1994).
5   Roy Bhaskar, Dialectic: The Pulse of Freedom, (Verso 1993), p15.
6   Ulrich Beck, Risk Society: Towards a New Modernity, (Sage Publications Ltd 1992), p162.
7   Davie, Religion in Britain since 1945, p43.
8   Ibid., p74.
9   James A. Beckford, Religion and Advanced Industrial Society, (Unwin Hyman Ltd 1989), p171.
10   Ibid., p171.
11   Anthony Giddens, Modernity and Self-Identity, (Polity Press 1991).
12   John Reader, Local Theology: Church and Community in Dialogue, (S.P.C.K. 1994), p139.
13   Gilles Kepel, The Revenge of God: The Resurgence of Islam, Christianity and Judaism in the Modern World, (Polity Press 1994).
14   Kepel, The Revenge of God, p55.
15   Ibid., p23.
16   Ibid., p133.
17   Anthony Giddens, Beyond Left and Right: The Future of Radical Politics, (Polity Press 1994), p84.
18   Giddens, Beyond Left and Right, p84.
19   Ibid., p8
20   Reader, Local Theology, p21.

Chapter Two

1   K. Marx and F. Engels, Collected Works VI, p487.

2   Alex Callinicos, Against Postmodernism, (Polity Press 1989), p31.
3   Jean-François Lyotard, The Postmodern Condition, (Manchester 1984).
4   M. Gottdiener, Postmodern Semiotics, (Blackwell Publishers 1995), p119.
5   Francis Fukuyama, The End of History and the Last Man, (Penguin Books 1992).
6   J. Richard Middleton & Brian J.Walsh, Truth is stranger than it used to be: Biblical Faith in a Postmodern Age, (S.P.C.K. 1995), p188.
7   Lesslie Newbigin, The Gospel in a Pluralist Society, (S.P.C.K. 1989), p90.
8   David Tracy, On Naming the Present: God, Hermeneutics and Church, (S.C.M. 1994), p8.
9   Stanley Hauerwas, After Christendom, (Abingdon Press 1991), p35.
10   Zygmunt Bauman, Postmodern Ethics, (Blackwell Publishers 1993), p240.
11   Douglas Kellner, Jean Baudrillard: From Marxism to Postmodernism and Beyond, (Polity Press 1989), p157.
12   Anthony C. Thiselton, Interpreting God and the Postmodern Self: On Meaning Manipulation and Promise, (T & T Clark Ltd 1995), p12.
13   John Atherton, Christianity and the Market: Christian Social Thought for our times, (S.P.C.K. 1992), p239.

Chapter Three

1   Jean-François Lyotard, The Postmodern Condition, (Manchester University, 1979).
2   Jean-François Lyotard, Notes on the Return of Capital, Semiotext vol 3, no 1, p53: quoted in Steven Best and Douglas Kellner, Postmodern Theory: Critical Interrogations, (Macmillan Educational Ltd 1991), p156.
3   Jean-François Lyotard, The Inhuman, (Polity Press 1993), p25.
4   Richard Rorty, Philosophy and the Mirror of Nature, (Blackwell Publishers, 1980.)
5   Ibid p5.
6   For instance, Lesslie Newbigin, The Gospel in a Pluralist Society, (S.P.C.K. 1989); Don Cupitt, The Time Being, (S.C.M. Press Ltd, 1992): J. Richard Middleton and Brian J. Walsh, Truth is stranger than it used to be: Biblical Faith in a Postmodern Age, (S.P.C.K. 1995).
7   Richard Rorty, Philosophy and the Mirror of Nature, (Blackwell Publishers, 1980), p389.
8   Paul Feyerabend, Against Method, (Verso, 1978).
9   Richard Rorty, Objectivity, Relativism and Truth,: Philosophical Papers Volume 1, (Cambridge University Press, 1991), p37.
10   Ibid., p98.
11   For instance: Don Cupitt, What is a Story?, (S.C.M. Press Ltd, 1991), p76: Don Cupitt, The New Christian Ethic, (S.C.M. Press Ltd, 1988), p38ff: Anthony Thiselton, Interpreting God and the Postmodern Self: On Meaning, Manipulation and Promise, (T & T Clark Ltd, 1995), p134: J. Richard Middleton and Brian J. Walsh, Truth is stranger than it used to be: Biblical Faith in a Postmodern Age, (S.P.C.K. 1995), p50: Charles Davis, Religion and the Making of Society: Essays in Social Theology, (Cambridge University

Press, 1994), p159.

12 Jean Baudrillard, Oublier Foucault, (Editions Galilee, Paris, 1977).

13 David Macey, The Lives of Michel Foucault, (Hutchinson, 1993), Chapter 15.

14 Ibid., p. xiv and p458.

15 Michel Foucault, Afterword: The Subject and Power, published in Hubert L. Dreyfus & Paul Rabinow, Michel Foucault: Beyond Structuralism and Hermeneutics, (Harvester Press Ltd, 1982), p208.

16 J. Richard Middleton & Brian J. Walsh, Truth is stranger than it used to be: Biblical Faith in a Postmodern Age, (S.P.C.K. 1995).

17 Michel Foucault, Madness and Civilization: A History of Insanity in the Age of Reason, (Tavistock Publications Ltd, 1967): Michel Foucault, The Birth of the Clinic: An Archaeology of Medical Perception, (Tavistock Publications Ltd, 1973): Michel Foucault, Discipline and Punish: The Birth of the Prison, (Peregrine Books, 1979).

18 Michel Foucault, The Archaeology of Knowledge, (Tavistock Publications Ltd, 1972).

19 Michel Foucault, The History of Sexuality: Volume 1. An Introduction, (Penguin Books, 1990).

20 Michel Foucault, Afterword: The Subject and Power, published in Hubert L. Dreyfus and Paul Rabinow, Michel Foucault: Beyond Structuralism and Hermeneutics, (Harvester Press Ltd, 1982), p219ff: also Michel Foucault, Power/Knowledge: Selected Interviews and Other Writings 1972-1977 edited by Colin Gordon, (Harvester Press Ltd, 1980).

21 Jean Baudrillard, Simulations, Semiotext, New York, 1983, p147.

22 Jean Baudrillard, The Reality Gulf, The Guardian, 11th January 1991.

23 Christopher Norris, Uncritical Theory: Postmodernism, Intellectuals and the Gulf War, (Lawrence and Wishart, 1992).

24 Jean Baudrillard, Les strategies fatales, (Grasset, Paris, 1983).

25 Richard Rorty, Is Derrida a Transcendental Philosopher, published as Chapter 11 in ed. David Wood, Derrida: A Critical Reader, (Blackwell Publishers, 1992).

26 Christopher Norris, Derrida, (Fontana Press, 1987), p159.

27 Anthony Giddens, The Consequences of Modernity, (Polity Press, 1990), p139.

28 Ibid., p36ff : also Anthony Giddens, Living in a Post-Traditional Society, published in Ulrich Beck, Anthony Giddens, Scott Lash, Reflexive Modernization, (Polity Press, 1994).

29 Anthony Giddens, Modernity and Self-Identity, (Polity Press, 1991).

30 Ibid., p209ff.

31 David Held, Introduction to Critical Theory: Horkheimer to Habermas, (University of California Press, 1980).

32 Stephen K. White, The Recent Work of Jürgen Habermas: Reason, Justice and Modernity, (Cambridge University Press, 1988), p58 and William Outhwaite, Habermas: A Critical Introduction, (Polity Press, 1994), p4.

33 Jürgen Habermas, The Philosophical Discourse of Modernity, (Polity Press, 1987), p303.

34 Jürgen Habermas, The Theory of Communicative Action: Volume 2 The Critique of Functionalist Reason, (Polity Press, 1987), p153ff.

35 Jürgen Habermas, The Philosophical Discourse of Modernity, (Polity Press, 1987), p303.

Chapter Four

1 Nicholas Lash, The Beginning and the End of 'Religion', (Cambridge University Press 1996), p199.
2 Ibid., p201.
3 Ibid., p11.
4 Ibid., p18.
5 Ibid., p246.
6 e.g. Jean-François Lyotard, Lessons on the Analytic of the Sublime (Kant's Critique of Judgement 23-29), (Stanford University Press, Stanford, California 1994).
7 The Cambridge Edition of the Works of Immanuel Kant, Opus postumum, (Cambridge University Press 1993), p241.
8 Ibid., p241.
9 Ibid., p200.
10 Jürgen Habermas, Knowledge and Human Interests, (Heinemann Educational Books 1972), Chapter 9.
11 Cornelius Castoriadis in conversation, Conversations with French Philosophers, (Humanities Press International, Inc, New Jersey 1995), p32.
12 Jean-François Lyotard in conversation with Willem van Reijen and Dick Veerman, Postmodernism: Theory, Culture and Society, (Sage Publications Ltd 1988), p277.
13 Ibid., p277.
14 Jean-François Lyotard, Le Differend, (Minuit, Paris 1984).
15 Jean-François Lyotard in conversation with Willem van Reijen and Dick Veerman, Postmodernism: Theory, Culture and Society, (Sage Publications Ltd 1988), p278.
16 Ibid., p279.
17 Ibid., p280.
18 Jean-François Lyotard in conversation, Conversations with French Philosophers, (Humanities Press International Inc., New Jersey 1995).
19 Ibid., p74.
20 Ludwig Wittgenstein, Philosophical Investigations, (Basil Blackwell, Oxford 1972), p8.
21 Terrence W. Tilley, Postmodern Theologies, (Orbis Books, Maryknoll, U.S.A. 1995), p94.
22 George Lindbeck, The Nature of Doctrine, (Westminster, Philadelphia 1984).
23 Stanley Hauerwas, The Peaceable Kingdom: A Primer in Christian Ethics, (S.C.M. Press Ltd London 1984), p. xxiii.
24 Stanley Hauerwas, After Christendom, (Abingdon Press, Nashville 1991), p15-16.
25 Ibid., p33.
26 Ibid., p25.
27 Ibid., p26.
28 Ibid., p14.
29 Mark S. Cladis, A Communitarian Defense of Liberalism: Emile Durkheim and Contemporary Social Theory, (Stanford University Press, Stanford California 1992), p169.
30 John Milbank, Theology and Social Theory: Beyond Secular Reason,

(Blackwell Publishers 1990).

31 Ibid., p1.
32 Ibid., p1.
33 Ibid., Chapter 5.
34 Ibid., p380.
35 Ibid., p381.
36 Steven Best and Douglas Kellner, Postmodern Theory: Critical Interrogations, (MacMillan Education Ltd 1991), p172.
37 Ibid., p172.
38 ed. R.S. Sugirtharajah, Asian Faces of Jesus, (S.C.M. Press Ltd 1993).
39 Ibid., p258.
40 Jürgen Habermas, Moral Consciousness and Communicative Action, (Polity Press 1992), p94.
41 Seyla Benhabib, Situating the Self: Gender, Community and Postmodernism in Contemporary Ethics, (Polity Press 1992).
42 Ibid., p190.
43 John Reader, Local Theology: Church and Community in Dialogue, (S.P.C.K. London 1994), p12-14.

Chapter Five

1   John Macquarrie, Principles of Christian Theology, (S.C.M. Press Ltd 1966), p4.
2   Zygmunt Bauman, Modernity and the Holocaust, (Polity Press 1989).
3   Ibid., p17.
4   Ibid., p17.
5   Ibid., p18.
6   Alasdair MacIntyre, After Virtue: A Study in Moral Theory, (Duckworth, London 1981): Alasdair MacIntyre, Whose Justice? Which Rationality?, (Duckworth, London 1988): Alasdair MacIntyre, Three Rival Versions of Moral Enquiry: Encyclopaedia, Genealogy, Tradition, (Duckworth, London 1990).
7   Alasdair MacIntyre, After Virtue: A Study in Moral Theory, (Duckworth, London 1981), p6.
8   Alasdair MacIntyre, Whose Justice? Which Rationality?, (Duckworth, London1988), p346.
9   Ibid., p348.
10 Ibid., p348.
11 Ibid., p352.
12 John Henry Newman, University Sermons: Fifteen Sermons Preached before the University of Oxford 1826-1843, (S.P.C.K. London 1970), p312ff.
13 Alasdair MacIntyre, Whose Justice? Which Rationality?, (Duckworth, London, 1988), p355.
14 Ibid., p359.
15 Alasdair MacIntyre, Three Rival Versions of Moral Enquiry: Encyclopaedia, Genealogy, Tradition, (Duckworth, London, 1990).
16 John Milbank, Theology and Social Theory: Beyond Secular Reason, (Blackwell Publishers, 1990), p327.
17 Ibid., p326.

18 Ibid., p327.
19 Ibid., p328.
20 Ibid., p259.
21 Ibid., p259.
22 Ibid., p260.
23 Ibid., p260.
24 Ibid., p262.
25 Ibid., p278.
26 Richard J. Bernstein, Philosophical Profiles, (Polity Press, 1986), p135ff.
27 Ibid., p138.
28 Alasdair MacIntyre, After Virtue: A Study in Moral Theory, (Duckworth, London, 1981), p111.
29 Richard J.Bernstein, Philosophical Profiles, (Polity Press, 1986), p140.
30 Ed. John Horton and Susan Mendis, After MacIntyre: Critical Perspectives on the Work of Alastair MacIntyre, (Polity Press 1994), essay by John Haldane, p95.
31 Simon Critchley, Jacques Derrida, Ernesto Laclau & Richard Rorty, edited by Chantal Mouffe, Deconstruction and Pragmatism, (Routledge, London 1996).
32 Richard Rorty, Objectivism, Relativism and Truth: Philosophical Papers Volume 1, (Cambridge University Press 1991), p37.
33 Florian Rötzer, Conversations with French Philosophers, (Humanities Press International Inc. New Jersey, 1995), interview with Jacques Derrida, p43ff.
34 Ibid., p43.
35 Ibid., p44.
36 Ibid., p45.
37 Ibid., p48.
38 Ibid., p49.
39 Ibid., p50.
40 ed. David Wood, Derrida: A Critical Reader, (Blackwell Publishers, 1992), essay by Christopher Norris, p168.
41 Jürgen Habermas, Moral Consciousness and Communicative Action, (Polity Press, 1990).
42 Ibid., p93.
43 Jürgen Habermas, Justification and Application, (Polity Press, 1993), p35ff.
44 Ibid., p105.
45 Jürgen Habermas, Between Facts and Norms: Contributions to a Discourse Theory of Law and Democracy, (Polity Press, 1996).
46 Ibid., p157.

Chapter Six

1 David H. Kelsey in ed. Hodgson and King, Christian Theology: An Introduction to its Traditions and Tasks, (S.P.C.K., 1983), p141.
2 see Genesis Chapter 2.
3 see Mark C. Taylor, Erring: A Postmodern A/theology, (The University of Chicago Press, 1984), p38, where he argues that it was St Augustine who first recognized and defined the principle of subjectivity.
4 Paul Tillich, Systematic Theology, Part 3: Existence and the Christ, (S.C.M.

Press Ltd, 1978), p33ff.

5   Joshua Cooper Ramo, Finding God on the Web, (TIME Dec 16th 1996, New York), pp44-49.
6   Zygmunt Bauman, Postmodern Ethics, (Blackwell Publishers, 1993), p240.
7   Ibid., p241.
8   Douglas Kellner in ed. Lash & Friedman, Modernity and Identity, (Blackwell Publishers, 1992), p142.
9   see John Macquarrie, An Existentialist Theology, (Pelican Books, 1973), p65.
10 Douglas Kellner in ed Lash & Friedman, Modernity and Identity, (Blackwell Publishers, 1992), p144.
11 Anthony C. Thiselton, Interpreting God and the Postmodern Self, (T & T Clark Ltd, Edinburgh, 1995).
12 Ibid., p11.
13 Ibid., pp11-12.
14 Ibid., p12.
15 Charles Davis, Religion and the Making of Society, (Cambridge University Press, 1994), p160ff.
16 Hubert L. Dreyfus & Paul Rabinow, Michel Foucault: Beyond Structuralism and Hermeneutics, (The Harvester Press Ltd, 1982), p184.
17 Michel Foucault in ed. Paul Rabinow, The Foucault Reader: An Introduction to Foucault's Thought, (Penguin Books, 1991), an interview between Rabinow and Foucault entitled 'Space, Knowledge and Power', p239.
18 Ibid., p248.
19 Ibid., p249.
20 Ibid., p249.
21 Michel Foucault, The History of Sexuality Volumes 1, 2 &3, (Penguin Books, 1990 and following).
22 Michel Foucault and Richard Sennet in ed. D. Rieff, Humanities in Review, Volume 1, (Cambridge University Press, 1982), and quoted in Steven Best and Douglas Kellner, Postmodern Theory: Critical Interrogations, (Macmillan Education Ltd, 1991), p61.
23 Best and Kellner Ibid., p65.
24 Alison Assiter, Enlightened Women: Modernist Feminism in a Postmodern Age, (Routledge, 1996), p10.
25 Ibid., p22.
26 Seyla Benhabib, Situating the Self, (Polity Press, 1992), p214.
27 Michael Jacobs, Towards the Fullness of Christ: Pastoral Care and Christian Maturity, (Darton, Longman and Todd, 1988), Chapter 2.
28 Ibid., p29ff.
29 James Fowler, Stages of Faith: The Psychology of Human Development and the Quest for Meaning, (Harper and Row, San Francisco, 1981).
30 Jürgen Habermas, Moral Consciousness and Communicative Action, (Polity Press, 1990), pp33-41 also pp119-133.
31 Carol Gilligan, In A Different Voice, (Cambridge, Mass., 1982).
32 John Reader, Local Theology: Church and Community in Dialogue, (S.P.C.K., 1994), p22.
33 Ulrich Beck, Anthony Giddens, Scott Lash, Reflexive Modernization: Politics, Tradition and Aesthetics in the Modern Social Order, (Polity Press, 1994).
34 Ulrich Beck, Risk Society: Towards a New Modernity, (Sage Publications, 1992),

p135.

35 see Will Hutton, The State to Come, (Vintage, 1997), p26.

36 Scott Lash in Reflexive Modernization, ibid., p135ff.

37 Anthony Giddens, Modernity and Self-Identity: Self and Society in the late Modern Age, (Polity Press, 1991).

38 Ibid., p190.

39 Ibid., p190.

Chapter Seven

1 David Tracy, The Analogical Imagination, (S.C.M. Press Ltd 1981), p5.

2 Rebecca S. Chopp & Mark Lewis Taylor eds, Reconstructing Christian Theology, (Fortress Press, Minneapolis, 1994), p3ff.

3 Ibid., p4.

4 Laurie Green, Lets Do Theology, (Mowbray, 1990); Chris Rowland and John Vincent eds, Liberation Theology U.K., (Urban Theology Unit, Sheffield 1995); John Reader, Local Theology: Church and Community in Dialogue, (S.P.C.K., 1994).

5 Rebecca S.Chopp & Mark Lewis Taylor eds, Reconstructing Christian Theology, (Fortress Press, Minneapolis, 1994), p8.

6 Article by Margaret Goodall and John Reader on Creating Spaces, Chapter 7 of eds Ian Ball, Margaret Goodall, Clare Palmer and John Reader, The Earth Beneath: A Critical Guide to Green Theology, (S.P.C.K., 1992).

7 John Reader, Local Theology: Church and Community in Dialogue, (S.P.C.K., 1994), pp14-16.

8 John Milbank, Theology and Social Theory: Beyond Secular Reason, (Blackwell Publishers, 1990), p207.

9 Ibid., p208.

10 Ibid., p218.

11 Gavin D'Costa editor, Christian Uniqueness Reconsidered: The Myth of a Pluralistic Theology of Religions, (Orbis Books, New York, 1990).

12 John Hick and Paul F. Knitter, The Myth of Christian Uniqueness, (Orbis Books New York, 1987).

13 Gavin D'Costa editor, Christian Uniqueness Reconsidered: The Myth of a Pluralistic Theology of Religions, (Orbis Books, New York, 1990), the chapter by John Milbank entitled 'The End of Dialogue', p174.

14 Ibid., p175.

15 Ibid., p178.

16 Ibid., p180.

17 Ibid., p189.

18 Ibid., p189.

19 Ibid., p190.

20 Ibid., p98.

21 Richard J. Bernstein, The New Constellation: The Ethical-Political Horizons of Modernity/Post-Modernity, (Polity Press, 1990), chapter 7.

22 Ibid., p59.

23 Ibid., p66.

24 Ibid., p72.
25 Ibid., p72.
26 Ibid., p74.
27 Ibid., p75.
28 John Reader, Local Theology: Church and Community in Dialogue, (S.P.C.K., 1994), pp12-14.
29 Ibid., p14.
30 Gavin D'Costa, Christian Uniqueness Reconsidered: The Myth of a Pluralistic Theology of Religions, (Orbis Books, New York, 1990), essay by John B. Cobb Jnr, p84.
31 Ibid., pp85-86.
32 Ken Wilbur, A Sociable God: Toward a new understanding of Religion, (New Science Library, Shambhala Publications. Inc, Boulder, Colorado, 1983).
33 Roy Bhaskar, Dialectic: The Pulse of Freedom, (Verso, 1993).
34 Andrew Collier, Critical Realism: An Introduction to Roy Bhaskar's Philosophy, (Verso, 1994).
35 Ibid., p57.

Chapter Eight

1 Peter Dews, The Limits of Disenchantment: Essays on Contemporary European Philosophy, (Verso, 1995), p9.
2 Jürgen Habermas, Postmetaphysical Thinking, (Polity Press, 1992), p51.
3 Jürgen Habermas quoted in Peter Dews, Ibid., p11.
4 Jacques Derrida, On the Name, (Stanford University Press, California, 1995), the chapter 'Sauf le Nom (Post-Scriptum)', pp35-85.
5 Ibid., p68.
6 Ibid., p71.
7 Daphne Hampson, After Christianity, (S.C.M. Press Ltd, 1996).
8 Ibid., p2.
9 Ibid., p3.
10 Ibid., p5.
11 Ibid., p101.
12 Ibid., p104.
13 Ibid., p111.
14 Ibid., p230.
15 Ibid., p239.
16 Ibid., p260.
17 Ibid., p251.

Bibliography

Alison Assiter, Enlightened Women: Modernist Feminism in a Postmodern Age, (Routledge, 1996).

ed Ian Ball, Margaret Goodall, Clare Palmer and John Reader, The Earth Beneath: A Critical Guide to Green Theology, (S.P.C.K., 1992).

Jean Baudrillard, Cool Memories, (Verso, 1990).

Jean Baudrillard, Les strategies fatales, (Grasset, Paris, 1983).

Jean Baudrillard, Oublier Foucault, (Editions Galilee, Paris, 1977).

Jean Baudrillard, Simulations, (Semiotext, New York, 1983).

Zygmunt Bauman, Intimations of Postmodernity, (Routledge, 1992).

Zygmunt Bauman, Modernity and the Holocaust, (Polity Press, 1989).

Zygmunt Bauman, Postmodern Ethics, (Blackwell Publishers, 1993).

Ulrich Beck, Risk Society: Towards a New Modernity, (Sage Publications, 1992).

Ulrich Beck, Anthony Giddens, Scott Lash, Reflexive Modernization: Politics, Tradition and Aesthetics in the Modern Social Order, (Polity Press, 1994).

James A. Beckford, Religion and Advanced Industrial Society, (Unwin Hyman Ltd, 1989).

Seyla Benhabib, Situating the Self: Gender, Community and Postmodernism in Contemporary Ethics, (Polity Press, 1992).

Richard J. Bernstein, Beyond Objectivism and Relativism, (Blackwell Publishers, 1983).

Richard J. Bernstein, Philosophical Profiles, (Polity Press, 1986).

Richard J. Bernstein, The New Constellation: The Ethical-Political Horizons of Modernity / Postmodernity, (Polity Press, 1991).

Roy Bhaskar, Dialectic: The Pulse of Freedom, (Verso, 1993).

Roy Bhaskar, Philosophy and the Idea of Freedom, (Blackwell Publishers, 1991).

Roy Bhaskar, Plato Etc: The Problems of Philosophy and their Resolution, (Verso, 1994).

Alex Callinicos, Against Postmodernism, (Polity Press, 1989).

eds Rebecca. S. Chopp & Mark Lewis Taylor, Reconstructing Christian Theology, (Fortress Press, Minneapolis, 1994).

Mark. S. Cladis, A Communitarian Defense of Liberalism: Emile Durkheim and Contemporary Social Theory, (Stanford University Press, California, 1992).

Andrew Collier, Critical Realism: An Introduction to Roy Bhaskar's Philosophy, (Verso, 1994).

Grace Davie, Religion in Britain since 1945: Believing without Belonging, (Blackwell Publishers, 1994).

Charles Davis, Religion and the Making of Society: Essays in Social Theology, (Cambridge University Press, 1994).

ed Gavin D'Costa, Christian Uniqueness Reconsidered: The Myth of a Pluralistic Theology of Religions, (Orbis Books, New York, 1990).

ed Mathieu Deflem, Habermas, Modernity and Law, (Sage Publications Ltd, 1996).

Jacques Derrida, Margins of Philosophy, (Chicago University Press, 1982).

Jacques Derrida, On the Name, (Stanford University Press, 1995).

Jacques Derrida, Writing and Difference, (Routledge and Kegan Paul, 1978).

Peter Dews, Logics of Disintegration: Post-Structuralist Thought and the Claims of Critical Theory, (Verso, 1987).

Peter Dews, The Limits of Disenchantment: Essays on Contemporary European Philosophy, (Verso, 1995).

Hubert. L. Dreyfus & Paul Rabinow, Michel Foucault: Beyond Structuralism and Hermeneutics, (The Harvester Press, 1986).

Michel Foucault, Discipline and Punish: The Birth of the Prison, (Peregrine Books, 1979).

Michel Foucault, Madness and Civilization: A History of Insanity in the Age of Reason, (Tavistock Publications Ltd, 1967).

Michel Foucault, Power/Knowledge: Selected Interviews and other writings 1972-1977, (The Harvester Press, 1980).

Michel Foucault, The Archaeology of Knowledge, (Tavistock Publications Ltd, 1972).

Michel Foucault, The Birth of the Clinic: An Archaeology of Medical Perception, (Tavistock Publications Ltd, 1973).

Michel Foucault, The History of Sexuality, Vol 1: An Introduction, (Penguin Books, 1990).

Michel Foucault, The History of Sexuality, Vol 2: The Use of Pleasure, (Penguin Books, 1991).

Michel Foucault, The History of Sexuality, Vol 3: The Care of the Self, (Penguin Books, 1992).

Michel Foucault, The Order of Things: An Archaeology of the Human Sciences, (Tavistock Publications Ltd, 1990).

James. W. Fowler, Stages of Faith: The Psychology of Human Development and the Quest for Meaning, (Harper & Row Publishers, San Francisco, 1981).

eds James. W. Fowler, Karl Ernst Nipkow and Friedrich Schweitzer, Stages of Faith and Religious Development: Implications for Church, Education and Society, (S.C.M. Press Ltd, 1992).

Francis Fukuyama, The End of History and the Last Man, (Penguin Books, 1992).

Anthony Giddens, Beyond Left and Right: The Future of Radical Politics, (Polity Press, 1994).

Anthony Giddens, Modernity and Self-Identity: Self and Society in the Late Modern Age, (Polity Press, 1991).

Anthony Giddens, The Consequences of Modernity, (Polity Press, 1990).

Anthony Giddens, The Transformation of Intimacy: Sexuality, Love & Eroticism in Modern Societies, (Polity Press, 1992).

Carol Gilligan, In a Different Voice: Psychological Theory and Women's Development, (Harvard University Press, Cambridge, Mass., 1982).

Jürgen Habermas, Between Facts and Norms, (Polity Press, 1997).
Jürgen Habermas, Justification and Application, (Polity Press, 1993).
Jürgen Habermas, Moral Consciousness and Communicative Action, (Polity Press, 1990).
Jürgen Habermas, Postmetaphysical Thinking, (Polity Press, 1992).
Jürgen Habermas, The Theory of Communicative Action: Vol 1. Reason and the Rationalization of Society, (Beacon Press,Boston Mass, 1984).
Jürgen Habermas, The Theory of Communicative Action: Vol 2. The Critique of Functionalist Reason, (Polity Press, 1987).
Jürgen Habermas, The Philosophical Discourse of Modernity, (Polity Press, 1987).
Daphne Hampson, After Christianity, (S.C.M.Press Ltd, 1996).
Stanley Hauerwas, After Christendom? : How the Church is to behave if freedom, justice, and a Christian nation are bad ideas, (Abingdon Press, 1991).
Stanley Hauerwas, The Peaceable Kingdom: A Primer in Christian Ethics, (S.C.M. Press Ltd, 1984).
David Held, Introduction to Critical Theory: Horkheimer to Habermas, (University of California Press, 1980).
eds John Hick and Paul Knitter, The Myth of Christian Uniqueness, (Maryknoll, N.Y: Orbis Books; London, S.C.M. Press Ltd, 1987).
eds John Horton and Susan Mendus, After MacIntyre: Critical Perspectives on the Work of Alasdair MacIntyre, (Polity Press, 1994).
Michael Jacobs, Towards the Fullness of Christ: Pastoral Care and Christian Maturity, (Darton, Longman and Todd, 1988).
Immanuel Kant, Opus postumum: The Cambridge Edition of the Works of Immanuel Kant, (Cambridge University Press, 1993).
Douglas Kellner, Jean Baudrillard: From Marxism to Postmodernism and Beyond, (Polity Press, 1989).
Douglas Kellner, Critical Theory, Marxism and Modernity, (Polity Press, 1989).
Douglas Kellner and Steven Best, Postmodern Theory: Critical Interrogations, (Macmillan Education Ltd, 1991).
Gilles Kepel, The Revenge of God: The Resurgence of Islam, Christianity and Judaism in the Modern World, (Polity Press, 1994).
Nicholas Lash, The Beginning and the End of 'Religion', (Cambridge University Press, 1996).
eds Scott Lash and Jonathan Friedman, Modernity and Identity, (Basil Blackwell Publishers, 1992).
George Lindbeck, The Nature of Doctrine, (Westminster, Philadelphia, 1984).
Jean-Francois Lyotard, Le Differend, (Minuit, Paris, 1984).
Jean-Francois Lyotard, Lessons on the Analytic of the Sublime: Kant's Critique of Judgement 23-29, (Stanford University Press, California, 1994).
Jean-Francois Lyotard in conversation in Postmodernism: Theory,Culture and Society, (Sage Publications Ltd, 1988).
Jean-Francois Lyotard, The Inhuman, (Polity Press, 1991).
Jean-Francois Lyotard, The Postmodern Condition, (Manchester University, 1979).
David Macey, The Lives of Michel Foucault, (Hutchinson, 1993).
Alasdair MacIntyre, After Virtue: A Study in Moral Theory, (Duckworth, 1981).
Alasdair MacIntyre, Whose Justice? Which Rationality?, (Duckworth, 1988).
Alasdair MacIntyre, Three Rival Versions of Moral Enquiry: Encyclopaedia, Genealogy, Tradition, (Duckworth, 1990).

J. Richard Middleton & Brian J. Walsh, Truth is stranger than it used to be: Biblical Faith in a Postmodern Age, (S.P.C.K., 1995).

John Milbank, Theology & Social Theory: Beyond Secular Reason, (Blackwell Publishers, 1990).

ed Chantal Mouffe, Deconstruction and Pragmatism: Simon Critchley, Jacques Derrida, Ernesto Laclau & Richard Rorty, (Routledge, 1996).

Christopher Norris, Derrida, (Fontana Press, 1987).

Christopher Norris, Uncritical Theory: Postmodernism, Intellectuals and the Gulf War, (Lawrence & Wishart Ltd, 1992).

William Outhwaite, Habermas: A Critical Introduction, (Polity Press, 1994).

ed Paul Rabinow, The Foucault Reader: An Introduction to Foucault's Thought, (Penguin Books, 1984).

John Reader, Local Theology: Church and Community in Dialogue, (S.P.C.K., 1994).

Richard Rorty, Contingency, Irony and Solidarity, (Cambridge University Press, 1989).

Richard Rorty, Objectivity, Relativism and Truth: Philosophical Papers Vol.1, (Cambridge University Press, 1991).

Richard Rorty, Philosophy and the Mirror of Nature, (Basil Blackwell Publishers, 1980).

Florian Rotzer, Conversations with French Philosophers, (Humanities Press International Ltd, New Jersey, 1995).

Mark C. Taylor, Erring: A Postmodern A/theology, (The University of Chicago Press, 1984).

Anthony C. Thiselton, Interpreting God and the Postmodern Self: On Meaning, Manipulation and Promise, (T & T Clark Ltd, 1995).

Terrence W. Tilley, Postmodern Theologies: The Challenge of Religious Diversity, (Orbis Books, Maryknoll, New York, 1995).

David Tracy, On Naming the Present: God, Hermeneutics, and Church, (S.C.M. Press Ltd, 1994).

David Tracy, The Analogical Imagination: Christian Theology and the Culture of Pluralism, (S.C.M. Press Ltd, 1981).

ed. Stephen K. White, The Cambridge Companion to Habermas, (Cambridge University Press, 1995).

Stephen. K. White, The recent work of Jürgen Habermas: Reason, Justice and Modernity, (Cambridge University Press, 1988).

Ken Wilbur, A Brief History of Everything, (Gill & Macmillan Ltd., Dublin, 1996).

Ken Wilbur, A Sociable God: Toward a New Understanding of Religion, (Shambhala Publications Inc., Boulder, Colorado, 1983).

Ken Wilbur, Up From Eden: A Transpersonal View of Human Evolution, (Routledge & Kegan Paul, 1983).

ed David Wood, Derrida: A Critical Reader, (Blackwell Publishers Ltd, 1992).

Index